TREATMENT IN AMERICA:
Her Life Matters

By Jacqueline White-Ivey

DISCLAIMER

This is a book based on my memoirs. Names of characters and some locations have been changed to protect those who would prefer to remain anonymous. While liberties were taken reconstructing some of the dialogue, most conversations were quoted word for word, because you can't make that shit up.

CREDITS

Cover picture: Taylor Murray
Developmental editing under working title, The Gift: Lori Garside
Copy editing: Jerry Ivey
Read/critique: Susan Hedges

ALL RIGHTS RESERVED

First edition copyright © 2020 Maemo Publishing, LLC. Written permission must be secured from the publisher to use or reproduce any part of this book, except for brief quotations in critical reviews or articles.

For Anabelle

Chapter One

Our family is gathered around our dining room table. We are celebrating Thanksgiving at home in Brookhaven, Mississippi. Angela, my oldest child, her fiancé, Jason, and Susan, my second oldest child, drove two hours from New Orleans to be with us. They sit on one side of the table while Jackson, my third child, and only son, sits on the opposite side with Jenny, my baby. Jackson is home on pass for the holidays from Tinker Air Force Base in Oklahoma. Lance, my husband, sits at the head of the table with me across from him. Just as we finish eating our holiday dinner, Angela stands up and starts tapping her water glass with her butter knife getting everyone's attention.

"Jason and I have something we need to share with you. Next year we will need another chair at the table!" Angela says with the biggest smile you ever saw.

"Oh my god, are you saying that you are having a baby?" I scream with equal enthusiasm, excited at the thought of our first grandbaby.

"That is what I'm trying to tell you. We are going to have a baby, due in July," she glows as she shares the news.

The whole table erupts in cheers and laughter at the good news. Jason and Angela were childhood sweethearts and they reconnected while Angela was living in the South of France teaching in a program the French government has for teacher assistants. They have recently moved back to the United States, to New Orleans, into an apartment located downstairs in the same Victorian, four-plex on Magazine Street her sister Susan lives in. It's a neighborhood where you can walk to the grocery store, corner bar, or a restaurant and never have to drive your car.

Susan moved to the city a year earlier after graduating from the American InterContinental University in London, England, where she studied design. Her first job was working with a local designer before recently taking a position in the growing New Orleans film industry. She is starting out as a costumer, hoping to work her way toward her ultimate goal of designer. My two older daughters are as much alike as they are different. They share a special bond with each other. Sisters by birth and best friends by choice.

"So, I finally get to be an Uncle!" Jackson chimes in. Our third born and only son spends most holiday meals waiting for one of his sisters or myself to take a breath, so he can get a word in edgewise.

"That is such good news!" Lance, my husband, their stepfather says beaming. He joined our family when Angela and Susan were teenagers, Jackson was five years old and Jenny was just one year old.

"I can't wait to be an Aunt!" our youngest daughter, Jenny shouts, "I am going to spoil that baby!" Jenny is as country as a mayonnaise sandwich, strong willed, but just enough sweetness to balance it out. We keep her busy with softball, tennis, soccer, basketball, swim team, gymnastics and cheerleading in hopes she is too tired to find trouble. That has been my basic method of raising four children, and so far, it is working.

We stay up late playing charades and drinking wine (except no wine for Angela). The competition is fierce causing a vote from the family to keep Angela and Susan from being on the same team. They seem to be able to read each other's minds giving them an unfair advantage.

The next morning, I get up early to begin preparing for the day. I make a pot of coffee and put a pan of biscuits in the oven. I take a cup of coffee and go sit at the table on the back screened porch to have a moment of calm before the gang awakes. The birds are singing as rays of sunlight pass through the thick foliage from the pine trees that shade our large fenced back yard.

Last night after everyone went to bed, my husband was asking me questions I didn't know the answers to. Are they going to get married? Why hasn't Jason given her a ring yet? He is very protective, like a papa bear, when it comes to the children. I think he fell in love with being called daddy as much as he fell in love with me. I am interrupted from my thoughts as the door creeks open and Angela comes to join me.

"I thought you might sleep late?" I ask.

"I wanted to have you all to myself before everyone wakes up! I took the biscuits out of the oven, the timer was about to go off, and they were looking ready," she smiles as she tells me.

"Thank you, sweetheart! How are things now that a baby is on the way? You guys getting married? No pressure from me, I'm just wondering," I ask gently.

"You know he has been asking me to marry him for the past three years, but I wanted to wait. Now I am not sure if we should get married before the baby or after," Angela tells me, "I don't want to get married now just because we are having a baby. I want it to be special."

"It will be special no matter what. You decide whenever you feel ready and I'll help you anyway I can!" I say before changing the subject, "How is the wine bar?"

"It's still as busy as when we opened. We are going to be in an article in *Garden and Gun Magazine,* a national publication, the March issue. They are covering new places to visit when in NOLA." Angela tells me. She and Jason opened Salutations, a wine and cheese dive, six months ago. Salutations is located on the second floor above Feelings restaurant on Chartres Street in the Marigny.

"That is fantastic! How are you going to teach school, work at Salutations and take care of a baby?" I ask.

"I'm your daughter. I will find a way. If the business keeps doing so good, I may not have to teach once the baby is born. I can hire some help for home and the wine bar so I can be Super Woman just like you!" she says laughing, trying to ease my concerns.

"I could come down on the weekends and help with the baby," I gladly volunteer without hesitation.

"See, we are working it out already!" she glows.

"Come on, let's go inside and finish making the rest of breakfast. You have a baby to feed!" I suggest.

Treatment in America: Her Life Matters

Chapter Two

I am at work doing home health when I get the call.

"Mom, it's happening...we are having a baby today!" she gushes on the phone.

"OH MY GOD! I'M ON MY WAY!" I scream into the receiver. I know the first baby doesn't come quickly but I'm two hours away. This is my first grandchild. It is impossible for me to concentrate on my patients, so I go to my office and turn in my paperwork. I head home to speed pack and get on the road. If all goes well, I will be there when our angel arrives!

Angela and Jason have already been admitted to the labor and delivery ward by the time I get there. Angela is smiling with her make-up applied and a flower in her hair.

"I'm only four centimeters. I requested the birthing tub, but someone was already in there. We are next in line," she explains. I think to myself, four centimeters, you have a long way to go before we get to ten and the pushing starts. We have lots of time.

The birthing tub is designed to allow the baby to be born in a more serene environment, leaving the waters of the womb to emerge gently in a tub of warm water. One of the stipulations for using the tub is that no anesthesia can be used. It must be all natural. My thoughts on the subject are to let her get in that tub ASAP, so if the pain becomes too unbearable, there will be time for her to change her mind on the natural childbirth route. I can hardly bear to watch my grown baby suffer. I fear anesthesia will be needed if she is like me. I attempted the Lamaze natural childbirth experience when I had her thirty-one years ago but, in the end, I was begging for anesthesia or for them to mercifully just kill me. I had discussed my experience with her but like me, she had her own ideas of wanting to do it all natural. I already know there is no magic in that birthing tub that can take away the pain of childbirth but until she gets in there and tries it, we will have to endure watching her suffer.

Our labor and delivery nurse, a slender, British woman, who seems as nervous as a cat on a hot tin roof, in need of a sedative herself, finally returns telling us we can transfer to the birthing tub suite. I am relieved as Angela's discomfort level is rising.

"Here we go," she says as she unlocks the wheels and begins pushing the bed with Angela out of the room and down the hall. Jason, his mother, sister, father, and I follow behind. She rolls her two doors down the hallway to the large room housing the whirlpool tub with birthing stool centered inside. She positions the bed across from it and locks the wheels before turning to head back out the door. Just before disappearing she instructs, "Don't get into the tub just yet."

Angela's pain level is steadily increasing as the contractions start to come closer behind each other. She takes slow deep breaths through her nose and exhales slowly through pursed lips in attempts to relax and ease the pain. Jason is by her side rubbing her back and giving her encouragement.

"Mom, can you call the nurse and see if we can get in the tub yet?" she asks in between contractions.

"Of course, darling," I say as I press the call light.

"Yes, can I help you?" a small voice emerges from the wall mounted speaker.

"My daughter wants to know if she can get in the tub. Her pain level is becoming intense," I say in my nice controlled voice.

"I will check with her nurse," the voice responds without the answer we hoped for. It seems like an eternity passes as I watch the clock slowly tick. Fifteen minutes, twenty minutes, still no word from the nurse. Angela's ability to control the pain with her breathing is diminishing. I call the nurses station again.

"Yes, can I help you?" the same small voice from the wall speaker asks.

"I am checking to see if we can help Angela into the tub now. She is beginning to hurt more and needs some relief," I ask again explaining the urgency.

"Her nurse is with another patient now. I will ask her to come to your room as soon as she is available," click and she is gone along with my patience.

Angela's moans are getting louder and closer together as the contractions begin coming faster. I glance at my watch. It has been thirty minutes since I began calling the nurse for permission to use that miracle tub. I decide it is better to ask for forgiveness than permission. I go over to the oversized tub and turn the water on. I let the water get warm before putting in the plug and returning to Angela's side to help her get out of the bed. Jason's mother, father and sister opt to leave and wait outside.

"Here we go my baby," I say as I help her sit up on the side of the bed, "You think you can walk and get in the tub?"

"Yes, Mama," She says as we get up and begin making our way to the tub. She is moving slow and continues to do her rhythmic breathing as she steps into the warm swirling water. Slowly she eases down onto the birthing stool and begins to recline back. Our nurse walks in just as the warm water envelops Angela.

"What are you doing?" she demands with her British accent.

"Well, you disappeared for quite a while. I have called for you for over thirty minutes now. We tried to wait for you to return before getting in the tub, but her pain level is getting worse and I gave up on you. It's been hours since you even checked to see if her dilation is progressing, so we don't even know how close we might be to delivery," I say defiantly in a stern voice that surprises the nurse and myself.

About this time Angela's pain level peaks to the point of get me pain medication or kill me and she can't stand it any longer.

"I want the epidural," Angela moans between breaths.

"Will you please examine her to see if it's time to call the doctor for the delivery. We also need to get an anesthesiologist up here as soon as possible. Angela has changed her mind and can no longer endure this," I ask emphatically.

Nurse Britain finally examines Angela, calls the doctor and gets things moving in the right direction. We are moved from the birthing tub room and placed inside a small, windowless delivery room, but one with an anesthesiologist, who gives Angela sweet relief with an epidural. I don't care what the nurse thinks of me. I only care that my daughter isn't in pain anymore.

The doctor arrives just in time to deliver our angel. Lottie Mae is born without complications. The only concern I have is about the lack of a loud cry from our new little one. The doctor assures us that all is fine, giving her a high Apgar score. I am overwhelmed with emotion. I leave the room to make calls to the rest of our family and to allow Angela and Jason to bond with their precious little one. As I walk down the hospital corridor to the waiting area, something in my gut won't stop nagging me. After delivering four healthy babies, I can't stop thinking about how soft Lottie Mae's first cries were.

Chapter Three

Two months later, my fears start becoming confirmed. I get a call from Angela and the nagging feelings haunting my thoughts start to come back.

"Hey Mom," Angela begins, "Do you think you can come with me to Lottie Mae's two-month check-up? Jason has to work at the store that morning and open *Salutations* that night, not to mention pick up the baguettes in between."

"What day is that?" I ask knowing I will work my schedule to be there no matter what day it is.

"Next Tuesday," she tells me.

"I will be there. I'll just move some of my patients, no worries," I say not letting her know it is sort of a big deal to change the schedule. My rule is family first.

"Thanks Mom! You're the best!" she gushes.

I keep my word and arrange my work schedule to accommodate the request. I wake up early to make the two-hour commute to New Orleans so that I get in town before the morning rush hour traffic. I make it to Angela's by 7 a.m. without any trouble. She has just finished breast feeding when I arrive. I take our sweet baby in my arms and tell Angela to take her time getting ready.

I study our little angel as I rock, while Angela gets ready. She looks smaller than she did when she was born. Her skin color looks slightly yellow. Angela had told me she was having loose bowels but that is typical with breast feeding. I am not prepared for how thin and gaunt

Lottie Mae's little body is looking. I am grateful we are headed to see the doctor.

On the way to the pediatrician, Angela tells me her regular doctor is on vacation and we will be seeing one of her partners. I don't upset Angela and keep my fears to myself. No need to cause extra anxiety before we see what the doctor has to say.

The pediatrician is a young woman, with facial expressions that she cannot mask.

"How often does Lottie Mae eat?" Dr. Welch asks as she carefully examines Lottie Mae.

"Every two to four hours," Angela answers.

"She has lost weight since her last check up," the doctor says as she continues her exam. "I am filling in for Dr. Ward and I apologize but it seems that Lottie Mae is failing to thrive. Has Dr. Ward voiced any concerns?"

"No," Angela answers timidly.

"Are you giving any supplemental formula feedings or strictly breastfeeding?" the doctor asks as she continues to gather history.

"I am just breastfeeding...she falls asleep while nursing sometimes," Angela adds.

"I know I'm not her regular pediatrician, but I am very concerned with her weight. I think we need to see what is going on with her, because she is at a critical point with weight loss," the doctor sternly informs us, "I am going to call Children's Hospital and see if we can have Lottie Mae admitted for a few tests. I recommend a GI specialist along with a geneticist to see if we can determine why she is not gaining weight."

She leaves us to make the phone calls.

"Mom, do you think she thinks I'm not feeding Lottie Mae enough?" Angela ask looking confused and hurt as she turns to me.

"No way, sweetheart! She just thinks that something may be interfering with her weight gain and she wants to find out what it is, as soon as possible, so they can fix it," I say reassuring my daughter.

"I am so scared, Mama," Angela says looking to me for support.

"I know, sweetheart. I think she is doing the right thing. They have good doctors here. Everything is going to be alright," I say trying to calm her. I am also scared to death, but don't want to make things worse.

After a few minutes, Dr. Welch returns.

"I want you to take these (she hands Angela a stack of papers) and go directly to Children's Hospital on Henry Clay Avenue. I have called ahead. They will be expecting you. Go to the admission's office and give this to the attendant. They will probably have to keep Lottie Mae for a few days to complete all the tests."

We are in shock that this is happening, even with the red flags, we find ourselves beyond words. Angela cries once we get to the car. I want to cry, too, but I hold it together as I hug her, and tell her, we are doing the right thing. I drive us the three miles to Children's Hospital while she calls Jason to let him know what is going on.

Treatment in America: Her Life Matters

Chapter Four

Lottie Mae is admitted to Children's Hospital for an intense week of medical tests. The problem with all the tests is the amount of blood needed to perform each test. Ultrasounds are performed resulting in findings of cysts on her heart and kidneys. Cardiologist, nephrologist, GI specialist, geneticist, and many others are in line for blood to perform the many tests needed to diagnose her. It is difficult to hold her still as the nurse probes her for the multiple blood tests. Our sweet baby doesn't understand what is happening. I begin to appreciate the skilled hands of a seasoned phlebotomist that can draw blood with little discomfort to our angel.

The geneticist is the one doctor that breaks it down to a level of understanding that makes it clear what is to be our fate. He gives us a thirty-page report on Zellweger Disorder. Zellweger, it reads, is a biogenesis cell disorder, where one to three enzymes are missing in every cell of her body. Enzymes that affect her ability to absorb nutrition and the ability for each cell to eliminate waste so that toxins don't build up. The bottom line is that there is no cure.

It is three days into Lottie's testing when the geneticist comes to talk to us about the preliminary findings.

"Hi, I'm Dr. Stone," the tall elderly man with a bow tie extends his hand to Angela as he introduces himself, "I left some information about what I feel Lottie Mae has. Have you had an opportunity to read over it?"

"Yes, I've read it and I have been researching the internet about Zellweger," Angela nods as she answers.

"There are ten different levels on the spectrum of Zellweger syndrome, with various life expectancies and complications with each. I will need to do another test that must be sent to a lab in the Midwest for analysis. It will take approximately two months before we have the final test results to diagnose where she falls on the Zellweger spectrum," he solemnly states.

I read the stack of information that broke my heart into a million pieces. It is terminal, no cure, no hope. It is in every cell of her body, from the moment she was conceived, she had this. This beautiful little angel that still smiles as she looks into my eyes. I understand the literature. From my experience working in healthcare, my brain is able to understand it, but not my heart. I am also holding my breath as I watch my daughter's heart break as we discuss her only child's fate.

"I understand in the most severe case life expectancy is for maybe one year and the least severe case she may live to be a teenager?" I ask trying to clarify what I read.

"Yes, but we won't know which type Lottie Mae has until we get the results from the final test," he adds.

"I have been reading online where there is research in Amsterdam about different treatment approaches for Zellweger. Have you heard anything about this?" Angela interjects, asking for hope.

"I am available for your questions if you should have them later," he says, not commenting on the Amsterdam question, brushing it aside as he exits. He seems to know it will take some time for us to allow the information to sink in.

The GI doctor makes rounds with resident doctors in tow. Earlier, they asked permission to include Lottie Mae on their rounds for training their doctors in the residency program to study her case of Zellweger. Every morning the group filters into our small room. This morning, I stay during their round. Lottie Mae had been given a nasal gastric feeding tube our second day at the hospital, allowing her to be fed slowly to accommodate the slow rate of absorption. She started having blood in her bowel movements shortly after. The group of interns are discussing Lottie Mae's newest problem along with the type of formula being given.

The GI doctor leading the group begins lecturing using medical jargon describing deficiencies in Lottie Mae's ability to form clots as a complication of the disease. Angela is listening intently, but not fully understanding the complicated terminology. I understand. She keeps interrupting him as he discusses the case with the group.

"How will you know when something is wrong with the clotting?" she asks pressing his patience.

"Well, blood will be coming out of every orifice," he callously answers. Then he smirks and is laughing as he quickly turns and leads the group on to the next room.

I am furious and in disbelief at his response. I can't just let this go. I jump up as the group is exiting and grab one of the young interns by the arm and I pull him aside.

"I want you to know what I think of your instructor, Dr. I Don't Give a Shit. He obviously has no compassion or empathy and needs to choose another field of endeavor. I don't think my daughter fully understands what we are dealing with, but regardless that was uncalled for. I hope you will be a more considerate and compassionate doctor with your bedside manner than your instructor!" I say, looking him dead in the eyes as we stand just outside the door to our angel's room. He just nods, looking like a deer in the headlights, before apologizing and rejoining his group.

Later that day, the head of pediatrics comes by.

"Miss McMillin, Lottie Mae seems to be stabilizing. We have more tests to run but need to stop and let her platelets build back up. We are limited in the amount of blood we can draw for test each day and must pace and coordinate the test in order to not take too much blood at one time," he explains, "you have the option of staying here in the hospital as we do this, or you can take her home and we will send home health to draw blood for the test."

"I think we are ready to go home," Angela decides, "she may be able to rest better there."

"Alright, I'll have the nurse come take the information to set up home health, so you can go home tomorrow," the doctor reiterates before leaving the room to make the discharge arrangements.

"Oh, Mom, I'm so glad we get to take our angel home! She must be doing better, or they wouldn't let her go," Angela says looking to me for encouragement as she begins to tidy the tiny hospital room that we've turned into home for the past week. "Do you mind if I go home to get things ready for tomorrow?"

"That's why I'm here, sweetheart. I'll gladly stay," I tell her. Angela gathers her bag of dirty laundry and kisses me before heading to the apartment.

I gently pick up our sweet baby. I arrange her NG tube and grab the IV pole and we make our way to the rocking chair in the corner of the hospital room. I look into her sweet trusting eyes as we slowly rock. I begin to sing the song I made up for her, "Lottie Mae and Maemo, Maemo and Lottie Mae..." she smiles wide then drifts off to sleep. I pray for mercy and a miracle as I try to memorize the details of her face.

Chapter Five

Thirty-four percent charge left on my iPhone and I can't leave my post on the front porch of Angela's fourplex on Magazine Street, two blocks west of Tracy's Bar and Grill, uptown New Orleans, Louisiana. It's 8:35 p.m. and I'm waiting on Lottie Mae's feeding pump to be delivered. I'm anxious about the whole situation. I have never heard of a medical company delivering equipment this late, and on a Friday night at that. I am new to these needs.

The traffic is flowing, a constant trickle, and every now and then a small group of people walk by laughing, enjoying a Friday night out in the city. A jogger runs past plugged into her phone as I sit on our front porch. The air is cool, sixty-eight degrees, October in the South. The phone signals a text message.

"Pump in route," it reads from Angela.

Well thank you baby Jesus, Mary and Joseph! I sigh a little relief. It's only now I feel the temperature dropping. I leave my watch to adjust the thermostat. Phone chimes again.

"We are leaving the hospital," the text from my mother reads. She arrived yesterday and spent the night at the hospital with Angela. She retired from her part time job at the Ace Hardware store that she had been working at since my father's passing. My father was a Baptist minister, but the real minister should have been my mother. She is narrow minded, and her strict religious views often make it a challenge to be around her.

Angela, Nanna, and Lottie Mae, pull up at the same time the medical delivery van arrives. I meet them curbside and help unload Lottie Mae's supplies and luggage. We get the feeding pump started and leave Lottie Mae in Angela's care. Jason is running Salutations, along with the newly hired help and won't be home until after midnight. Susan is working twelve to fourteen hour days on set, so for the most part, the upstairs apartment is vacant and available. We decide to let Nanna stay upstairs.

I carry her luggage and crotchet bag upstairs. I check the apartment for serial killers and rapist, looking under beds, inside closets and behind the shower curtain. It's a family tradition.

"All clear," I say as I smile and kiss her on the cheek good night and return downstairs.

Angela has pulled the baby crib next to her bed and they both are sleeping. I tiptoe past their room and crash on the futon in Lottie Mae's room and I am asleep before my head hits the pillow.

The next morning, I awake to the smell of coffee.

"Good morning Maemo," Angela smiles, "you want some coffee?'

"Would love some!" I reply.

She fixes breakfast for us and we prepare the grocery list. Lottie Mae is sleeping soundly still, giving us a little time to prepare for the next few days.

"My friend, Mary, from the Lycée Francais de la Nouvelle-Orleans School, where I taught last year, is bringing by a macaroni casserole for us. I was thinking about making meat loaf to go with it. Maybe you could go to the store a little later, after I finish making the grocery list?" Angela asks.

"Sure, sweetheart! I'll wait until Nanna wakes up and comes downstairs, then I'll go," I offer.

"Do you know what Nanna did at the hospital in front of Jason's mom night before last?" she asks, grinning ear to ear.

"I'm afraid to ask," I admit.

"Well, I guess she and Jason's mother hit it off. She felt comfortable enough to strip off her shirt and bra and walk around the hospital room topless as she changed into her nightgown, instead of changing in the bathroom, like anyone else would have done," she says, as a matter of fact.

"Oh my god!! What did Dana do?" I venture.

"Nothing, she just kept talking and crocheting, as if nothing was out of the ordinary," she tells me.

"Well, you know Nanna always walked around the house naked while she got ready to go somewhere, but I never thought anything about it. At least I am sleep walking when I go nude," I joke. I have been known to sleepwalk before.

It's not long before Nanna joins us. After breakfast, we all hover over our angel. I get the bath water ready. Angela picks out the outfit for the day and Nanna is preparing our girl for her bath. As I come around the corner to Lottie Mae's changing table, I see her eyes wide open, arms flailing wide, Angela grabs the battery powered suction machine and begins suctioning her mouth, clearing her airway. Her little arms relax as she takes a deep breath. I think, dear God, no child should go through this. The fear in her eyes cuts my soul.

Angela is calm and measured as she takes control of the situation. She is such a good mother.

"This was happening at the hospital. Sometimes she gets a mucus plug that she can't clear. They gave us a hand bulb to use at first, but this one works much better," she says, pointing to the battery-operated device. Little Lottie Mae relaxes into her mother's arm as we finish with her bath.

The day goes by quickly. I venture to Walmart alone. I am country come to town. I am fearful, but I put those thoughts out of my head and do the shopping. I am conquering a lot of my fears, simply because I have no choice. I find the city less threatening the more I am forced to go out alone on a regular basis.

I try to accomplish as many errands as I can for her today. I must return to Brookhaven tomorrow to go back to work. We have our weekly home health Monday morning meeting at 8 a.m. I also need to sit down with my boss and tell her the latest on Lottie Mae. So far, I have been able to come down on Wednesdays after work and stay through Sunday. I have been scheduling to treat patients this way since our nightmare began, so I can be here when Angela needs me.

In the evening, we make popcorn and settle in the living room on her long-oversized couch and start watching a Doris Day movie from long ago. It's something all of us can watch without offending Nanna. I excuse myself to sit on the back porch for a glass of Pinot Noir and a smoke.

Just as I inhale, the door opens slowly and my mother peers through the crack.

"The baby just went to sleep, and we laid her down. Now would be a good time for you to take your bath," she suggests.

"Thanks, Mom. I'm going to sit out here and take a little decompression break," I explain.

"A good hot bath would help you decompress," she says, still trying to persuade me.

"Please Mom, just a little alone time," I plead. After all, how old does one have to be in order to be in control over their own decisions? Fifty? Sixty? Ninety years old? Maybe, when I'm ninety, I can choose my own bath time.

She relents and closes the door. I try to be patient with her. I stay until the wine is gone. For just a moment, I release a little tension and listen to the sounds of the city, as I sit in the courtyard, staring at the moon that's almost full. I am frightened of the future, but I keep it to myself. I must be strong for Angela.

I return to the living room where Doris Day and Rock Hudson are entertaining on the television. My mother is glued to the set. I think back to when I lived at home. She wouldn't let me watch *The Golden Girls* television program because she thought they talked too dirty. I don't think she knows about Rock Hudson or she wouldn't be watching this movie. She likes taking, what she believes, is a moral stance. I don't share her beliefs, and this has been a difficult thing for her to accept.

"Are you going to take your bath now?" she asks again.

"In a little while, after the movie is over," I patiently answer.

"You would feel so much better..." she continues.

I just ignore her. Our angel is sleeping soundly in her crib. I cuddle Angela in my arms and Nanna cuddles her from the other side.

"I was just going to stay down here until you got your bath so I could help Angela with the baby," unrelenting my mother continues.

"Is the baby still sleeping?" I ask.

"Yes," she answers.

"Then I guess you can go, and we will be OK," irritation obvious in my tone by this point.

She retreats to watching the movie. I learned a long time ago to be kind with Nanna, but firm about whatever I want to do. As the credits begin to roll across the screen, I give Nanna her wish.

"OK, Mom, I'm going to take my bath now," I grin and wink.

"Well," she pauses, "only if you want to."

By the time I emerge from my bath, she has gotten her things together and is waiting for me to escort her upstairs. I hold the flashlight as we make our way up the steep narrow stairs. I am more afraid of her falling and breaking a hip, than I am of someone waiting to attack us in Susan's apartment. I hold onto her waist and guide her, like I would with a therapy patient. We both go in and I help her search the apartment.

"No serial killers, all clear!" I say as I walk up to her and give her a kiss and hug good night.

"I love you, Mom," I say looking down at this tiny woman that raised me.

"I love you, too, my darling!" she says, smiling back.

Treatment in America: Her Life Matters

Chapter Six

I glance down at my phone vibrating in my hand, 8:16 a.m., the text reads, "Call when you can." It's from Angela. I sit wedged in the middle of a ten-foot-long conference table, lined with co-workers, gathered for our weekly Monday morning home health conference meeting. I can't take it any longer and I whisper my apologies, down the row, leading to the door. My thoughts and heart are in New Orleans, not this meeting, I can't help it. I finally make it outside, where I call Angela and hold my breath unconsciously.

"Hi Mom," Angela answers in her soft whispery voice, "Lottie Mae was sick all night. She kept spitting up. Now, she is so lethargic. It is scaring me."

"If you need to take that baby to the ER, then take her darling!" I say anxiously, "Is Nanna still with you?"

"Yes, I'm waiting on her to come downstairs, so we can go. I just wanted to tell you what is going on. I've called the doctor's answering service. We are waiting for the doctor to call back. I'm not sure if she will send us to her office, or to the hospital," she whispers, so not to disturb the sleeping baby in her arms.

"I want you to call me whenever you need me," I begin, "I have patients scheduled for the next three days, then I'll be down there, but I can change my schedule anytime you need me," I add, hating myself for being poor and worried about my job, or to be specific, just eating and keeping a roof over our heads.

"Nanna is here. We will be OK. I'll call you as soon as we speak with the doctor, or if anything else changes. I promise. Don't worry, Mom! I love you!" she assures me.

I have seven patients scheduled back to back today. I skip my lunch break and opt to eat my packed lunch while I drive between homes. I love caring for my patients. It is also a distraction from the constant worry that is on my mind and in my heart.

I meet my husband and youngest daughter for dinner at our hometown Mexican restaurant. I am too exhausted to cook. Jenny is excited about playing softball, telling us about her teammates, the life of a fifteen-year-old. I try to stay present and feel her enthusiasm. My heart still aches as I wonder how things are going with our angel.

As we pull in the driveway, I get a call from Jason, my common-law-son-in-law.

"Hey, this is Jason, we are at the emergency room. They started IV fluids and medication. She has lost more weight since coming home from the hospital. It looks like they are going to admit her," his voice cracks. He sounds like he is crying.

"Are you OK?" I ask. I think of Jason as my own son. I admire how he loves my daughter and their child.

"I am tired, but I'm OK," he lies.

"Thanks for letting me know. Keep me updated. Please let me know if you need me before Thursday," I offer, knowing this is not enough. I hang up the phone.

Like a robot, I gather my things from the car, and make it into our home. I find Lance in our bedroom. I was hoping Jenny would not be near, so we could talk freely.

"You know this could be something she can't survive?" I say, looking directly into his eyes.

"I know," he says and begins to sob, so hard, his huge frame shakes. He is a gentle giant. I just hold him in my arms. I can't cry. I feel like this is a bad nightmare, and any minute, I am going to wake up, and let out a sigh of relief. We say nothing else. We retreat to our usual separate spots in the house. He watches news stories of the day on the living room couch. I am in the computer room, with a full glass of Captain Morgan spiced rum and diet coke, while I enjoy a smoke. I find relief, relaxation, playing computer solitaire, and listening to the radio. Each of us waiting on the next phone call about Lottie Mae.

7:30 a.m. my phone rings. I check caller ID. It's Angela. I immediately answer it.

"Angela?" I ask as my anxiety level rises.

"Hey Mom, I wanted to give you an update," she says with a happy note to her voice, "Lottie Mae is doing better. We had a little scare last night. She seemed to have an allergic reaction from the pacifier the hospital gave her. It was shaped like her Nuk, but it was brown. She began to swell up on half of her face and so they gave her some Benadryl through her IV and she is fine now. I am so tired. I have been up two nights in a row with her. Nanna is here, but she's no Maemo."

I smile at her kind words, "Maemo wishes she could be there."

"It's OK, Mom. You do what you have to do for your job. Lottie Mae's doing well now. She even drank two ounces from a bottle," Angela reports, always optimistic and kind.

"Well, I hate not being there. This is one of those times, again, I wish to be rich," I say hating the limitations of our circumstance.

"Really, Mom, you've done so much already. Anyway, Nanna is here, and Jason's Mom is coming over from Lake Charles. I want you to stay and work, so you can cook and bring Thanksgiving dinner," she says. Always the planner, even in the hospital tending to her sweet Lottie Mae. She continues to persuade me, "Papa Joe, Jason's dad, is smoking a turkey, Granny Dana is making the dressing. I thought you could make dessert and a couple of sides. Could Dad bring some chairs from the country club?"

"Yes, sweetheart. OK then, sounds like you have it all worked out," I concede before hanging up the phone.

Later that night, I try to fall asleep, but my thoughts won't let me rest. I get out of bed and stop trying to fight the insomnia. Angela had said the baby was improving a little. Still, the geneticist report about Zellweger, is heavy in my thoughts. I take a cigarette from my silver, engraved case, light my Virginia Slim, inhale deep. I take a sip of diet coke and Captain Morgan spiced rum. I turn on the radio, then the computer, then click solitaire. I try to zone out. I try to escape my feelings of constant worry about Lottie Mae...is she going to survive this? I take a sip of sweetness and reassure myself, remembering that she is doing a little better, Angela had said as much.

On the radio, several stations are talking about Thanksgiving that is fast approaching in two days. I wonder how I am supposed to work, take care of my home, cook a holiday meal and drive to New Orleans within forty-eight hours. That's depressing. My next thoughts return to being thankful for every moment I've spent with Lottie Mae. Just three short months and she has touched my heart in a life transforming way. I will never be the same.

Chapter Seven

I begin my day early on this Thanksgiving eve. I have six patients, from the Walthall County line, to Hazlehurst, Mississippi, on my schedule today. I make a homemade egg and cheese English muffin for breakfast and pour my coffee to go. I bring a packed lunch, water and soft drinks to help me through the day, without having to stop. Before leaving home, I fax my previous day's work and head out the door. I push my emotions aside, compartmentalized to do what needs to be done.

Steady day of occupational therapy, successfully making the most of my time. After I leave my last patient's home, I circle around to my office. I update my boss on Lottie Mae's current hospitalization, followed by awkward silence. My new boss is as cold as ice.

Once home, I rush to prepare my grocery list. I have a banana split pie, asparagus casserole, and English pea salad to prepare before I head south. Jenny joins me and I let her drive us to Walmart with her new driving permit. We make a game out of the task, dividing our list in half and then speed shopping.

Returning home, we work together to complete each dish and arrange them in the refrigerator, until time to load up. I lay down on the floor, in the middle of the kitchen, after placing the last casserole dish in.

"My back is in spasms. I need to lay here for just five minutes," I explain to Jenny, as she looks down at me, on the floor, with a concerned look on her face.

"I want to ride down with you tonight. If that's OK?" she offers.

"Of course, it's OK," I answer surprised, "I just thought you were hanging out with your friends tonight and coming down tomorrow with Lance."

"I was going to hang out with Madison and Haley, but I want to be with you, more," she says, still leaning over me and smiling.

"Awe, that is so sweet! Get packed and we'll get on the road about 8 p.m.," I say as she leaves me resting on the floor. The spasms finally subside, allowing me to finish packing for the trip, and to return to Lottie Mae. I manage to take a few minutes to relax my mind with a quick smoke on the back porch, compliments of Jason. Just a little Cannabis to take my anxiety level down and allow the knots between my shoulders to disappear, and I get my second wind. Just fifteen minutes of nothingness, no responsibilities, a little boost for my mental health that helps tremendously. It's not long before the break is over, and we are on our way.

We arrive slightly before 10 p.m. We find a spot to parallel park on Magazine Street. As we unload our things, I see a small frame female walking around the corner.

"Mom? Jenny?" a familiar voice calls out.

"Susan?" Jenny and I say at the same time.

"I was just hanging out with my moped gang friends at Parasol's," Susan begins as we group hug on the sidewalk. "I've been working some crazy hours." Susan's career in fashion design has landed her working in the design department, on her first feature film, as a SAG (Screen Actors Guild) member.

"I understand! It's good to take a break from life every now and then!" I continue, "Can you help us get this stuff in. I brought some casseroles and dessert for tomorrow. Lance is driving down tomorrow with some chess pies, wine, and chairs from the country club."

We unload the car and make our way to our assigned rooms. I am sharing a bed with my sister, who is visiting from North Louisiana. I tiptoe in, trying not to wake her. She is passed out, motionless, as I fumble with my bags. I check to see if she is breathing. Yes, she is breathing. I worry about the self-medicating practices she has employed in the past and her battles with bipolar disorder. I tiptoe out of the room. Susan is with Jenny in the kitchen. As I join them, she hands me a gift bag.

"This is from Angela," Susan tells me, "she said to call her, before you open it."

I call Angela and put her on speaker as I prepare to open my surprise package. I proceed to remove the tissue paper hiding a Rudolf the red nose reindeer robe inside. I slip it on and squeal with delight as Susan takes my picture.

"I LOVE IT!" I scream, "by the way, you are on speaker, and Susan is here."

"Your picture is hilarious!" Angela giggles at the image Susan sent her, "Is Nanna or Aunt Lynn up?"

"No, looks like everyone but Susan, me and Jenny are asleep," I reply.

"OK, well, can you clean the courtyard in the morning, Susan?" Angela ask, "Mom, can you come to the hospital around 10 a.m. to help me with Lottie Mae? I want to come back to the house to get everything ready?"

"Of course, darling," I reply.

"Hi Angela," Jenny chimes in as she heads up the stairs to find her assigned spot, sleeping next to her grandmother, on a cot, in Susan's apartment.

After finalizing the schedule for tomorrow's Thanksgiving meal, we hang up the phone. Susan and I retire to the balcony of her apartment to talk. She drinks her Pabst Blue Ribbon beer while I smoke a little cannabis. Our conversation runs deep. We comfort each other. We both agree that we are so blessed to have a good family. We have each other no matter what the future holds.

Treatment in America: Her Life Matters

Chapter Eight

I wake up ten minutes before my 7 a.m. alarm sounds. I look around the room trying to remember where I am. I slowly recognize Susan's apartment and my sister as she starts to show signs of life.

"Hi," she says as she rolls over, "what time did you get here?"

"It was late. You were passed out. I checked to see if you were breathing," I say half picking, still seriously concerned. Several years ago, I confronted her about prescription vials of pain medications I found, when she shared an apartment with Angela, in Lafayette. She is an adult. There is little influence I have on her, so I choose not to get into it with her now.

"I didn't hear you. I am just coming off a week of nights," she explains her nursing schedule, "I was t-i-r-e-d! (she spells out loud) What are you doing?"

"I am going to the hospital. Angela planned the whole day. She asked if I would come stay with Lottie Mae at the hospital, so she can come home and prepare the house for Thanksgiving. I brought my casseroles last night and put notes on each one, listing how long to cook, and what temperature to set the stove. I stacked them in the refrigerator. Do you want to stay here and help organize or come to the hospital with me?"

"Dear god, how many are we fixing for?" Lynn, my baby sister asks.

"Jason and his mom, dad, sister, brother and sister-in-law with their three children are coming. All of mine, except Jackson, will be here. Jackson is stationed in Oklahoma and won't have leave for a while. Angela even invited Garry and his new girlfriend," I say, trying to count them all in my head, as I do a roll call.

"Why, in the hell, are you doing all this?" Lynn asks.

"Angela wants to. I am just trying to help make her feel better. I am exhausted myself. I don't think this is a good idea, but it's already done. Angela says she wants to keep things as normal as possible. At least Jason's mom and dad are bringing the turkey and dressing," I add.

"I will go with you to the hospital. I am so sorry I haven't been around to help you," she looks at me, waiting on my reaction.

"It's OK," I lie, "I know you have the girls that keep you busy."

"I know, but I want to be there for you," she says, and I believe her, but I know they are empty words. It was only a couple of years ago, when she was hospitalized twice for her breakdown. I dropped everything to take care of my nieces and her. There have been times when her illness has made her into a liar. She has thrown me under the bus, more times than I can count, but I know it's not her, it's her bipolar disorder. I love her, anyway.

I grab my clothes and take my turn in the bathroom getting ready. Once dressed, I gather the load of baby laundry that I finished last night. We wave at Susan in the backyard, before heading to where my car is parked, on Magazine Street.

As I drive, I keep thinking to myself, this is so bizarre to have a big celebration, when our Lottie Mae is in the hospital. Angela is trying so hard to keep everything normal, but it isn't normal. I didn't tell her not to do it. If this family get together makes her feel better, then I see no harm in going along with her plans. I am only risking total exhaustion.

Granny Dana, Jason's mother, and his sister-in-law are visiting at the hospital when we arrive at 8:45 a.m. His sister-in-law, Connie, is rocking Lottie Mae and offers to let me hold her. I eagerly accept, taking my little angel gently in my arms. She begins stirring a little. She smiles at me and my heart skips a beat. My Lottie Mae is still able to smile.

The doctor walks in doing rounds, as Angela is gathering her bags, preparing to run home, just a couple of miles from our new world of hospital tests.

"How is our little one and mother doing today?" he asks.

"Hi," Angela begins in her soft poised voice, "I am glad I get to talk to you! We are still having trouble with her rest being interrupted for the blood test. The other doctors don't seem to be communicating and are not coordinating the tests very well."

"Yes, we are working on that," he assures her, as he takes our angel and begins doing his assessment. He is receptive and encouraging, saying as he exits, "I will be meeting with the team to correct this!"

I gently pick up our angel and sit in the rocker. Angela and I finish going over the list of instructions for cooking the casseroles, as I rock Lottie Mae.

"Thanks Mom," Angela whispers in my ear as she hugs me good-bye.

"Don't worry about anything," Granny Dana adds, "Papa Joe cooked a turkey, and I made some dressing, along with some other sides. We are going to have a good meal!"

"Thank you, Dana," I tell her. I think that at least this is bringing us together. We are all here, because of our love for this precious angel.

Soon the room is quiet. Jason's family heads to the house with the turkey and dressing. My sister decides to ride with Angela, as I assure them that I will be fine alone with my sweet grandbaby.

"Lottie Mae and Maemo, Maemo and Lottie Mae," I sing, "We love each other, everyday!" She smiles wide as I continue rocking, praying in my head, a thank you prayer, and begging God to heal her. I believe God can do anything. I am just not sure it's in his plan. I can't help but pray and hope he has mercy on us. The time flies as I hold this innocent bundle of love. I walk with her on my shoulder, nuzzling my nose into her lavender scented hair. She is weak and doesn't do much kicking. She tries to hold her head up, but she is too weak. It's not long before she is sleeping sweetly. I look down from our hospital room window. I can see a tennis center and ladies playing. I think how my life is changing. I am sad and afraid, but I don't want to waste the precious moments I have with her worrying. I go back to the rocking chair, careful to arrange the feeding, oxygen and catheter tubing, so it doesn't pull on her, as we sit and rock.

After a couple of hours solo, Jason returns with his father, Joe.

"Hi Jamie, it's time for the men to take over," Jason says, smiling as he enters the room, "Angela is waiting for you. We already ate. She has it arranged so we can eat in shifts. You know your daughter, always planning. How is my princess?"

"She has been sleeping for the most part," I smile and say, "I haven't put her down." I gently place her in her dad's arms and head back to Magazine Street.

When I get to Angela's apartment, I follow the sound of music coming from the courtyard, in the rear of the complex. As I open the back door to the courtyard, I see a washtub full of ice and drinks. There is a side table with a red checkered tablecloth, holding Angela's replica antique turntable, playing a Johnny Cash LP. The food table is full. Turkey, dressing, sweet potato casserole, string bean casserole, banana split pie, and chess pies cover the center table. There are little round patio lights strung overhead. The banana plants that line the perimeter of the courtyard complete the feel of a tropical oasis for our holiday meal. I recognize the white folding chairs and look for Lance. We smile at each other.

Garry, my first husband, Angela's biological father, arrives with his new girlfriend. They bring biscuits. I am not too thrilled with this one. I had become friends with his second wife and felt sad that she had been replaced. This one is a nurse that he had dated years ago, before we were married. I am civilized and Southern, so I just smile and say, "Bless your heart!" Everyone knows that is Southern for "Fuck you!" Despite the circumstances, the day is good. We visit and share a meal.

"What are your plans?" Lance leans in and asks as he takes my hand.

"I am going to stay with Angela at the hospital tonight. Susan is going to help Jason at the wine bar. Jenny has been asking when you are leaving to take her back?" I say.

"Well, she can wait a little while longer," he begins, "I think I'm going to head back in a couple of hours."

"I know. She said she needs to go to her grandmother's," I explain, "I told her, it will be OK. Surely, they will understand. She's just being a teenager."

My nephew, Trent Purvis, shows up after his shift as Director of Nurses on the third floor of Touro Hospital, that is less than two miles from our apartment.

"Hi Aunt Jamie," Trent says as he kisses my cheek.

"I'm so glad you were able to make it! Do you have to work every holiday?" I ask.

"Seems that way. I have been wanting to stop by and check on you. How are you holding up?" Trent asks.

"I take it one day at a time. I am still working home health but have been able to schedule all my patients Monday through Wednesday, so

I can come down, and help Thursday through Sunday. Jason's mom has been staying here on the days I am working. She has a special needs daughter, so her time is limited also. The doctor's preliminary findings are discouraging. They believe she has a biogenesis cell disorder called Zellweger. They are going to replace her NG tube with a permanent feeding tube, before she can come home, because she can only absorb nutrition at a slow rate. I am so happy you stopped by! I miss you!" I tell him as we make our way to sit on the front porch.

"Do you ever hear from my dad?" he asks.

"No, not a word. Since he started dating Jane, it's like he has disappeared," I reply.

"I don't know why he is like that Aunt Jamie," Trent says as he looks at the ground, "I can't imagine not being there for my sister."

"Well, don't you worry about it, sweetheart. I am just happy you are here!" I say, changing the subject. I don't know where to begin in telling him how my relationship with his father, my brother, has always been damaged. I don't have the energy for it. I am grateful that my nephew is a kind soul and I choose to focus on our relationship instead. We continue to visit for the next half hour, before he says his good-bye.

"Hey sweetheart, I am about to go," Lance says as he joins me on the porch, "Jenny has been asking to leave every fifteen minutes."

"I appreciate you taking care of her," I tell him.

"I know," he says, "she misses you."

"I miss her too, but I can't help it. I need to be here for Angela. I don't think she could make it without me," I explain.

"Tell them they can come stay with us," Lance offers.

"But sweetheart, all the specialists are here. They wouldn't know what to do for her back home in Mississippi," I say.

"Jenny needs you, too," he doesn't relent.

"Well, Jenny is a healthy fifteen-year-old. She will be fine. Besides Jason's job is here. Their business is here. It's not my choice where they live," I am beginning to become agitated, "I am too tired to have this conversation."

"I'm sorry," he says as he relaxes his stand, "I miss you."

"I am sorry, too," I say as we hug, "I have to be here. We will make it through this."

Treatment in America: Her Life Matters

Chapter Nine

I sleep at the hospital with Angela and Lottie Mae. Jason and Susan are working at Salutations, Angela and Jason's wine and cheese dive, located in the Faubourg Marigny neighborhood, of New Orleans. The three of us went to sleep around 9:30 p.m. and didn't wake until 3 a.m., when the nurse came in. Lottie Mae fell back to sleep, after Angela changed her diaper, and turned her. By 5:45 a.m., she is up again, and ready to play.

"Go back to sleep, sweetheart. I'll take the first shift this morning," I whisper to Angela, as she peers with squinted eyes, from underneath her sleep mask. She lays back down as I make my way to Lottie Mae's crib. Our little angel makes eye contact with me as I lean over to change her diaper. Oh no, I see more bright red droplets in her diaper. I press the nurse call button and say, "Angela, there is more blood in her diaper. I'm calling the nurse."

The nurse comes prepared and takes a specimen to send to the lab and calls the doctor. Garry arrives with pastries and coffee, just as the nurse exits the room.

"Good morning! I brought breakfast," he says smiling as he enters the room. "Angela, do you want to go for a run with me this morning, before the doctors make their rounds?"

"That is a good idea!" I say with encouragement.

Angela has been reluctant to leave Lottie Mae's side, except for short periods of time. When she first became ill, Angela would barely even go to the cafeteria. She decides a run might be helpful to fight the dark depression she is beginning to experience.

Just as they return from their jog, the GI specialist arrives.

"It's spotty, not clotty," the elderly doctor with a blue checkered bow tie explains, "As long as it's spotty, things should be fine. Her labs look good this morning. I may let her go home tomorrow."

"But she lost weight?" I ask, questioning his decision to send her home so soon.

"I stopped the IV fluids last night. A small weight loss is to be expected," he adds.

"I think it's too early," I blurt out.

"I am so excited we can go home," Angela's face brightens as she adds, "I am ready to get out of here!"

I still think it's too early to be discharged, but I'm just Maemo. Angela is excited and I don't want to ruin her mood. I've already said how I feel, so I try to let it go. It's hard to trust the doctor, after the third hospital admit, in the past two months, under his care.

"I think I will go home when Jason gets here. I want to clean the apartment, wash all the clothes, get some groceries and prepare for Lottie Mae to come home," I say, trying to keep things positive, "I'll come back to spend the night."

"I can stay with Angela, until he gets here," Garry offers.

"Thank you! I guess I'll go ahead and leave, so I can get back before it's too late," I say.

I return to Angela's empty apartment. Everyone has left and returned to their respective houses. It is quiet, except for the steady sound of cars passing outside, on Magazine Street. I begin cleaning. It's therapeutic for me. I try not to think of what we are going through. I try to keep faith, but it is hard. I pray to God and beg for a miracle. I cry as I clean. It feels hopeless. I know I must be strong now for Angela.

"RING, RING, RING," the doorbell summons my attention from my mental anguish.

"Hi, I'm Margaret. I met you at Lottie Mae's baby shower. Angela teaches my daughter at *Lycée Francais de la Nouvelle*. Some of the other mothers and I want to help. We love your daughter. She has been such a great teacher and so sweet. We want to take turns bringing food. I brought you a Mexican casserole," says the smiling, short, stout lady holding a covered dish.

"Oh my! That is so sweet! Come on in," I say as I hold the door wide for her.

"We organized it so that we rotate nights. A different parent will be coming by, every other day," she tells me as she comes inside.

"I don't know what to say. Thank you, so much! You are so kind and thoughtful," I gush, feeling the hot stream of tears beginning to brim in my eyes. Kindness has always moved me.

She places the dish on the dining room table.

"Stephanie will be coming Monday," she quickly adds, as she makes her way back to the front door. We hug. "We want you to know, we are here for you!"

"I appreciate this more than I can say!" I shout, as she hurries down the walkway, to her car. I finish folding the last load of clothes and pack my overnight bag. One smoke break before I head back to the hospital.

As I get closer to Lottie Mae's room, I hear a guitar and an angelic voice singing. I ease the door open to find Cindy, Angela's friend, that regularly performs at her wine dive. She is serenading Lottie Mae, Angela, Jason, and Susan. Such a sweet and unexpected gift. She is performing at Salutations tonight and took time out of her day for a special private concert. Her voice holds me mesmerized, so soft and perfect pitch. Lottie Mae smiles in response as Angela holds her near.

"That was beautiful," I tell the small framed lady with the guitar.

"Yes, thank you so much Cindy!" Angela joins in.

"My pleasure! I'm about to head over to Salutations, but I wanted to see Lottie Mae first," she answers, smiling at Lottie Mae.

"I'm heading out, too," Jason adds, "I have a new hire coming to help."

"Yes, I hired a new girl, Tina, to fill in, since I'm at the hospital, and can't be there as much," Angela tells us, "she reminds me of myself."

"OK, Maemo is here. So you guys do whatever you need to do," I tell the small group. Jason and Cindy leave to make the twenty-minute drive across town.

"Mom, do you mind if I take Angela to a movie?" Susan asks.

"I think that is a good idea," I say. I had a hard time consoling Angela this morning. She has been crying most of the day. Maybe a movie can give her a little break from reality.

Soon the room is quiet. Just me and Lottie Mae. She is sleeping in the hospital crib, with small string lights woven around the dowels and rails, illuminating with soft light, the curves of her face. I pull the rocking chair near her crib so I can see her better. There is nowhere else I'd rather be.

The next morning the GI doctor's plans change.

"We are going to keep her a little longer," Dr. Grant begins, as he makes his morning rounds, "She has lost another pound and the bright red streaks of blood are persisting."

"We have to stay?" Angela interrupts in her small soft voice.

"I think we need to take a step back, decrease the rate of formula, start Pedialyte and antibiotics to kill some of the bacteria in her intestine's that may be causing her to have a high metabolism," he dryly explains.

I hope he knows what he is talking about. I am relieved he is keeping her. She is so weak. Her skin color is yellowish to me, but he won't discuss this when I ask about it. I still think he is an asshole.

Angela is visibly upset as the doctor leaves. I just hold her as she sobs. My heart is breaking for her.

"Hey," Garry says as he opens the door, "what's going on?"

"You just missed the GI specialist. We are staying a little longer," I say. I get him caught up on the details as Angela composes herself.

"Why don't you and Angela go for a walk and get some sunshine?" I ask, hoping it might help her to get outside for a little while.

They leave to take a walk outside and hopefully find comfort from being in nature. I go to the crib where my heart is. I bend down and gently take sweet Lottie Mae into my arms. Her eyes are partially open. This is how she sleeps. I make sure to hold the feeding tube, so that the weight of the tubing, doesn't pull on the tape, holding it to her delicate skin. I kiss her cheek as we settle into the rocking chair.

The humidifier blows a misty cloud that leaves condensation forming on the bed rails. The humidity helps her breathe easier. I scan the bedside table for the suction bulb, just in case her secretions become too thick, and she chokes. I pray to myself, "Dear God, please forgive me of my sin, and have mercy, and hear my prayer. My sweet Lottie Mae needs a miracle and you're the only one that can do this. Please, please heal her. Lord she is suffering so much, and Angela is hurting...it's more than I can bear...I don't mean to question you God, but I don't understand, and my heart is breaking," as tears flow from my eyes.

Angela seems a little more composed after she and Garry return from walking. As they take turns washing their hands, there is a knock at the door. I stop gathering my belongings and open the door. It's Angela's best friend, Krista, and her husband, Dave, from Hattiesburg, Mississippi.

"Oh Krista, it's so good to see you!" I say as I hug her neck. "Thank you both for coming!"

"I had to come," she says, squeezing me hard.

"I hate to leave, but I have to work in the morning. I wish I didn't have to go," I say as I resume gathering my overnight bag and straightening the room.

Garry offers to help me with my bag. We leave our daughter with her childhood best friend and see her spirits are lifted by Krista's visit.

"You're a good mother Jamie. I'm glad Angela has you," Garry says as he puts my bags into my SUV.

"You're a good father, too," I say right back and mean it.

I drive the two hours home to Mississippi without the radio on, lost in thought. I am concerned for my sweet baby. All I can think about is that I may never get to hold her again.

Treatment in America: Her Life Matters

Chapter Ten

Monday, workday, goes by as usual. The day is steady with one patient after another. The weather is rainy and cold. It fits my mood. My heart and thoughts are at Children's Hospital, room 314. The room that has photos covering every wall and door, with balloons and Christmas lights decorating the crib. Angela has transformed the cold sterile environment into a cozy place to heal.

I call her between patients, but my call goes to voice mail.

"Hey sweetheart. It's Maemo. I'm just checking on my babies. I'm working today, love you, will catch up with you later." I speak into my phone.

I hang up the phone and continue with my day. I get to my next appointment. Just as I just finish checking my elderly patient's blood pressure, I get a text.

"New GI doctor wants to test her poop and check with the nutritionist about the Pedialyte/formula ratio, to see if he has any recommendations. She gained weight today, but acts like her tummy hurts," Angela's message reads.

I read it quickly, then compartmentalize the information. I can't think too much about the seriousness of the situation. It is time for faith and so I pray and pray and pray. Every time I think of Lottie Mae, I pray, which turns out, is about every two minutes. I work hard to just focus on my patients, one at a time. As I head home, my phone begins to ring.

"Mom, can you meet me at Bebe's? I need a dress for the athletic banquet tonight. Maddie's mom said she could drop me off," Jenny asks.

I glance at my car clock, 5:05 p.m.

"Ok, I am on my way. I'll be cutting it close, but I should be there by 5:25 p.m.," I say, knowing they close at 5:30 p.m. Jenny has always been low maintenance. I've been so busy with Lottie Mae that it's been hard for me to spend a lot of mother-daughter time. I ask, "Do you need shoes?"

"No, I have some I can wear. I just don't have any dresses that fit," she explains.

I make it to the store in time to buy her dress before they close. At the banquet, Jenny won a trophy for best offensive player, leading the team with a .567 batting average. She also made all district player. She is beautiful and grown up on the outside, but on the inside, she is still my little girl, just a Freshman in high school. It's so challenging to be there for her and still be there for Angela, as I split my time between them.

Tuesday's work schedule takes me toward the Country Club area. Lance encourages me to go see my friends and play tennis after work. It is one evening we aren't scheduled to be at a hospital or a ballfield. I have been missing my two best friends, so I decide to go. It has been our routine, to play tennis, and then go sit at the bar, on the terrace, to discuss life, and catch up.

"Did you hear what that Tammy said to me?" I say to my two besties.

"I heard her," Suzy says, "She questions everything you say."

"Always," I add.

"What did she say?" Betsy asks as she comes to the table carrying two beers and a rum and diet coke.

"Sam, our new tennis pro, was asking me about Lottie Mae when I got to the court. I told him about Zellweger Disorder and what we are dealing with. Then Tammy butts in and tells me I'm exaggerating. It probably isn't that bad," I tell my sympathetic listeners, "I didn't have the energy to set her straight."

"She's always a bitch," Betsy states adding, "Don't even think about her. You've got enough to deal with."

"It's so good to see you two. I've been missing you both. I don't have the patience to deal with these country club bitches!" I say as we laugh and try to distract ourselves from what I am going through. I have been friends with these two for ten years and I like the witty banter we share.

On my way home, I call Angela to catch up.

"Hey, are you still up?" I ask Angela as she answers her phone.

"Yes, I'm glad you called," she begins, "They decided to go ahead with the surgery tomorrow to replace the nasal gastric feeding tube with a peg tube."

"Should I come down there to be with you?" I ask, knowing I'm needed, but my job is keeping me tied here.

"It's OK, Mom. Jason is here with me. I want you to come down when you finish up your work week. Jason's mom and dad are coming. I will be OK, I promise," she assures me.

"Let me know when she's out of surgery. I love you darling. I'll talk with you tomorrow," I say as I hang up the phone.

I get up an hour earlier than usual the next morning.

"Lance, the baby is having surgery today. Angela said to wait and just come down tomorrow, but I don't know how I'm going to make it through the day," I tell him.

"I have a board meeting I'm getting ready for today. Let me know when you hear from them. I'll be putting packets together," he says. He has been the general manager at Fernwood Country Club for twelve years. Not an easy task with the changing economy and members with champagne taste and beer budgets. I have been jealous for years of all the time devoted to the country club that didn't seem balanced to the time devoted to making our life together.

"Also, Jenny has a soccer game tonight," I add as we try to get on the same page.

"I will meet you there. I may be running a little late," he says, heading out the door.

I push all my thoughts aside, and once again, take one patient after another, until finally number seven, and I head to West Lincoln school. While in route the call comes.

"Mom, the surgery went well. She is in recovery. The doctors are saying she can come home tomorrow," Angela informs me.

"Tomorrow? That soon?" I ask in disbelief.

"I think she can rest better at home," sweet Angela says, trying to make me feel better.

"Well, I'm so glad the surgery went well. I will try to come down after my last patient, tomorrow. I should get into the city around 8 p.m.," I say, trying to get our plans coordinated, while we have a moment to talk.

"Thank you, Mama. I love you!" she tells me.

"I love you, too!" I say as I hang up the phone and pull into the parking lot beside the school's soccer field.

It is forty degrees. Cold for the South. I put on my gloves, hat, two coats, grab the folding chairs and head to the visitor's side. I see Lance waiting for me, with a propane tank on a dolly, with a heater mounted on top. First quarter, Jenny and a West Lincoln player are both running full speed for the ball. Jenny drops her shoulder and drives the opponent, who goes flying ten feet before landing on her side. A yellow flag follows. Penalty called. At least sports give her an outlet for all the pent-up emotions. Mental note to self, talk to Jenny about her feelings.

Chapter Eleven

The next morning, I get up two hours before my alarm goes off. I can't stop thinking about Lottie Mae. After tossing and turning, for most of the night, I quit fighting it. I pack my clothes for the weekend, organize my work folders for each patient scheduled, pack my lunch, and head toward my first patient's home, before the sun rises.

I get a text from the office cancelling my last appointment, my patient is unavailable, so this frees up my afternoon. I am so happy to be on my way to see our Lottie Mae. If the traffic is not bad, I should be there by 4 p.m. I feel so helpless being two hours away. I should have been there yesterday for her surgery. I am interrupted from my thoughts by the ringing of my cell phone.

"Hi Jamie," she greets me, "this is your mother."

"Hi Mom," I answer.

"I went to the doctor about my shoulder this morning," she says, "He wants to do surgery."

"What?" I ask. I am upset, because she won't listen to my recommendations, for easing the pain. I was hoping she would postpone the surgery, until after we get through this difficult time with Lottie Mae. She won't even try.

"He said I could send you the report, so you can see why I need to have it done," she goes on to say.

"Mom, it's not that. I know you have been hurting, but I need you now. I want you to postpone it, while Lottie Mae is sick," I try to explain.

"I am going to mail it to you," she interrupts, "I can't put it off."

"Mom, I'm a therapist. You might want to take advantage of that. I think, if you let that arm rest, limit how you…," I repeat the instructions, trying to persuade her, but she is relentless.

"I'm sorry, I can't even hold the baby now," she interrupts, raising her voice.

"You have two arms. You can just be here for emotional support. It's terrible timing, Mom. We don't know how much longer we have," I continue trying to convince her but to no avail. This awakens old wounds from my youth.

I excuse myself and hang up the phone. I am so upset with her. She is stubborn and inflexible. It is useless to keep explaining. I think about my mother as I drive on auto pilot down the interstate. I think back to when I asked her and dad to come help me, when I was married to Jenny's father. He had beaten me mercilessly, held a shotgun to my head, and threatened to kill me, and the kids. He kidnapped me, and I had to jump from his truck, on Highway Eighty-Four, to get away from him. I called my parents, and asked them to come help me, but she said they couldn't come, because she had to teach Sunday school class, and Dad must preach. I survived that nightmare. I will survive this, too.

When I reached Angela's, she is getting Lottie Mae ready for an outing.

"Mom, so glad you're here! Wow, you made great time. I was just about to take her around the block for a stroller ride," she says, smiling as she opens the door.

"Sounds wonderful! Let me kiss that baby first!" I say as I pick Lottie Mae up into my arms. I breath the sweet scent of her hair as I kiss her cheek. She opens her little mouth, like a baby bird, she turns her head toward me, giving sweet kisses back. My heart melts.

After unloading my weekend luggage, we take off west, on Magazine Street. The air is perfect, sixty-five degrees. A gentle breeze blows through the tree top canopy over our heads. Lottie Mae smiles as the sunlight caresses her face. She loves strolling. We have her feeding pump, in her backpack, hanging on the stroller. I wonder if people can tell our baby is sick, as we pass strangers, on the sidewalk.

"We have a new pediatrician. Her practice is based at Tulane Medical Center. She is a specialist for children with rare diseases. She is supposed to help us manage her care from home, utilizing home health, instead of going to the ER," Angela explains. I am glad to hear this.

"When is Lottie Mae's next appointment with her?" I ask.

"Next Thursday." She answers, just as a small beeping sound begins to emit from the backpack, carrying the feeding pump.

"What is that noise?" I ask, as I watch her unzip the backpack, and start pressing buttons on the control panel of the small square device housing tubing, connecting our angel to a bag of formula.

"It's the pump. Sometimes, it must be reset," Angela says, placing the feeding pump back in the backpack. Little Lottie Mae begins to grunt, letting us know she doesn't like stopping for long. I admire how she gently repositions Lottie Mae, adjusting her little pink crocheted hat with yellow ribbon. "I think this is enough stimulation for one afternoon. Let's head back."

"Nanna called and said she is going to have shoulder surgery," I share my news, as we turn the corner, to walk back down the tree lined row of one-hundred-fifty to two-hundred-year-old southern homes, with meticulously maintained, manicured lawns. "That's going to have her out for the next three months or so."

"Oh no," Angela says, "Well, at least we have Maemo! We better hurry back to the house. I forgot one of my former student's mom is bringing a casserole by."

We make it back just in time to see Jason, my common-law-son-in-law, as he makes a quick clothing change from his day job uniform at Breaux Mart, to his evening chef's uniform, before heading to Salutations. They hired a new waitress a few weeks ago, Angela describes her as her "mini me." This will allow Angela to stay home with Lottie Mae.

I meet Tiffany, another parent from Lycée Francais Elementary School, as she drops off spaghetti and garlic bread for our dinner. She and her two daughters stay for a short visit. I am touched by her kindness and sweet words, as she shares how much her daughter loves being in Angela's class. We are very grateful. My phone rings as we say our good-byes.

"Lance?" I ask, reading caller ID.

"Hey sweetheart," he begins, "how is our sweet angel doing?"

"She has had a good day, Paw-Paw," I answer, "Is everything OK?"

"No. Our house was broken into. Jenny came home from school with her friends and saw the garage door halfway open. Instead of calling the police, they armed themselves with softball bats and a golf iron and proceeded inside to get the burglar," he says, with frustration.

"Oh my god! I guess I haven't taught my child anything. Doesn't she know a bat is worthless, if the burglar has a gun? Is she OK? Anything missing?" I ask, in shock.

"She is OK. No one was there, thank God. She is just scared and shaken up. It looks like they kicked in the back door, then tried to go out the garage door, but were too stupid to press the button to open it. All I can see missing is the TV from the living room and our big jug of coins we had in our bedroom. I talked to her about how dangerous it was to go inside. I told her if this ever happens again, go to the neighbor's house, and wait for the police. The person, or persons, could still be inside, armed and dangerous. Speaking of police, you want to hear what they said when I called?" he asks.

"I'm afraid to ask," I say.

"I call down to the station and say I want to report a burglary. They said, 'What do you want us to do about it?' I told them, you're the damn police department. I just told you someone broke into my home. What do you think I want you to do? Go over to my house and see if they are still there. I am at work, thirty minutes away, and will be there as fast as I can."

"That is why people talk about the South," I interject.

"I had already told Jenny to go over to the Smith's, our neighbor, and wait there, until I get home. I know the chance of finding out who did this is slim to none, but that is beside the point. Anyway, they finally came and did a report. Jenny is too scared to stay here tonight and is going to her grandmother's house. I just propped a chair against the door, until I can get it fixed, tomorrow," he explains.

"Can we please get an alarm system? I can come home tonight, if you need me to," I offer.

"I will get an alarm system, so you don't worry. I'm fine. There's nothing you can do. Just take care of our little one and give Angela my love. I love you," he says.

"I love you, too!" I say, before hanging up. My head is reeling. How much bad luck can one person have?

The rest of the weekend, we spend taking more walks uptown, singing along with Thomas the Tank Engine musical book, and rocking our angel. Angela is relentlessly researching the internet for any helpful information for fighting this disease. She joins the Global Foundation for Peroxisomal Disorders, so she can connect and communicate with other families, that are also fighting this nightmare disease.

"I'm going to talk to our new pediatrician about the suggestions of vitamin K, to help with clotting, and fish oil, to help with her brain functioning. I am still not giving up on that study in Amsterdam," she shares her thoughts with me as I eat my breakfast, and prepare to leave and head north, to be back in time to work on Monday.

"I would definitely talk to the pediatrician before doing anything different, just in case it might interfere with her medications. About that study in Amsterdam, it takes a large control group to yield valid results. I thought it was only three children in that study and that isn't enough. I hate leaving you," I say, as I gather my plate and place it in the sink.

"I know. Granny Dana should be here around noon. We have an appointment with the geneticist this week. He has the blood test results from two months ago, that will tell us a little more about where she falls on the spectrum. Other than that, we will just be here, waiting for you to come back," she updates me, before I leave to head back to my other life.

Treatment in America: Her Life Matters

Chapter Twelve

As I sit in the circle around the office conference table, I feel irritated as I listen to my supervising OTR complain about her life. I keep quiet and work on my charting. Our director comes in and starts our weekly meeting. As she goes through the list of patients scheduled for case conference, I think about how life has changed. Just a few months ago, I was begging for patients, and even volunteered to help with marketing. Today, I hope they don't assign more patients. I just want to meet my responsibilities, without adding to my schedule. Life has become a balancing act between helping with Lottie Mae, in Louisiana, and taking care of my family, and job, in Mississippi. As the meeting ends, the director asks me to stop by her office before I leave. This is not good, I think to myself.

"Hi Mrs. Joyce," I greet her, as I settle into one of the chairs, paired in front of her desk, "how are you?"

"Hi Jamie," she looks up from her stack of papers, "Can you shut the door?"

Oh god, here it comes. I get back up and close the door as instructed.

"What is going on with your grandbaby?" she asks.

"She is doing a little better. They placed a peg tube last week. She has Zellweger Disorder. It's a biogenesis cell disorder where she is lacking three enzymes that affect her ability to digest food and for the cells to clean out toxins. It is a progressive disease, with no cure. They aren't certain how severe her Zellweger is on the spectrum. We will get the final test results back from the geneticist later this week. She is home now, with home health coming twice a week. We are taking it one day at a time," I update her, hoping she will be kind.

"Keep me posted. I can get someone to fill in from our Jackson office, if you need to take some time off, to be with your family," she offers.

"Thank you," I say and quickly leave. I was recently forced to switch from our office in McComb, to our office in Hazlehurst, Mississippi. Our company is reorganizing and closed my hiring office as we downsize. The director of the new office is not as warm as my former boss. It's hard to know what to say. Yes, I need this job. Yes, my family needs me. My best choice of action is to keep it short and sweet and get out of there.

After leaving the office, I make it through my heavy stacked day of patients. On the way home, I call Angela to check on our sweetheart.

"Hey Mom. I was going to call you. I wasn't sure when you were going to be finished with work. Lottie Mae has been sleeping most of the day. I am a little worried. Dana is here rocking her in the living room, and I was just about to get in the bathtub," Angela states.

"Oh no! I hope she isn't getting an infection. Is she still taking antibiotics?" I ask.

"We are still on them. Tomorrow is the last dose," she adds.

"Hopefully, she is OK. Maybe, she is just growing. Babies do sleep a lot," I offer hope.

"I hope that's all it is. I'll call you in the morning. I love you!" she says.

"I love you too!" I respond, before hanging up the phone.

The next morning, I am awakened by my phone ringing. I glance at the screen, 5:03 a.m. It's Angela.

"Hey Mom, we are heading to Tulane's ER," her voice cracks, as she takes a deep breath, and continues, "She is so lethargic. I'm scared." She begins to cry.

"OK darling. I am so sorry. I am glad you are taking her to the hospital. I will call work, and rearrange my schedule, so I can come be there with you. Hopefully, I should get to the hospital before lunch. I am going to let you go, so I can start getting ready," I say, as I start getting out of bed.

"OK Mom," she sobs, as she answers.

"I will call you, when I'm on my way. I love you!" I tell her. I hang up the phone and hit the floor running.

By the time I shower and pack my overnight bag, the sun is starting to peek through the darkness. I begin making my calls to the office, to each patient expecting me to show up for therapy, and finally to Angela to say I am on my way.

I reach the parking garage on South Villere Street, and find a space on the third floor, near the pedestrian bridge. I notice it's 11:45 a.m. on my phone, as I send Angela a text.

"Hey, I made it to the parking garage. What's the room number?" I press send.

"Room 4130. Jason is going to meet you at the pedestrian bridge," she texts back.

I leave my overnight bag in the car. I am prepared to stay if needed, but I don't know if Jason is planning to stay tonight with them, or if he must work. My stomach is turning cartwheels, as I try to contain my nerves and push all my fears of Lottie Mae's fate to the side. I try to focus. I grab my phone, purse, keys and head to the pedestrian bridge, connecting the parking garage and the hospital. It's another ten minutes, before I see Jason's familiar small frame walking toward me.

"Hi Jason, how is our baby?" I ask, as I hug him.

"She is very sick. The doctor thinks it's Sepsis. We might be here for a while. She is on IV antibiotics and they want to change her formula to an enzyme based, predigested, non-dairy type. She is a little fighter, hanging on," his voice begins to falter, as tears start rolling down his cheeks.

"We are going to get through this. She is strong for such a tiny little thing," I say, trying to reassure him. "Now, take me to see our angel."

It's a ten-minute walk down long halls, turns, and an elevator ride, before we make it to our destination. Angela is holding Lottie Mae, rocking her when I arrive. I glance around the room. It is smaller than the room at Children's hospital. There is only one chair that converts into a bed, a rocking chair, and a baby bed, along with a bedside table. I bend down and kiss my sweet Angela on the forehead, before kissing little Lottie Mae.

"Hey Sweetheart, how is our little one?" I whisper, so I don't wake up our baby.

"She is very sick Mama. I'm so scared," she says, and starts to cry.

I just hold her as she sobs and shakes. I have read all the information. I know this could very well be the end. There aren't any words to make it better. There is nothing more I can do but hold her.

"I'm scared too, sweetheart," I agree, as tears roll down my cheeks.

"I am going to run some errands while your mom is here," Jason says, bringing us back to the present, as he begins to gather his things.

I wash my hands and take our sweet baby in my arms. She has oxygen tubing, as well as the peg tube attached to the feeding pump. They have a tiny splint, on her left foot, where an IV has been started, to fight this terrible infection. I carefully take Angela's place in the rocker and adjust all the tubes.

"I am so exhausted. The doctor said we will be here for at least a week, maybe longer. I didn't sleep much last night," Angela tells me.

"Is Jason going to be able to stay with you tonight or does he have to work?" I ask.

"He is going to close Salutations for tonight, and open tomorrow night, so he can stay with us. He was up most of the night, as well," she explains.

"OK," I say and start thinking of a plan. "I will go back home tonight. I still need to make up the visits, for the patients, I had to move off my schedule today. I'll drive back here after work tomorrow, so I can stay with you, while Jason opens Salutations."

"You know, Christmas is next week, and I haven't been able to go shopping. I did decorate a little on Monday, after Granny Dana came. I was hoping we would be home, "she says, with a sadness in her voice.

"Why don't you lie down, and take a nap, while I'm here," I encourage.

"I am so tired. It's hard to shut off all my thoughts and sleep," she says, pulling out the convertible sleeper chair, turning it into a single bed. She straightens the pillow and blanket she had brought from home and lies down.

"You don't have to go to sleep. Just close your eyes, and rest," I say trying to help.

Within minutes, she is out cold. Every hour or two, a nurse comes in, and takes Lottie Mae's blood pressure, and temperature, and checks to see if she has any emissions. Angela is so exhausted; she doesn't wake from the intrusions. I lay our little angel down in the bed. I am afraid all my holding her, might make her sore.

It's around three hours before Jason returns from picking up clothes, from their apartment. He also went to put up a sign at Salutations, notifying patrons of a family emergency, and that the wine bar will be closed for the evening.

"Hey Jason. I'm going to head out since you're back. Lottie Mae has been sleeping most of the time. The nurse came in and checked her a couple of times, but no significant changes. Angela must be exhausted, because she has slept almost the entire time you've been gone," I inform him.

"Well, we had a rough night. No one slept well. Thanks for coming," he tells me.

"I'll be back tomorrow, after I see my last patient," I say, "Angela said you are going to try to work tomorrow night, at Salutations, and go to work at Breaux Mart in the morning."

"Yeah, I just closed the wine bar for tonight. I didn't know if Lottie Mae was going to be OK. I didn't want to be away from her. I think she is looking better, now. So, I need to work, while I can," he explains.

"I understand. OK then, I'll see you all tomorrow," I say, and begin to gather my things. I go to the crib and kiss Lottie Mae on her forehead. Her eyes are half closed as she sleeps. She looks so thin and frail. My heart is full of love and sadness at the same time. I go to where my daughter is resting and bend down to kiss her on her forehead. She barely stirs.

I make it home by 8:30 p.m. Jenny is spending the night with a friend. Lance is in the living room, getting caught up on CNN. We visit and get each other caught up on our lives. I am so exhausted that I can barely move. I go and pour myself a stiff drink and head to my computer to take a moment to zone out and play solitaire. I don't want to think about anything, for just an hour or so, as I try to unwind, from all the pressure. I play a Counting Crows CD, that lets me feel the sadness, in rhythmic melodies I find soothing. The spiced rum lets me forget, for just a little while, that my world has changed.

Treatment in America: Her Life Matters

Chapter Thirteen

"Hi Sweetheart," I whisper, as I enter the small hospital room and walk over to where Angela is resting, on the pull-out convertible chair/bed.

"Hi Mama," Angela says, as she hugs me. "I'm so glad you are here."

"How is our little one today?" I ask, as I go to her crib, "Can I pick her up?"

"Yes, she is just waking up," Angela says, smiling as she joins me crib side.

I lean over and smile at our baby. I pick her up and place her on my shoulder. She is too weak to hold her head up. I make sure I am supporting her head and neck, as Angela helps me arrange the multiple tubing, so that they aren't pulling on her delicate body, as I ease down, into the rocking chair, by the bed.

"Have you been able to rest any?" I ask.

"I try. There is only this one sleeper chair. When Jason is here, it is difficult for both of us to sleep comfortably. Maybe, if we can pull the top cushions off the sleeper chair, and make an extra pallet in the corner, we each can sleep comfortably tonight, if you think that will work?" she asks.

"That's OK with me. I don't mind sleeping on the floor," I answer, as I take a deep breath, trying to take in the lavender scent from Lottie Mae's hair. "She smells so good!"

Later that afternoon, we get a knock on the door. Angela gets up and answers it. There are two women and a couple of children pulling a red wagon loaded with brightly wrapped Christmas presents.

"Hi, I am Marie Johnston," says the thin, tall lady leading the group. "We are giving Christmas presents today. Do you have a little girl or boy?"

"Oh, that is so sweet," Angela answers her, "We have a little girl, Lottie Mae. She is five months old."

The other lady accompanying her takes one of the gifts from the wagon, gives it to one of the young children in their group, and instructs her to give it to Angela.

"My little one was in this same room," she says, beginning to choke up, as tears swell in her eyes. "I'm sorry, I didn't know I would react like this."

"It's OK," her friend tells her, as she puts her arm around her for support. Then she turns to Angela and explains, "It's been a year since we lost our little one. We know what you are going through and just wanted to send a little love to you."

"That is so kind of you! Thank you so much for coming by," I say, as they gather around their grieving mother, touching her arm, leading her down the hall, to another hospital room, to the next child. I feel so sorry for this kind family. I wonder if the plaque, on the rocking chair, bears the name of their lost angel.

It's not too much longer, before another group comes by. This time, it's the fire department, leaving a stuffed Dalmatian fire fighter dog, as their Christmas gift.

"What if we are here for Christmas?" Angela asks.

"Well, if we are, we will just celebrate here," I say, trying to cheer her up. Truth is, I want to skip Christmas all together. I can't think of much, except making it through today. "I am going to get a few things for Jenny, since she is just fifteen. I am handing out gift cards for everyone else."

"I just want her first Christmas to be special," Angela adds.

It seems so odd to hear her talk about making it special. I have always admired the way Angela decorates and celebrates holidays. It's just that Lottie Mae is so sick. We aren't even sure if she will make it to Christmas. Sepsis will be hard to survive in her weakened state. Angela never talks about the possibility that Lottie Mae may not live very long. I read the same material the geneticist gave us that she read. I am so depressed. I can barely eat. I have lost fifteen pounds, since we learned of her terminal illness.

Lottie Mae is beginning to rest better, now that the antibiotics are beginning to fight the infection. The nurses make rounds, every two hours, and in between, we try to sleep. We took the cushions off the chair and made a pallet. I was sleeping soundly on the floor, when the eleven o'clock shift change occurs.

"Ma'am, I am sorry to wake you, but you can't have the cushions on the floor," a stern voice says. I blink my eyes twice and wipe the drool off my cheek. As I begin to focus, Angela raises up from the sleeper chair.

"What's the problem?" Angela asks, removing her sleep mask with the owl face.

"The fire code prohibits blocking the doorway," the new nurse says, "that is why you need to pick all this up. We have sleep rooms available, if you need a place to rest."

"I know. I checked them out. There are around thirty chairs in one room, fluorescent lighting overhead, and not to mention, no way to lock the door, or feel safe, making it impossible to sleep," I say in a direct manner.

"I am sorry, but you need to get this off the floor, pronto," the unsympathetic caregiver orders.

We do as we are instructed. I know they have a job to do. I just wonder if this woman, barking orders, has any idea how important it is for us to be near our baby, and still take care of ourselves? I would guess not. I have enough experience in life to know when to just be quiet, and just hope the next nurse will be nicer. We make do sleeping on the one bed, hugged close to each other, and try to time our turning, left and right, to each other's turning schedule.

The next morning, I feel like I haven't slept at all. I look at my watch, 6:04 a.m. I decide to just get up, and wash up, before the doctors start making their rounds. I tiptoe to my bag, and grab the remaining sweat suit, and fresh underwear. Sleeping in sports clothing is comfortable and helps to keep warm. It feels like it's fifty degrees inside this hospital. Angela wakes as I exit the bathroom.

"Hey, I hope I didn't wake you. I was hoping you might sleep some more, with me out of your bed," I say, as I organize my belongings, preparing for when I head back to Mississippi later this afternoon.

"I haven't really slept much," Angela confesses, "every time I close my eyes, it seems like the nurse is coming in to check her blood pressure."

"I hear you. I feel like I was awake all night myself," I add, "now look who's awake?"

"You want to hold her while I get dressed?" Angela asks.

"Of course!" I say with enthusiasm.

I go to the crib and peer over the railing. Sweet Lottie Mae has her eyes open and is looking at me. She is still able to move her little arms and kick her little legs some. I take her into my arms, adjusting the tubes myself this time. I feel a little more comfortable managing all the medical equipment.

Lottie Mae and Maemo, Maemo and Lottie Mae, we love each other, everyday! I sing the little song I wrote for her, as I rock her in the provided chair. Lottie Mae still opens her little mouth as I sing. She still smiles and my heart flutters. I see a little life in those sweet eyes. I feel hope that she is getting better. At least for now, she seems stronger than when I first arrived.

"What time are you going home?" Angela asks.

"I'm thinking around noon, whenever Jason gets here to be with you. I'm going to do some speed shopping for Jenny on my way home. If Lottie Mae is still here by Wednesday, we will come to spend Christmas with you here," I say making my plans as I tell them.

"I think Jason's family is coming tomorrow to stay at the apartment. You, dad and Jenny can stay there, too, if you want," she offers.

"Lance has to work tomorrow, so we will drive down Christmas morning, and just drive back that night," I explain.

Just as we were making our plans, Jason arrives in time for the doctor's rounds. A group of white coat professionals file in and semicircle the crib. Familiar with the routine, I slowly stand up and take Lottie Mae back to her crib for the doctor to examine.

"Good Morning. I am Dr. Turner," the young female doctor introduces herself, "This is my partner, Dr. Morrow, and Dr. Stone, our geneticist. How is Lottie today?"

"Hi, I'm Jamie, the grandmother," I introduce myself. I am so glad I am here to hear their prognosis. They politely nod and proceed to examine our precious baby. Jason and Angela join the circle of medical doctors and answer their questions. I quietly listen and try not to get in their way.

"She is responding positively to the antibiotics," Dr. Turner tells us, "She has lost a pound since she was admitted, but seems to be tolerating the new predigested, non-dairy, enzyme formula much better."

"Do you think we could go home for Christmas?" Angela asks.

"I feel she needs to stay for at least another week. We need to see that she isn't continuing to lose weight," Dr. Turner says, speaking in layman's terms. The doctors continue with their examination, checking her head to toe.

"We want to schedule a family conference for Thursday at 1 p.m. We will have all our test results by then," Dr. Stone tells us.

"That will be fine," Jason agrees, as the three doctors leave our room.

"Don't worry, sweetheart," I say, as I put my arms around Angela, "We will still make it special."

"Yes, we will," Jason says, as he joins in the group hug. We remain still and silent, for a few moments, before breaking apart.

"I guess I'll go ahead and get on the road. Jason, I'll call your mom, to see what her plans are for Christmas, so we can work out the details," I say, as I get up and start retrieving my bags, preparing to leave. I go over to Lottie Mae. She is looking directly into my eyes as I lean over to kiss her little forehead, "Maemo loves you! I will be back soon!"

Treatment in America: Her Life Matters

Chapter Fourteen

It's been a long time, since I waited to shop, until the day before Christmas Eve. The store is busy with Christmas music playing overhead, while frantic, last-minute, shoppers scurry down the superstore isles. I hate this store. I am surely not feeling the holiday spirit, but when you have the obligation of making your child's experience special, you suck it up, and do what you must do. Jenny has been so understanding and kind to me through this. She never complains about my helping with Lottie Mae, or my missing most of her soccer games, the past three months. When Lance and I met, Jenny was only a year old. I am lucky that he is such a wonderful father to her. He has taken her to all her sporting events in my absence.

"Hey, I'm home," I shout, as I make my way into the living room, where Lance is sitting, watching political shows.

"Hi Sweetheart," he says, as he rises to kiss me.

"Where is Jenny?" I ask.

"She is over at her friend Haley's house. She should be back soon," he informs me.

"Good! I went shopping for her and want to get it all wrapped before she gets home," I say, before hurrying to unload my shopping bags, pull the Christmas wrapping paper storage bin out, and begin my mother's work. It's not much, but at least she will have a little something to open. I also plan to give her some shopping money, to make up for the few gifts. I forget, I haven't called Jason's mom yet. I pull my cell phone out and call, putting it on speaker, so I can multitask.

"Hello Jamie?" Dana asks, looking at caller ID.

"Hey Dana, sorry for the late call. Have you had the chance to talk to Jason and Angela today?" I ask.

"Yes. They told me they are going to be in the hospital a little longer," she answers.

"That's right. I am calling to see what your plans are for Christmas. Do you want us to bring food like we did for Thanksgiving? I have to work a couple of hours Christmas eve morning. We are planning to drive down Christmas Day for a few hours," I ask, hoping we just do the minimum.

"Well, we are going to come over, and bring some food to the apartment, if you want to join us," she offers.

"No, no, that's OK. This Christmas is so hectic with work, Jenny's schedule, and Lottie Mae in the hospital. I think we would be less stressed, if we just ate on our own. I just wanted to touch base with you," I explain.

"Our son, and his wife, and my other three grandbabies, are coming to town from Tennessee, so I wanted to do something. Of course, I am retired, so I have a little more time to cook," she tells me.

"We will probably see you at the hospital. Merry Christmas!" I say, as I hang up the phone.

Monday morning, Christmas Eve, I get up and head into work for our weekly meeting. We review a few case conferences and the patients whose scheduled visits are being moved until after Christmas. It is hard to focus at work. My every thought is filled with Lottie Mae. At least today it's just a two-hour workday, because of the abbreviated holiday schedule.

Jenny is still sleeping when I get home. I go to her room and cuddle with her, until I drift off to sleep beside her.

"Mom," Jenny whispers, "I hate to wake you Mama, but my grandfather is here to pick me up, to go see my dad."

"OK sweetheart," I say, as I yawn and stretch, "Are you coming back tonight? We are going to see Lottie Mae in the morning at Tulane."

"Yes ma'am," she says, as she kisses my forehead.

I roll back over and fall back to sleep. When I wake, it is pitch black dark outside. I wonder how long I've been asleep. I go to the living room and see Lance sleeping, sitting on the couch, with the remote control still in his hand. I don't wake him. I begin getting things ready for our day trip tomorrow. It doesn't seem like Christmas. My heart is broken in a thousand pieces. I get my pajamas on, put some Counting Crows on, and pour myself a stiff drink. I don't want to think about anything for a few hours.

The house is so quiet for Christmas morning. This is the first year that only the three of us are here. Normally, all the kids are home, laughter would fill the air, as we drink mimosas, and challenge each other playing tennis on the Wii. How fast life can change. I take an hour for my meditation and morning ritual. I am not much on formal religious rituals, but I pray and worship my own way. I cry as I pray, begging God to intervene and heal our Lottie Mae.

It's not long before everyone is awake, and we are on our way. Jenny sleeps the whole two-hour drive to Tulane Hospital. When we get to Lottie Mae's room, Angela has her dressed in a beautiful Christmas gown, with little lace stockings, and matching head band.

"Merry Christmas!" I say, as we enter our grandbaby's room.

"Merry Christmas!" Angela greets us with hugs as we come in. Jason, rocking our sweet little one, nods and smiles.

"How is Paw-Paw's little girl?" Lance asks, as he leans down, and kisses our little one.

"She has been awake a lot more. We didn't sleep much last night. She's a little night owl," Angela says.

"Let me get a kiss, too," I say, squeezing in between Lance and Jason to get to Lottie Mae.

"I am so glad you came! Are you going to come to the apartment and eat later?" Angela asks.

"No, we will probably eat at the Hibachi restaurant, on the way home. They are usually open on Christmas. I thought we would just come down to spend a few hours with you all and drive back after. If you want, you two can go eat with Jason's family, while we are here to stay with Lottie Mae," I offer.

"Thanks mom. I think we might go later. The nurse said Santa is supposed to make a round on the children's wing sometime this afternoon. I want to stay and get some pictures of Lottie Mae and Santa," Angela says.

"How is the sleeping going?" I ask.

"Not very well," she admits.

"Maybe you can take a nap at the apartment this afternoon, while so many helpers are in town," I suggest.

"I'll try. I hate being away from her. It's hard to rest when I'm here, and hard to rest when I'm at the apartment, because I worry something might happen while I'm gone," she shares her struggle.

We each take a turn holding our precious baby. Jason's brother and wife arrive after we have been there a couple of hours. We visit with them for a short while and decide to head back north. I feel so many emotions. I am grateful for whatever time we have with Lottie Mae. I am mourning the expectations we had of a healthy grandbaby. I am sad as I watch my daughter suffer with the pain of her sick child she loves so much. I am bewildered as to how God can let this innocent child suffer so much. I sit in silence on the ride back home, lost in my thoughts.

I hit the ground running Wednesday to see all my patients and then try to get the house caught up with cleaning and laundry. It's obvious I've been gone. I try not to complain too much about the condition of our home. I know it's hard to take care of a teenager and a home while working full time. So, I put my earphones in, crank up the music, and start cleaning. My reward afterward is a few cocktails while playing Solitaire. I know tomorrow, I'll have to get up, and do it all again.

The next day is going as good as could be expected. I see all my scheduled patients without any complications. Just as I make it home from my workday, I get a call.

"Mom, Angela is in the ER," I hear Susan's voice crack as she tries to relay the message, "I think she is having a breakdown."

Chapter Fifteen

I find myself pausing and trying to make sure I heard correctly. I can't comprehend it. I am speechless.

"Mom, are you still there?" Susan asks.

"Did you say Angela is in the ER, having a breakdown?" I repeat, asking for clarification. It isn't sinking in.

"We had the family conference today. I was off work, so I went, too. Basically, they told us that Lottie Mae is terminal, and not expected to live more than a year. They said, we can take Lottie Mae home Friday, and home health will start seeing her, again. Mom, Angela isn't accepting it. She keeps talking about some study done in the Netherlands," Susan explains.

"How did she end up in the ER?" I ask, in shock, as I try to understand what is going on.

"After the meeting, she said she was going to run an errand. Next thing I know, Jason is calling, telling me that a doctor found her on the roof of the parking garage acting strange, and they are taking her to the ER," Susan tells us the sequence of events, "I am on my way there now. I just wanted to let you know what was happening."

"Thank you for letting me know. I'm going to throw some clothes in a bag, and I will text when I am on my way," I tell her, as I hang up the phone, and call Lance.

"Hey, Susan just called. Angela is in the ER. They think she is having a mental breakdown. I am going to pack a bag and head that way," I tell him, as I walk around gathering suitcases, and clothing.

"Oh no," he replies, "Look, I just got off work and am heading home. Wait for me, before you leave."

I hang up the phone and continue methodically packing enough clothes to make it through a week. I don't know how long she will need me there. All I know, is that I must get there. I am almost finished packing, when I hear the familiar sound of his car pulling into the driveway. I am searching through the stack of stretchy, workout clothes, when he opens the door to our closet.

"Jamie, I'm so sorry," Lance says as he takes me in his arms and holds me tight, "What are you going to do about work?"

I pull my head back to look directly in his eyes as I think about my response. I am defensive. When it comes to one of my babies, I am like a lioness.

"I will tell them, I'm experiencing a family emergency, and they will have to deal with it. I can't worry about work, now," I say, annoyed with his question, pulling away from his arms.

"OK, well, I guess I'll stay here, and take care of Jenny. You know, she has a soccer tournament this weekend," he tells me, following me from our closet, to the bathroom.

"You need to back off. What the hell do you think I should do? Jenny is healthy and fine, Angela is not. You are here to take care of Jenny. I have to go! I really don't appreciate this shit, when I am under so much pressure!" my voice rising, as I glare at him, with a sideways look.

"You are right. I'm sorry. You need to be there. Just let me know when you make it there," he reluctantly resigns his argument.

I arrive at Tulane's Emergency Room. I am familiar with the location. This is where Lottie Mae was first seen, when she was admitted here. At the ER, I explain who I am, and ask if I may see my daughter. I am led through the locked doors by a quiet, heavy-set nurse. She then directs me toward the south hallway. Psychiatric patients are easy to identify here with their red color hospital gowns. The nurse explains that Angela is being observed for now, and the doctor will be by soon, to ask me some questions about her medical history.

Angela is dressed in red, sitting on the side of her hospital bed, in front of a glass wall facing the nursing station. She is rocking back and forth, chanting in rhymes. Susan is seated beside her, with her head hanging down, shoulders rolled forward, while she stares at the floor deep in thought. As I enter the room, Susan looks up. Her watery, red, eyes tell me all I need to know, without a word. Angela looks my direction and there is a lull in her continuous rambling poetry, as she begins to recognize me.

"I just want to go to sleep and they won't let me get in bed and sleep," Angela tells me.

"Honey, you are in bed right now," I say, still in shock, and stunned by her condition. Angela has always been dependable and responsible. Never has there been even an inkling of mental illness.

"I'm fucking tired! They said they were taking me to find a place to rest and I'm still here," she says, as she swings her legs back in forth, as she sits on the side of the bed. "I'm in a goddamn prison here, when ALL I WANT TO DO IS SLEEP!"

I am again without words. The rhyming is disturbing, but not as much as the type of language she is screaming at me. It is totally out of character. As her agitation increases, she shifts her verbal attack toward her sister.

"You should be here, not me. This is so fucked up!" Angela yells at her sister.

"I'm going to check on Lottie Mae," Susan says, getting up, ignoring the insult, and exits the room.

"Can I at least go to piss," our once soft spoken, southern belle, queen of politeness, yells toward the nurse's station.

The heavy-set nurse calmly gets up and begins to escort her to the bathroom.

"Are you my fucking jailer?" she continues to harass the quiet nurse, who doesn't react to her taunts.

A few minutes pass, before Angela returns from the bathroom. She walks with her nurse escort, back to her bed, and sits down. Just as the nurse settles back at her desk writing notes, with a quick motion, Angela climbs, and stands on top of her bed. She turns toward the nurse's station and starts yelling at the observing medical staff.

"I just hid a lighter in the bathroom. You are all so STUPID! You thought you took everything away from me, but you didn't! FIRE DRILL!" Angela shouts, smiling, pleased with herself.

The staff that had been quietly observing her, jumps up from their charting, and quickly run to check the bathroom for the hidden lighter, that their newest, disturbed patient claims to have left there. While the nurses go one direction, two large attendants come and make her sit down, and stop yelling. I am in shock, as I sit quietly, a witness to the unraveling.

The nurses return from their search empty handed. Angela is quiet for the next few minutes, smiling, and mumbling to herself. I don't know how to help her. I can't believe this is happening. I am afraid to say anything to her. It would be pointless. Nothing seems to penetrate her reality.

A half hour passes, Angela asks the nurse to go to the bathroom again. This time the nurse brings a urine specimen cup and hands it to her.

"We need to run a test. If you can, pee in the cup this time, and hand it to me when you finish," the nurse instructs. She seems unphased by Angela's antics.

Angela takes the cup and carries it high in the air, like it is a prize she just won at the fair, as she sashays to the bathroom, in her red gown. After a few minutes, she emerges from the bathroom, holding the urine specimen cup, that now holds a red Bic lighter.

"See, I told you. YOU ARE ALL STUPID!" Angela laughs, and shouts, like a mad woman who proved her point.

Everything is surreal. I stare at my daughter and I don't recognize this stranger before me. Her mania is escalating, as well as her agitation. I remain quiet, sitting in the chair, beside her bed. Jason rounds the corner to where we are and takes the other vacant chair, where Susan had been sitting. I look at him and nod. I am frozen in place. I am afraid any movement or words will set her off. It reminds me of when my sister had her breakdown.

"I hate you," Angela begins to attack him, "You are the worst lover I have ever had!"

"I love you Angela! Please don't do this," he says, trying to reason with her.

"Get out! GET OUT!!!" she yells, taking a swing at him. The observing nurse motions to the large orderlies to come to our cubicle once more.

Jason is crying uncontrollably as he hangs his head, and moves toward the door, out of her reach.

"Angela, we need you. Lottie Mae needs you. I can't live without you," he sobs.

"Are you as stupid as the rest of these idiots, that couldn't even find a lighter? Get the fuck out!" she continues to demand, until he relents. He is crying, as he leaves to return to Lottie Mae's room, on the fourth floor.

Angela climbs back on top of her bed and shouts at the top her lungs, "STELLA! STELLA!"

The two buff guys in scrubs grab her, wrestling her down from her perched stance on the bed, and quickly subdue her. The nurse joins them. They begin to apply leather straps to her wrist and tie her to the bed. It's the only way to keep her from harming herself, as she becomes more aggressive. I get out of the way and exit to stand behind the glass wall, by the nurse's station.

"YOU ARE A TERRIBLE MOTHER!" Angela shouts my direction.

Tears pour down my cheeks, as I stare in horror and disbelief. My heart was already broken. Now, I feel a sense of hopelessness, that is beyond anything I have ever experienced.

"Hi, I am Dr. Mason, the psychiatrist that examined your daughter when they brought her in," the young ER physician introduces himself as he joins me.

"Hi," I numbly answer, continuing to stare at my daughter, while she struggles.

"Has she ever had this happen before?" he asks gently.

"Never," I whisper, without turning my head to face him.

"Do you have a moment? I would like to ask you a few questions that may help me better understand what is going on," the tall thin doctor persists.

"Of course," I answer, finally pulling my eyes from my precious daughter, that is falling apart before me.

Treatment in America: Her Life Matters

Chapter Sixteen

I follow the young intern to the conference room, a few steps from where my sweet Angela is falling apart. I take a seat at the empty oblong table as he arranges his clip board and notes preparing for the interview.

"Hi, Mrs. Thornton," he begins, "I am trying to get a baseline for her medical history. I appreciate you taking time to answer some questions."

"I want to help any way I can," I affirm.

"Has anyone in your family had mental illness before?" he continues.

"My sister was diagnosed with Bipolar Disorder during her thirties. She was hospitalized twice. I have depression and I attempted suicide as a teenager, but that was a long time ago," I answer, pausing to think hard, trying to answer honestly.

"Have you ever noticed any behavior in Angela over the years that might have indicated adjustment issues?" he asks, as he looks up from his notes.

"Not really. The only unusual behavior was that as a teenager, she would clean our home, organize our kitchen cabinets, and all without me asking. She is a college graduate. She is a French major and lived in France for three years, participating in a program the French government has for Americans to be French teacher assistants. She lived and taught in Lourdes, France, traveling to different elementary schools, in several small adjacent towns, as part of the program." I tell the doctor, as he continues to write his notes.

"What about recently," he looks up to ask.

"Well, before her pregnancy, everything was going great. She and Jason opened a very successful wine and cheese dive, on the edge of the French Quarter. She was teaching at Lycée Francais De La Nouvelle Orleans, before Lottie Mae was born. The children love her. Life was going really good," I answer, and drift off in thought about how life has changed, while the interviewing doctor continues to write notes.

"What about the past few days? Any changes?" he asks, pausing for my response.

"Well, I guess you are aware that her baby has been in and out of the hospital the past three months. Our sweet Lottie Mae has been diagnosed with Zellweger Disorder. It's a biogenesis cell disorder, where she is missing enzymes in her body's cells. Enzymes are necessary to break down, and absorb, nutrition properly. Each cell is also missing enzymes that clean out toxins, so there is a buildup effect over time. It's a rare and cruel disease and there is no cure. There was a family conference today. Angela attended the meeting with the pediatrician, gastrointestinal doctor, and geneticist, this afternoon. Her sister told me the medical team informed them Lottie Mae is terminal and not expected to live past her first birthday. Susan said Angela was acting strange at the meeting, not accepting the findings. That's enough to make any mother lose her mind," I say, as I begin to cry silent tears.

"Yes, they told us in report that she has a terminally ill child on the fourth floor. I want you to know what is happening to Angela is not your fault," the doctor adds, as if he is reading my mind. He goes on to explain his findings, "It's no one's fault. I feel she is suffering from Post-Traumatic Stress Disorder, causing the onset of Bipolar Disorder. She will need inpatient treatment in order to get her stabilized with medication. We are working on getting her transferred to a facility that will take her."

"Can I stay with her until she transfers?" I ask humbly.

"That will be fine. Thank you for your time. It helps a lot," the doctor answers, before escorting me back to my daughter. She is calm and resting from the heavy medications required to subdue her.

I text Susan what is happening. She texts back, asking me to let her know when they come to transfer Angela. She says she will wait with Jason and Lottie Mae, until we hear something. Then, she will ride with me to whatever facility takes her. It's taking a long time. I wonder if it's because she is uninsured.

It is eight hours of waiting, before the nurse comes to inform me the ambulance is here to transfer her to Community Care Hospital, on General Taylor Street, located Uptown. I am stiff and freezing, as I try to wake up from napping on the metal chair, beside her bed. I text Susan to meet me in the parking garage in ten minutes.

"Hey, how are you holding up, sweetheart?" I ask Susan, as she enters my SUV and wraps her arms around my neck.

"I don't know mom. I keep waiting to wake up from this nightmare," she says, as she relaxes her hug and looks in my eyes, "I'm so scared. I've never seen her like this."

"Me, too," I add, as I enter the hospital address into my GPS.

We leave the parking garage and follow her ambulance west on St. Charles Avenue. The streets are quiet with only a few cars traveling in the early morning hours. It's a short drive to the small, three-story, hospital that sits between an apartment building and a catholic church.

"What do we do?" Susan asks, as we find a parking place near the front entrance.

"I don't know. Let's get out and see what they tell us. We have come this far. The worst thing they can do is say leave," I answer, as I turn off the engine and grab my purse. I am trying to reach the front door, before they unload Angela from the ambulance.

We make it just in time, as the security guard pushes the double doors open.

"Ladies, the hospital is closed for visitors. You can come back at 4 p.m.," he yells our direction, as we get closer to the building.

"Sir, my daughter is in that ambulance. She is having a breakdown, because her baby is dying," I begin to tell him, trying to gain his sympathy, "I don't know what to do or who to talk to. I just need for her to know I am here, and I am not just abandoning her."

"You can stand right where you are," his voice softens, as he compromises on our position.

Susan and I huddle together. The ambulance beeps as it backs up to park in front of the building. We hold each other and watch as they open the back doors of the ambulance and pull out the gurney our Angela is strapped to. They wheel her through the front door of the facility. She raises her head as they enter the building, but quickly lies back down as they disappear behind the closing doors.

The security guard shows mercy and yells for us, before we return to our SUV.

"Ma'am, I have a number for you," the security guard says, waving a business card above his head, motioning for us to come to him. "This is Ms. Kathy's number. She's the nurse on duty tonight. She can give you the list of what your daughter can have while she's here and what times you can come to visit."

"Thank you, so much!" I say, as I take the business card and start crying, again. I am moved by the smallest acts of kindness. I return to where Susan is waiting, where we parked. We are exhausted and still in shock.

"We can call in the morning, well, later this morning," I tell Susan, as I hand her the card just given to me.

"Let's go try and sleep, Mom," she suggests, as she places the nurse's business card in my purse for me.

"Yes, nothing more we can do for now," I say, as I think out loud.

Chapter Seventeen

I wake up and stare at the light coming through the window of Susan's bedroom. I am not sure what time it is. It takes a few moments for the reality of yesterday's nightmare to return. I am alone with my thoughts. The bed is empty where Susan slept beside me. We got in around 4 a.m. and I couldn't fall asleep. I was so keyed up. So many complications. So many things out of my control. The exhaustion finally took over around 5 a.m.

I sit up and search for my phone and see that it's 1:58 p.m. I remember, I need to find out what I can bring Angela. I locate my purse, search for the nurse's business card, and dial the number.

"Hi, this is Kathy," the kind voice answers.

"Hi, this is Jamie Thornton. My daughter, Angela McMillin, was admitted early this morning. The security guard gave me your number. I am calling to see what I need to bring for Angela. I didn't know if you have rules on what items are allowed," I awkwardly ask the stranger.

"She just needs some comfortable, appropriate, clothing. No draw strings in hoodies or pants, no shoelaces, no belts, or anything she might harm herself with. We have two visiting times daily. The first time is 4 – 5 p.m. and the second time is 7:15 – 8:15 p.m. During the visit, you will need to leave your purse and keys behind. She is allowed only two visitors at a time. You will be required to sign in upon arrival, so you might want to come a little early," the nurse instructs.

I make mental notes on what is allowed.

"OK, that helps a lot. How is she doing?" I ask.

"She put you on her list of OK to share updates, in compliance with HIPPA. She is still very manic. It is going to take a few days, maybe even a couple of weeks, for some of the medications to reach their full effect," she reports.

"Please tell her we will see her at 4 p.m., and I love her," I ask, before hanging up.

I get dressed and make my way to Susan's kitchen to scavenge for food. I find a note on the refrigerator that reads, "Mom, I went to work for a few hours. Getting off at 3 p.m., Love, Susan."

I continue my mission. Eggs, bread, butter and coffee are spotted. I'm not hungry, but I need to make myself eat, to keep my strength up. I send a text to Susan to let her know Community Care's visiting hours and ask if she wants to ride with me.

I put the coffee on, bread in the toaster, and start the eggs cooking. I am not wanting to talk to anyone, but I need to call and let Lance know what is going on. I had several missed calls while I slept.

"Hey, I am sorry I haven't called earlier. I didn't get back to Susan's, until early this morning," I begin, as Lance answers the phone.

"I was getting worried. I tried calling all morning," he says, trying to hide his agitation.

"I know, I crashed about 5 a.m. and just woke up less than an hour ago," I say toward my phone on speaker, resting on the counter by the stove as I continue frying my eggs.

"Angela was admitted to Community Care Hospital uptown. I'm not sure how long she will be there. The doctor at the ER, thinks she has Post Traumatic Stress Disorder that has triggered the onset of Bipolar Disorder. They will need to keep her long enough to get her medications stabilized. I will let you know how it goes, when I go see her at 4 p.m.," I tell him.

"Are you going to try to come home tonight?" he asks, careful not to say anything upsetting.

"I probably will. I told work I would try to see the patients on my schedule this week, since no one else is available. I am thinking of driving back tonight, after the second visitation time. I'll get up early tomorrow to see my patients, so I can be back to the city before 4 p.m. I'll just drive back and forth," I say, as I try to figure a way to handle all my responsibilities in both worlds, two hours driving distance apart.

"I worry about you," he sincerely states, "you can't keep up this pace."

"I don't have a choice. I will call you when I'm on my way home tonight," I say, trying not to get into a debate on what I can or can't do, "I love you."

"I love you," he answers, before hanging up.

After eating, I call Dana to see how our little one is doing and tell her about Angela. She tells me that they are sending Lottie Mae home tomorrow, now that she is doing a little better. Then, I start making the long list of calls to reschedule my patients for the rest of the week. I also call my mother and sister to let them know what has happened. I am pushing myself to be strong and focus on what I must do, one thing at a time. I go downstairs to Angela and Jason's apartment and let myself in with my spare key. There are bags of clothes and hospital supplies lining the walls of their living room and spilling into their bedroom. I grab a suitcase from the coat closet and begin packing Angela's clothes for her hospital stay. I try to straighten up as I pack, but it is so overwhelming.

"Mom," Susan calls, as she enters Angela's apartment, "you ready to go?"

"Yes, just packing a few things for your sister," I say, as I meet her in the living room carrying the prepared overnight bag.

"Jason said he has to work late but will be able to go to the second visitation time. His mom is going to stay with Lottie Mae," she tells me, as we make our way to my SUV.

"I talked to Dana earlier. She said they are discharging Lottie Mae tomorrow," I tell her.

"Yes, that's what she told me, too, when I stopped by the hospital on my lunch break. By the way, she wanted me to ask if you can stay Monday with Lottie Mae. She needs to take her daughter, Janice, to a doctor's appointment in Lake Charles," Susan asks.

"I have a meeting Monday morning, but I can come down after, and be there before noon, if that helps. I will call her later today and work out the details," I offer.

"Sounds good. I finally told my boss what is going on. They were nice and understanding about it. I hate telling anybody anything. I don't want them to think I can't handle my job, because of my personal life. I want to be there for Angela and Lottie Mae, though. This job is so demanding. I'm afraid I will lose it, if I keep calling in," she vents to me.

"I understand, sweetheart. We can only do, what we can do. I'm not sure what's going to happen next. At least, we have each other," I say encouragingly, as we pull into the parking lot, of the grey stone building holding our sweet Angela. We hide our purses and phones under our car seats, grab the packed bag for Angela, and make our way to the lobby. We sign in on the clip board provided and wait to be escorted by the security guard. Several other visitors arrive and appear to be accustomed to the routine of signing in and waiting. It's five minutes past the hour, before the short stocky uniformed man gets up from his desk and begins to give instructions to the gathered group.

"Has everyone signed in?" the round officer asks looking across the room, as each individual nod yes. "OK then, let's line up single file, and go through the metal detector. No keys, purses, or bags allowed."

"I brought this bag for my daughter. The nurse said she could have these items," I speak up nervously, not sure of the system.

"I will take them," he states firmly, as he holds his hand out toward me, "Anyone else have something?"

No one speaks a word.

"The nurse will have to go through this to make sure there is nothing she can harm herself with," he explains, as he ushers the group to the elevator and presses the button to the third floor. I just look at Susan and keep quiet. I feel nauseated but push it aside. I know it's just my nerves.

When the doors open, another nurse is waiting to take over as group guide. The security guard hands her the prepared bag I had given him, then disappears behind the closing elevator doors. The group is then led past the nurse's station into the activity room. There sitting at a large square table, is our Angela. She is coloring a picture, still clad in her red hospital gown.

"Mommy!" Angela shouts, as she looks up from her coloring, "I am so glad you are here. They won't give me anything to wear. Did you bring me some clothes?"

"Hey Sweetheart," I greet her, giving her a long tight hug, "I gave the nurse a bag of clothes I packed for you. She must look through them to make sure everything is OK."

"I hate this place! You see that guy sitting in the corner?" she whispers, as she points to a young man, twenty-something, dressed in black pants, t-shirt and jacket, sitting at the end of the table. "He is the son of Jason's coworker, from Breaux Mart."

"How did you sleep last night?" I ask, changing the subject.

"I can't sleep here. They keep the lights on all night. Some woman came in and stood over my bed, until I woke up and made her leave...this place is not good," she answers, sounding irritated as she pauses from her coloring.

"Sweetheart, I know it's hard, but they are trying to get your medications right, so you can come home," I tell her, trying to reassure her that she is where she needs to be to get help.

"I made a picture for you," she says, jumping from one subject to another, as she pulls out a collage of magazine clippings that has my name colored at the top. "I made a list of some things I need. Can you get them for me?"

I take the mosaic picture of pasted magazine cuttings. On the back of her artwork is a note that reads:

> Dear Mom,
> Thank you for being here. I feel so special (smiley face). Before you go, I just need mascara, lip gloss, or lipstick, and long pink capri cigarettes. If you can't get anything, that's ok. I have money left over. I could really use quarters for the machine, because I have to buy snacks. You can probably bring me a soda, since both machines are completely empty. You are such a good mom, even if you are a little "wacky" at times. You are always there when I need you. I hope you know, I love you, even when I am mean to you! I really don't know what I am doing.
> Love you with all my heart!
> (heart symbol) Angela.

"I'll have to check with the nurse to see if it's OK," I answer her, after reading the long note.

"Do you want me to go get the nurse?" Angela says, beginning to get excited and jumps up from her coloring.

"Let's just visit for a little while," Susan says, stands up and takes her sisters hand and redirects her to sit and visit with us.

"We can talk to the nurse in a little while. Have you talked to the doctor today?" I ask.

"I have talked to so many different people. I can't keep up. I felt like I was able to leave my body last night and float up to the ceiling and see everything that is going on. I have been talking to God and I heard him talk back to me," she confides to us, as we sit and listen, stunned at what she is saying. It's hard to see her in this mental state.

"Jason is coming later to see you," Susan interjects, trying to bring her to reality.

"When is he coming?" She asks, as she switches to the new subject.

"The second visitation, 7:15 p.m. He has to work late at Breaux Mart," Susan answers, explaining why he couldn't be here now.

"Maybe he can bring me some of the things on my list," she says, thinking out loud about her wants.

"I doubt he has time. He said he is running by the hospital to check on Lottie Mae, before coming here. I will check with the nurse and bring what I can tomorrow," I say, cutting her off, "You are here to get well. It isn't a priority to have make-up, but we will get it for you, as soon as we can,"

"You can leave now! I just asked for a few things, Mother. I don't need this shit," she spits out her words angrily, changing her mood from happy to mad, in less than a few seconds.

"OK. I know it's the illness talking. I love you Angela. I'll let you visit with your sister and see you later," I say, getting up and hugging her, as I feel the hot stream of tears filling my eyes, betraying my attempt to be strong in front of her. I leave them and head to the nurse's station.

"Hi, I'm Jamie. May I speak with Angela McMillin's nurse?" I ask the two nurses, seated behind the glass opening at the nurse's station.

"Yes, I am Kathy. I spoke to you earlier today. I am the charge nurse for the unit," the small framed, blond-haired, lady answers.

"Do you mind telling me what medications she is on?" I ask, hoping she will take time to tell me.

"Let me get her chart and I'll review it with you," she answers, as she rolls on her chair to the row of charts behind her. She grabs Angela's chart and flips to medications, "Depakote 1000 mg every night for

Bipolar Disorder, Synthroid 25 mg daily for her thyroid, and Zyprexa 10 mg in morning and 15 mg at night for the mania, along with some multi vitamins, and Omega 3's."

"I work in therapy, so I'm just a little familiar with these medications. Angela has never been ill before. This is all new to us. She still seems very sick, easily agitated, and going from one subject to another," I share with the kind nurse.

"It's going to take some time for these medications to reach their effective dose. She will get better, when she has been taking her meds consistently for a few more days, and some, for several weeks, before they are working fully. The medications help level out her mood swings, as the medication level in her blood stream rises. She is still manic with grandiose delusions," she patiently explains.

"Yes, I am aware. Just like an antibiotic takes twenty-four hours to reach its effective dose to work fully toward curing an infection, the medications she is starting will need to be taken anywhere from several days, to several weeks, before they are working fully," I repeat to the nurse what I understand.

"That's right. Is there anything else you have questions about?" she asks.

"Not for now. Thank you for your time. I'm going to go downstairs to wait until her sister finishes visiting," I answer.

The nurse then replaces the chart and exits her locked glass enclosed nurses' station. She uses her key to activate the elevator to take me back downstairs. Shit, I forgot to ask about the make-up she requested, I think, as the elevator doors close. It doesn't matter. My strength is limited on what I can do.

I exit the elevator and take a seat in the lobby to wait for Susan. I need to be making calls, but I can't move or do anything else. I take a seat on one of the metal chairs that line the wall of the hospital entrance and stare at the gray speckled tiles on the floor. I am devastated as I realize, she will not bounce back quickly to her sane self. I am paralyzed by heartache.

Treatment in America: Her Life Matters

Chapter Eighteen

The next day, I juggle my work schedule to accommodate her visitation schedule. I reach Community Care Hospital parking lot at 3:45 p.m. Jason is joining me, but I don't see his scooter in the parking lot yet. I hide my purse under my car seat and get out to stretch before heading in. It's only five minutes, before Jason enters the glass doors and takes a seat beside me.

"Hey, how are you holding up?" I ask, as I hug his neck.

"I'm OK. How are you?" he asks.

"I'm OK," I lie. "How is our Lottie Mae? Is your mom with her?"

"We got home with her just a couple of hours ago. She is doing better. They gave us a couple of cases of the new formula they put her on. The home health nurse was just getting there, as I was leaving to come here," he updates me.

"I'm going to stop by and see her after our visit," I say, before the security officer gives the instructions for us to begin preparing for our visit.

We pass our screening and make our way to the day room where she is waiting. The room has two rectangular tables, placed end to end, with chairs circled around them. There is another row of chairs around the perimeter of the room, encircling the tables. Patients and their visitors are seated in this area, with empty chairs separating the different groups. Angela is wearing a red flower clip in her hair, looking more groomed and calmer, than before.

"Hi Mommy. Hi Jason," she says, stands and reaches to hug us.

We both take a turn getting a long hug from her, before settling into our seats around the designated visiting table. The nurses are monitoring through glass windows that line the day room. There is one attendant inside the room. He stands holding a clip board watching us, but not interacting.

"I feel really sleepy. The medicine they are giving me is not working," she complains.

"It's going to take a little while, before it is fully in your system," I say, trying to encourage.

"I don't think they know what they are doing," she continues, "They won't let me take a bath. I need to shave my legs. Look at them."

"We brought Lottie Mae home today," Jason tells her in a soft tone, changing the subject.

"Awe how is my little baby. I need to be with her. Do you think they will let me go see her?" she asks.

"We need you to get better first, sweetheart," I say gently.

"Maybe I can go out on pass," she adds.

"I don't think it's a good idea for now," I try to reason with her.

"Just forget it. Mom, can I visit with Jason, alone, for a little while," she asks, agitated with me.

"Sure," I concede, "I'm going to head on over to your place, Jason. I love you, Angela."

I wait until I get to my car, before allowing the wave of emotions to overtake me. The tears flow uncontrollably. I can't believe that this is happening. My sweet, first born, over achiever has changed, and I am afraid, she will never be the same. I take a deep breath, blow my nose, and drive the two miles to our other angel, Lottie Mae.

I ring the bell but get no answer at 2420 Magazine Street. I pull out my spare key and let myself in.

"Hi, it's Jamie. Anyone home?" I yell from the front door, down the hall of the shotgun apartment.

"Back here," a voice answers from the kitchen.

I make my way through the apartment to where our little one is swinging, in the portable battery-operated baby swing, in the corner. Jason's mom, Dana, is busy mixing baby formula. I quickly wash my hands and pick up our sweet Lottie Mae. I wonder if she misses her mommy. I kiss her on her cheek as I take her into my arms. She opens her little mouth in response and smiles a big smile. I need this. Pure love and innocence. I hold her and sway back and forth. She melts my heartache away for a few moments.

"How is Angela? Jason make it there?" Granny Dana asks.

"She is better. By that I mean she seemed a little calmer today. She is still very sick and changes from happy to see me, to asking me to leave, if I say or do anything that she disagrees with. I just hope they get her medications worked out soon. She is complaining about feeling tired and she doesn't want to take what they prescribed her," I share with Dana.

"I hope she gets better soon," Dana says, as she finishes making Lottie Mae's formula for her feeding pump. "I want to show you what I made for Lottie Mae."

I take the feeding pump backpack, and place it on my shoulder, allowing me to follow Dana through the narrow apartment, while holding our precious granddaughter. She leads me to Lottie Mae's room and pulls out a onesie she made and embroidered, reading "Maemo loves Me," with a little heart applicate, stitched on front.

"I love it!" I tell her, "You are so talented! You can sew anything!"

"See here," she says, pointing to the flap of material covering the opening on the onesie that allows the tubing from the feeding pump access to the G-tube placement site, on Lottie Mae's little belly. "I made it so she can wear clothes. I'm going to fix the rest of her little clothes, so they have a little pocket, too."

"I appreciate all that you do. That is going to work nicely," I say sincerely, as I trace my fingers over the raised embroidering.

"We love this baby and we love Angela," she says, "How are you doing?"

"I'm hanging in there. My job has been challenging. Before Lottie Mae was born, there were a bunch of changes, including a new office, new staff, and new town. The office I had been working in for the past year has closed, because our company is downsizing. I had been begging for more patients, but then all this happened, and now, I just try to see the minimum, so I can be here more," I say honestly.

"What about Garry? Have you talked to him since she has been hospitalized?" Dana prods, asking about Angela's birth father.

"Susan said she's been keeping him updated. Did you know he asked Angela if she had thought about funeral arrangements yet, while she was packing her bags to take Lottie Mae to the emergency room? He may have good intentions, but sometimes he is an idiot. I do need to check with him about our plans for her. I want to schedule a family conference for Angela at Community Care, so we can plan her discharge. So far, I haven't been successful in getting the social worker to call me back, after leaving several messages," I tell her.

"You know how men are. Sometimes they have no tact," she consoles me.

"I'll try to call him on my way home to see when he is available for the conference," I offer. I take a few more minutes rocking our baby and listening to Dana share about her challenges with her husband. She and I are beginning to bond with each other as we share the responsibilities and love of our granddaughter. I reluctantly hand our sweet one back into her arms and begin my trip north.

"Siri, dial Garry," I order my phone.

"Hey Jamie. What's up?" Garry answers.

"I am calling to see when you might be available for a family conference with Angela's medical team at Community Care Hospital?" I ask.

"I am offshore right now and won't be back until Tuesday, so any time after that. Then, I will be leaving on Monday of next week for vacation with Laura," he informs me. Laura is his new girlfriend, who was his old girlfriend from high school years ago, before marrying me.

"OK. That's all I needed to know. I'm waiting on the Social Worker to call me to tell me when we can meet. I'll call or text you, when I find out the date," I tell him, before hanging up. I want to keep him in the loop, but he seems more focused on his personal life. I make it home to Brookhaven around 12:30 a.m. It's another thirty minutes, before I find sleep.

Saturday morning starts early. I head out the door to see my first patient scheduled for 8 a.m. I am so exhausted, but I keep my nose to the grindstone. I get finished in time to drive the two hours south to Community Care and make visitation at 4 p.m. Angela asks about Lottie Mae more and seems to be better. She still thinks she hears God talking to her, and sometimes, she says, she feels the Devil is also talking to her.

So, I know, she isn't herself, yet. During the visit, the nurse tells me they have scheduled a discharge planning meeting for Tuesday at 3 p.m.

"Sweetheart, I won't be able to come tomorrow," I tell her, as we sit at the south end of the visitors table in the day room.

"It's OK. You have been here every day. I will be OK. When will you be able to come back?" she asks, sounding sad.

"I'll be back on Monday," I assure her, as I try to explain, "I just need one day to rest. I've been driving back and forth, working, seeing you and Lottie Mae when I can, but I'm so exhausted that I am afraid I'll fall asleep driving, if I don't take a time out."

"I need a few more things from the house, too. Can you get me some more stretchy pants and a sweater? It's cold in here at night. Also, can you get me some more cigarettes?" she says, beginning to get excited as she tells me her list of items.

"I'll do my best," I say, then change the subject, "have you been getting any counseling?"

"We have group sessions. This is not a good place, Mom. They don't care about you here," she says, beginning to act agitated, looking around the room. Her voice cracks, and tears begin to appear in the corners of her eyes as she pleads, "you have to get me out of here. I need to be with my baby."

"I promise you. I will do all I can. For now, this is the best place to get you well," I say. Looking around, I get it. The building itself is old and gray inside and out. They have everyone, male and female, housed on the same floor, which is not good. There aren't a lot of activities to structure their day. I must tell myself, that even if this isn't the best place, it's the only place willing to take her.

"There is someone I want you to meet," she says, beginning to smile, as she wipes her tears away, gets up from the table, and disappears down the hallway. I just remain seated and wait. After a few minutes, she returns with the young son of Jason's coworker, "Mom, meet Ricky."

"Hi," I say, awkward with my greeting. I remember him. She doesn't remember telling me who he was, "I am Jamie, Angela's mom."

"Hi," says the young man, dressed in black sweats and unkept hair, as he looks at his feet.

"Thank you for introducing him to me. I don't have much time to visit with you. Is it OK if I just hang out with you, Angela?" I ask, trying to limit my interactions with this disturbed young man.

"You don't have to be rude, Mom," she indignantly answers.

"I'm sorry," I say to the poor guy trying to follow Angela's instructions, "I don't mean to be unkind."

"Why don't you just go. I hate it when you act like this," she spits her words at me.

"OK. I'll go," I answer. I am hurt, but too exhausted to try to explain why I don't think it's a good idea for her to talk to him. "Jason and Susan will be here for your next visit. See you on Monday."

Angela goes and sits with her new friend as I leave. I swing by to see Lottie Mae. I decide not to mention Angela's new friend. I want to confirm with Dana our plans for switching days on Monday and get familiar with Lottie Mae's new medications and formula changes.

"How was your visit with Angela?" Dana asks, as I come through the front door.

"She is better, but is still easily agitated," I say, trying to keep it short and concise, "I was able to get a date for family conference, finally. The nurse said Tuesday at 3 p.m. I was going to ask Jason, Susan, and Garry to be there."

"I'll check with Jason for you. This one has been doing so much better. Yes, she has," Dana says, talking baby talk to Lottie Mae, "You ready to hold her?"

"Yes, please. I need some sweet love," I say, as I take Lottie Mae from Granny Dana. I look into our sweet little one's eyes and my heart leaps. She still opens her little mouth as I kiss her cheek. How I wish her mama was well to be here.

.

Chapter Nineteen

Sunday comes and so does rest. I sleep for twelve hours straight. The rest of the day, I spend lying in bed, napping between trips to the bathroom or kitchen. My phone has several unanswered messages from my two best friends. I am so overwhelmed with sadness. I can't find the strength to call them and update them on Angela and Lottie Mae. Jenny comes and cuddles with me for most of the afternoon. Lance tries to take care of me by cooking and bringing food to me as well.

Monday comes too soon. I get up early to prepare for the long day ahead. I pack my suitcase to return to Lottie Mae and Angela's. I fix my lunch to go and grab my charts and OT bag and head out the door. I dread going to my new office. I know I don't have a choice. No work means no eat to me.

I get to the office a few minutes before the scheduled weekly meeting. I check my mailbox on my way to the conference room. There is a memo about required continuing education for my company. Good luck getting me to do that right now, I think to myself. I take my seat by my new coworkers. My new supervisor seems so unhappy with her life. She is constantly complaining to the Physical Therapist sitting next to her. I don't think she knows true heartache, but she is young. I have little energy for trivial annoyances. After the hour and a half meeting, the director of our agency ask me to stay and see her before I leave. Good god, now what, I think to myself. I went to her office a few weeks before Lottie Mae's birth, asking if I could help with marketing and generating new referrals. I generated referrals, only to have her drop the ball getting them evaluated in a timely manner by an OTR. One of our nurses told me her frustration with the lack of follow up, after she gave her the referrals. Ironically, I am now trying to cut back on hours, so that I can spend more time with Lottie Mae, and now with Angela. I have no idea what she could want to talk about and neither does my stomach as it starts to do back flips. I hope they aren't firing me; I think as I knock on her door.

"Come in," the small framed blond-haired lady calls from her desk.

"Hi Mrs. Joyce," I nervously begin, "You wanted to see me?"

"Yes Jamie. Please come in and shut the door," she instructs me. "How is your granddaughter and daughter doing?"

"Lottie Mae was released from the hospital at the end of last week. She is doing better. Angela is still in the hospital. I have a family conference tomorrow, for her discharge planning, I scheduled patients for Wednesday through Friday, this week. I hope that's OK," I humbly ask.

"Yes, that's fine. I talked to my regional supervisor and we submitted you for a grant, from the T. H. Harris Foundation, our company has set up for catastrophic events for our employees. They have approved you for thirty-two hundred dollars," she smiles and hands me a check. I take it from her dumbfounded.

"Thank you so much!" I say, as I begin to cry tears of gratitude. "I don't know what to say. This is so kind and so needed."

"We know you are going through a very hard and challenging time. We want to help," she smiles as she tells me.

"I really appreciate this, Mrs. Joyce," I say, as I get up to hug her. Wow, that is so unexpected, and it couldn't happen at a better time. I have been spending so much on gasoline, driving back and forth. Along with the fewer patients on my caseload, I have been draining my savings account.

After the meeting, I put my lunch where I can reach it on the front seat beside me and drive the two and a half hours from Hazlehurst, Mississippi, to New Orleans, Louisiana. When I get to Angela's, I find Dana and the baby in the kitchen. Lottie Mae is in her swing she loves, while Dana looks like a chemist mixing formula.

"Glad you made it a little early. I have tried to organize everything, so it's easier for whomever is taking care of her. Look at what Jason helped me with," she says, pointing to the two by three foot dry erase board mounted on the hallway wall, between Lottie Mae's room and the kitchen. The board has a large chart showing the precise amount of formula, vegan DHA, fish oil, and Vitamin K, for mixing her complex baby formula. A second column lists her antibiotics and the times they are scheduled. "I also picked up a communication notebook, so we can write notes for any concerns we want to tell each other."

"Wow, you have been busy," I say, as I wash my hands, preparing to pick our little one up out of the swing, "How is my little princess?"

"She is doing OK. A few poopy diapers," Granny Dana says, as she continues preparing the formula for Lottie Mae's feeding bag.

Lottie Mae kicks her little feet and smiles as I kiss her all over her little face. I love her so much. She is still weak, so I make sure to support her little head. I look at this precious baby wondering if she is missing her mother. I miss her mother. My heart hurts that Angela can't be here, but I know it's important for her to get well.

"I hope your daughter is OK. Has she been sick?" I ask, referring to her doctor's visit scheduled for today.

"No, this is just a routine checkup for her," she answers.

"That's good," I say, thinking of how much I depend on Dana. "Tomorrow is the family conference at 2 p.m. Is Jason going to be able to be there?"

"Yes. He already made arrangements for getting off work early," she informs me, "I'll be back here around noon tomorrow, so you can go to the meeting."

"Thank you for doing that. I have been asking for a meeting, since she went into Community Care. She's better, but not back to her sweet Angela self, yet," I confide.

"How long do you think she will be in there?" Dana asks.

"I don't know. She still seems sick to me. The medicine she is on is getting in her system, but not working fully, yet. I hope they keep her, at least long enough for it to reach its full effect," I say concerned, "She still doesn't seem like her old self. She is still so sick."

"No need to rush it. We are all here to help and take care of Lottie Mae while she gets better," Dana adds, trying to give assurance.

Dana leaves me and our angel to the quiet of Angela's apartment. I spend most of the day rocking Lottie Mae and singing to her. She reaches up and touches my cheek as I look into her beautiful sweet eyes. I pray to God for mercy. I pray for healing for this precious child. I pray for healing for Angela. I tell God that he is all powerful and I believe he can do anything. I am heartbroken.

In the evening, Jason and I take turns going to visit. We decide he should go to the early visitation time, while I stay with Lottie Mae. Then, he watches Lottie Mae, while I go for the second visitation time. Angela still seems off. She has times when she seems lucid, showing concern, asking about Lottie Mae, but there are still signs of the mania. She has a stack of pictures she has colored with poems written on them. Occasionally, she talks about having magical powers. It is hard for me to see her struggling with reality. My stomach is in knots. I have lost ten more pounds this week, because I don't remember to eat.

The next day, Dana shows up on time, allowing me to go to the family conference. Susan meets me at Angela's apartment and rides with me to the hospital. Angela's father, Garry, is meeting us there. Jason is driving from Breaux Mart, after working the early morning shift.

We arrive at the facility and make our way inside. Garry and Jason are waiting in the lobby. The Social worker comes out and asks us to follow her to the conference room. She is dressed in jeans with frayed hemlines, t-shirt and tennis shoes. She is the most unprofessional looking social worker that I have ever seen. After getting us settled in our seats surrounding the large rectangular table, she exits to go get Angela. Within five minutes, we are all seated together.

"Hi, I'm Mary Johnson," she introduces herself, "thank you for coming. Angela has been doing well. We feel she is ready for discharge."

"What?" I ask in disbelief. "Did you just say she is ready for discharge? Ms. Johnson, I thought we were here to plan for a discharge. Not just discharge without a plan."

"We can talk about a plan," she goes on to say, like it isn't a problem. "Angela and I have been talking about what to do, if she starts to feel like she needs help again."

"Do you really feel she is ready to go home?" Garry asks, trying to prod the pace of the meeting. He is wanting to return to work. He keeps checking his phone.

"Yes," the social worker quickly answers.

"I am better now," Angela speaks up in her soft voice, "I need to get back home."

"One of the things we discussed is what to do if she feels like she is becoming sick," Ms. Johnson reassures us, then turns toward Angela, "What would you do, if you felt you were having a breakdown?"

"I would call 911," Angela answers the prepared response in a monotone voice.

"Has the medicine had time to fully work yet?" I ask this person, who looks like she is heading to a football game instead of work.

"The doctor feels she is doing so much better now and is ready to go home," she quickly answers.

"Where is the doctor? I thought he was to be here," I feel myself becoming upset, as I realize what is happening. They are sending her home, too early.

"The doctor usually isn't at discharge meetings," she casually states.

"When are you sending her home?" Jason asks.

"She can go home after the meeting," Ms. Johnson tells us.

Angela looks like the cat that ate the canary as she smiles.

"I already have my bag packed," Angela says, then still smiling, she gets up from the table to go get her belongings. The Social Worker also leaves, following her out the door.

"I think it's too soon," I say out loud to the gathered family members. I am feeling sick to my stomach and angry at the same time.

"Well, the doctor thinks she is OK," Garry interjects, as he gets up from the table. "I need to get back on the road. I have some more work to do, before we head out of town next week."

He gets up and kisses Susan, who has been quiet during the meeting, and starts toward the door. I am in shock at what just happened. I wanted to plan for going home. This was not the plan. How are we going to care for a dying child, and her mother, if they don't get her well, before sending her home?

Treatment in America: Her Life Matters

Chapter Twenty

The first week after being released from the hospital, Angela seems to be managing with the help of Dana and myself. I bring a pill organizer box to help her comply with her medication schedule. She and Jason decide that working at the wine bar is too stressful for her at this time. She is sleeping a lot and complains of lack of energy. I continue working, scheduling my patients for three days, and then I drive to the city to stay with Angela the other four days. When I go to visit, I try to get Jason alone to see how things are going. I see my opportunity when he takes a smoke break on the back porch.

"Hey Jason, Angela and Lottie Mae have gone to bed. Do you mind if I hang out?" I ask, as I sit down beside him on the back doorsteps facing the private fenced area. The backyard hosts an outdoor table and chairs, with strings of white lights overhead, banana plants lining the privacy fence perimeter, and flowers decorating the small, inviting courtyard.

"It's OK. Want a smoke?" he offers, as he extends his hand offering the small pipe filled with cannabis.

"Yes, thank you so much!" I say, before taking the pipe and taking a deep inhalation. "How are you holding up?"

"Well, I decided to go see a counselor. It's helping," he confides.

"How did you find one? Are they from your church?" I ask.

"No, no, no, I'm an atheist. My job provides insurance and they had a list of therapists that are on my plan," he clarifies.

"I didn't know you were an atheist," I say, as I take another hit from his smoke pipe and feel myself relaxing. "Your mom is Catholic. Is that how you were raised?"

"Yes, I was brought up going to church. I just had a change of heart, when I was very young," he answers. I hand him the pipe and he takes another toke.

"What happened?" I ask, curious about what could make him change so drastically.

"It was when I found out Santa Claus wasn't real. I know it sounds funny, but when I found out how they lied to me about Santa, I felt they had probably lied about God, too," he shares, also relaxed and more talkative than usual.

How ironic. My mother never let me believe in Santa as a child, because she was so hurt by the Santa lie when she found out he wasn't real. The difference is, she became so extreme with her narrow, dogmatic, religious views that over time it has become more of a mental illness, than faith. Two very different reactions spun from the Santa lie.

"I am not religious. My dad was a preacher and my mother is extremely religious. I don't share their same rigid beliefs, but I do feel God is real. I worship in my own way," I share. It's not up to me to judge anyone on how they believe, whom they believe in, or whom they don't believe in. I hate discussions about religion. I decide to change the subject and ask, "How do you think Angela is doing?"

"I see her trying. She has started complaining about her medicine making her feel tired and wants the doctor to change them," he tells me.

"I've been reading a lot of information about Bipolar Disorder. It's common for patients to want to stop or change their medication, because the mania makes them feel on top of the world, and the medicine slows them down. I will talk to her about it," I say, offering my support.

Jason is like my own son to me. I know it is hard for him. The illness has Angela behaving cruelly towards him at times. I hope he is strong enough for this storm they are going through. I begin to feel fully relaxed. I excuse myself from our talk and go back inside. I take a long hot soaking bath and go to bed while the magic of the cannabis is still working.

The next morning, I wake up to the smell of bacon cooking.

"Good morning, Maemo," Angela whispers to me, "Are you ready for breakfast?"

"That sounds good," I say, trying to wake up. I slept better than I have in months. "Are you cooking?"

"Yes, I made bacon, biscuits, and was just about to cook the eggs," she smiles, sounding like her old self.

"Is there anything I can do to help?" I ask, as I follow her to the kitchen.

"No, I've got it all under control," Angela states, with renewed energy.

"Then I'll pick this little one up and spoil her while you cook," I say, as I bend over and gently pick up our baby from her portable swing near the table.

"Oh, guess what?" Angela says, as she stops cooking and turns toward me, "Dad and Laura got married."

"What? When?" I ask.

"He and Laura went to the Bahamas and got married," she goes on, "It was a surprise to Susan and me, as well."

"It's just that he hasn't been divorced from Anna that long," I say, shocked by the news, "I can't believe it."

"Didn't he date her when he was in high school?" Angela asks, as she scrambles the eggs in the black cast iron skillet.

"Yes. Guess he never got over her. That explains his lack of effort in our marriage," I laugh and say. "It's too bad for Anna. I had just start liking her."

Angela seems more like her normal energetic self. Later that afternoon, my two best friends from Mississippi come to visit me in the city.

"Hey girl. You haven't been texting us back, so we decided to drive to see you! How are you?" Betsy asks.

"We've missed you!" Suzy adds.

"I know, I've been out of touch. It's kind of hard when you are living a nightmare. I haven't talked to anyone from home much," I apologize. It means so much that they came to see me. "What's been happening back home?"

"Same old same old," Betsy states, "Can we take you to lunch?"

"Sure. Jason is off work this morning, so he can stay with Angela and Lottie Mae. I don't like leaving her alone for very long," I tell them.

"We brought you something," Suzy says, as she smiles and hands me a small gift bag.

"What?" I ask, as I take the small bag and look inside, "Green fingernail polish?"

"Yes. We want you to paint your toenails green, so that every time you look down at them, you will know we are also with you in spirit," Betsy smiles and informs me.

"That is so sweet girls. I will do it!" I say, filled with gratefulness for good friends.

I've missed our drinks on the front porch of the country club. I didn't realize how much I missed them, until they were here. We go to eat at Parasols, where they make the best shrimp po'boy in the Irish Channel area. We eat, drink, laugh and cry. For a couple of hours, I feel normal in their company. They each take turns holding our angel and visiting with Angela when we return.

Two weeks go by with Lottie Mae maintaining her health with nurses visiting twice a week, PT and OT visiting once a week, and Granny Dana and I continuing our rotating schedule. Angela is soft spoken and attentive the first week. Subtle changes surface in the second week, as she becomes less attentive, and starts complaining more about her medications prescribed to her. During the third week post Community Care, I get a call from Jason's father, while I am doing home health.

"Do you have any control over your daughter?" Joe abruptly asks, as I answer my phone.

"Hi Joe," I answer, trying to remain calm, ignoring his tone. He is an odd little short man with strained social skills. I have heard all the stories about him from his wife. "What are you talking about?"

"She is getting out of control and you need to call and talk to her," he demands.

"I will find out what is going on," I say, measuring my response. I take a deep breath, and try to remain calm, "Thanks for calling and letting me know."

I quickly hang up the phone, before I react poorly to his tactless approach. I am in the middle of my workday, with two more patients to see. I'm lucky he caught me, while I am driving to my next patient's home. I pull over to the side of the road and start making calls. Susan is first on the list.

"Susan, I just got off the phone with Jason's dad. He asked me if I can control my daughter. Do you have any idea what he is referring to?" I ask.

"Yeah, I think she has not been taking her meds. She called one of her new friends that she made while at Community Care. He's a schizophrenic patient that is the son of one of Jason's co-workers that was hospitalized the same time she was. Evidently, she has been in contact with him," Susan explains.

"Oh my god, that's just great. I'll call Dana and see what's been going on with Joe," I tell her my plans.

"Thanks Mom, she doesn't listen to me," Susan says, with a sadness in her tone. The two of them have always been not only close as sisters, but best friends. I can hear the desperation in her voice. We say our good-byes and hang up the phone. I waste no time and dial Dana's number.

"Hi, this is Jamie, I just got a strange call from your husband asking me if I can control my daughter. What's going on?" I ask.

"I told him not to contact you. I can't tell him anything without him over reacting," she begins, "I think, she is not taking her medication. She has basically been ignoring Lottie Mae, and lately, she has had her new friends coming over. One of them is a patient she met while she was hospitalized, and it's starting to worry Jason."

"It's OK. I'm glad Joe called to let me know what was going on," I say, leaving out how angry his approach made me, "I'll see what I can do. I'm supposed to come down tomorrow after work to relieve you. Do you think I need to come tonight?"

"I think we are OK at the moment, but she is starting to talk in that voice she had when she was manic last time, cold and harsh, instead of her soft, sweet, normal voice," Dana shares.

"OK, I'll try to get an early start for work in the morning, so I can get there as soon as possible," I offer, before hanging up.

I sit there, on the side of Highway Fifty-One, just south of Hazlehurst, Mississippi, and cry my heart out. After a long while, I compose myself enough to make it through the rest of my workday.

Treatment in America: Her Life Matters

Chapter Twenty-One

When I arrive at Angela's the next day, I find her happy and full of energy. Not the way you would expect someone caring for their dying child. I am afraid she is becoming manic.

"Angela how are you feeling," I ask, as I kiss her on the cheek and wrap my arms around her.

"I feel better than I have in a long time," she beams. "I'm going to a party with some of my friends tonight, if you don't mind. I need a break."

"Which friends are you talking about?" I ask curiously.

"My new friend, Ricky. He is meeting me at Carrie's house later this evening," she informs me of her plans.

"I don't remember Ricky. Where do you know him from?" I prod.

"I met him when I was at Community Care," she explains, "he understands what I am going through, and I just need to get out of this house for a little bit."

"Have you been taking your medications?" I cut to the chase and ask.

"Yes mother. I have and I'm sick of everyone asking me this," she tells me, becoming agitated and raising her voice. I see Dana standing behind Angela, out of her sight, motioning for me to follow her.

"OK, I need to check with Dana on the baby's schedule, before she has to head back to Lake Charles," I tell her. I kiss Lottie Mae as she sleeps in the baby swing, positioned beside Angela in the living room, before going to find Dana.

"She has been seeing that guy she met from Community Care. Her friend, Ricky, is the one whose father works with Jason and whose family has been at their wits end, trying to keep him off illegal drugs and sane," Dana whispers to me, in the privacy of the kitchen.

"So, I see what you are talking about. She sure is acting like she hasn't been taking her medicine, for at least a week or so," I say anxiously, agreeing with her assessment.

"She has barely paid any attention to Lottie Mae. Not to mention, she didn't sleep a wink, last night," she continues whispering to me, so Angela can't hear from the next room.

"I will try to talk to her, however, when she's sick like this, she doesn't listen to me. I will call Garry and see if he can help," I tell Dana, as I think about our options out loud. Oh, this is just great. Just what Angela needs, another friend that has more issues than herself. I know I must put an end to this. It is like having a teenager, except this teenager is thirty-one years old, and there is little I can do to stop her. We go back to the living room and rejoin Angela, where she is rummaging around, getting ready for her departure.

"She's been awake all night, almost twenty-four hours, now," Dana tells me again, this time in front of Angela.

"Angela, have you been up all night?" I ask, preparing to confront her.

"I can't rest Mom. I just need a break and want to go out to a party with my friends for a little while," she states, like she is talking about lifelong friends, not someone she just met. I see her transforming, from not wanting to leave Lottie Mae's side, to this unrecognizable personality that appears selfish with no regard for others. Manic Angela is so far from how she normally behaves. I know it's the illness returning. I feel nauseated, afraid that she is getting worse.

"Well you are not going tonight. You need to rest and be here for your baby!" I say forcefully, hoping she will listen.

"You can't tell me what to do," she says, not relenting.

"I am here to help you. You must trust me on this. Lottie Mae needs you here," I say, trying to take a different approach as I lower my voice and try to speak with kindness and patience.

"Well, I guess I'll stay here, but I'm going to ask them to come over," she states, making a compromise.

"Angela, it's late and we don't need company. Besides that, two sick people can't help each other. It's not a good idea to continue this carrying on with someone that is more sick than you are. You aren't thinking this through. I love you sweetheart. You need to hear this," I tell her, desperately trying to reason with her.

"I can't deal with you right now. I'm going to take a bath," Angela says angrily, as she stomps out of the living room and heads toward the back of the apartment.

"Call me if you need help," Dana tells me, as she finishes gathering her things and heads toward the front door.

"I will. Thanks Dana," I say, as I close the door behind her.

I feel that everything was understood by Angela and accepted for the moment. I take sweet Lottie Mae out of the baby swing and carefully settle into the rocking chair with her. Jason comes through and heads out the door without talking. He is going to Salutations, their wine and cheese bar, to open for the evening. I am afraid to say too much to him. I have my own worries about Angela. I can't mask them to give words of comfort to him that she is going to get better.

Mardi Gras is in full swing. The street outside is full of carnival goers making their way to the parade routes. The apartment is quiet for a little while. I find Thomas the Tank Engine sing-along musical book and slowly turn the pages for Lottie Mae, as I sing the memorized verses. Lottie Mae responds with wide smiles, lifting my spirit for the moment. I kiss the top of her head and close my eyes as I continue to rock her. My heart is filled with so much love and sadness at the same time. I hold her close to me as I pray for her healing, for her mama's healing and for strength for myself.

After thirty minutes of spoiling our little one, I decide to lay her down to nap, so I can mix the formula for tomorrow. As I head into the kitchen, I hear music coming from the back courtyard. I check the bathroom. No Angela. She was supposed to be taking a bath. I open the back door to see that she has let three oddly dressed, wearing all black, young guys in through the side entrance. She is dancing, circling the three mental cases as they sit around the patio table, where she has set up a stereo blaring music.

"What the hell is going on?" I ask, all out of patience. She doesn't stop dancing. Ignoring me, she continues acting like everything is fine and dandy.

"Hi Mom! I want you to meet my friends," she begins, introducing crazy one, two and three. I cut her off.

"I thought I told you that this is not a good idea," I repeat myself.

"This is my house and I will do whatever I want!" she barks, with a cigarette dangling from the corner of her mouth, as she moves to Billy Idol's Dancing with Myself.

"Well, it's my house, too, while I'm here helping. You guys better start gathering your things, because you are leaving, now!" I demand, not giving a shit if I sound bitchy or not. Crazy one has the nerve to speak up, as he makes his way to the gate.

"All she needs is you to be a mother!" he says, as he passes me.

"This is what a mother does. Maybe if you were a responsible adult, you would know that. Now leave!" I say to her newfound idiot.

"Just fifteen more minutes?" Angela pouts and asks, like she's a thirteen-year-old.

"No. They leave now, and you get yourself inside. Have you forgotten Lottie Mae is ill? We need to rest, so we can take care of her," I tell her, feeling frustrated, angry and in disbelief. I am done with reasoning at this point. I go inside to check on our precious one, who is still sleeping. It takes a few minutes, but Angela reluctantly bids her demented friends good-bye and comes inside.

I finish making the formula as Angela gets her bath. It's a long night of her getting up and down, as I try to rest on the futon beside Lottie Mae's bed. I see Angela spiraling downward and there is nothing I can do to stop it. Jason gets home in the wee hours and he helps to calm her. Finally, she sleeps.

I get up early to bathe Lottie Mae. Lately, her muscles have increased abnormal tone, causing her to keep her little hands fisted, and arms extended. After her bath, I rub the lavender scented grapeseed oil gently on her legs and arms, working out the knots, leaving her relaxed and comfortable. There are two words our baby understands, "strolling and bath." Every time you say one of these two words to Lottie Mae, she smiles. I decide to let her mommy and daddy continue sleeping and take her for a stroll by myself.

We take the familiar route down Magazine Street, avoiding the bumps in the sidewalk. We circle past Coliseum Park, where I notice several homeless people sleeping. No one bothers us as we make our way past them. Lottie Mae's feeding bag is hung on the handle of the stroller, giving the only clue that something is different about our baby. She has little sunglasses on, and a bonnet, to help with her light sensitivity. She looks adorable. My head is so full of thoughts. Why has God put us on this path of sadness? I am feeling the weight of everything. First Lottie Mae's fate, now Angela's illness, not to mention the financial stress. I don't know how we are going to get through this. As we near the house, I try to push the negative thoughts aside and wipe the tears away that have been seeping from my eyes.

Our little one has been sleeping since that last block from home. I try to be quiet as I take her out of the stroller and place her in her crib. Jason and Angela are still sleeping. I tiptoe to the back porch to call Garry to see if he can come over and spend time with Angela.

"Hey Garry, Angela has not been taking her medications. She was up for over twenty-four hours. She is sleeping now, but not too soundly. Do you think you can come and spend some time with her today? Susan called me yesterday very upset with how Angela has been acting and wants to go to lunch with me today to talk," I explain.

"I can come over for a little bit, if you can go somewhere nearby to eat. I have errands I need to run today," he offers.

"Sure, just going to Joey K's," I tell him. Then I text Susan to let her know I can go with her in a couple of hours to eat and catch each other up on what is going on with Angela. As I return to nap on the Futon beside Lottie Mae, I am met by Angela, who is already back up, after less than two hours of sleep.

"Can you sleep upstairs with Susan, so I can sleep on the futon? Jason's snoring won't let me sleep," she says, as she rubs her eyes and motions towards Jason. He continues sleeping in, after closing the bar so late.

"You can sleep with me. I don't want to sleep upstairs. Susan is doing some work in her studio this morning, before I am supposed to go eat lunch with her," I tell her. The truth is, I am afraid to leave the baby in her care, while Jason sleeps. She is slipping and I feel the need to keep watch over Lottie Mae. I still have visions of her dancing around the three lunatics the night before. She reluctantly joins me. I wrap my arms around her as we spoon and try to nap while our baby naps.

Treatment in America: Her Life Matters

Chapter Twenty-Two

Jason is cooking when I wake up from my nap. Lottie Mae is still asleep and so is Angela, for the moment. I ease up, trying not to shake the bed. I am thankful that she finally is resting. I have a little time before I need to be ready for my lunch date with Susan.

"It smells wonderful in here," I tell Jason. He is concentrating while seasoning the meat cooking in the big cast iron skillet.

"I'm searing a roast," he breaks to tell me, "I decided to close the wine bar tonight. So many parades going on and Angela not doing well."

"I understand. I am about to have lunch with Susan. She is pretty upset with Angela. How are you holding up?" I ask, afraid of his response.

"It's been hard. I don't know if we are going to make it. I love her so much. I try to be there for her, but she keeps pushing me away," he tells me, as he stares straight ahead, tending the sizzling meat.

"I don't think she's been taking her medications. It's the illness Jason. She loves you. I know she loves you. I see her slipping away again, too. She is cruel to me also when she starts being unbalanced. At least Garry promised to come by today. Sometimes, he can talk to her and she listens better than when I talk to her. At this point, I will try anything," I tell him, trying to persuade him to keep trying with Angela.

"I hope you are right," he answers, sounding broken.

I leave him doing his therapeutic cooking, while I get ready to check on my second to oldest. It has been particularly difficult for her because she and Angela are best friends, as well as sisters. By the time I get changed, I hear her coming through the front door.

"Thanks for going to lunch with me today, Mom," Susan tells me, as she greets me with a kiss on the cheek. I grab my purse and we are on our way.

"Glad I can go. Your dad isn't here yet, but Jason is up, so I feel OK about leaving her. Between you and me, I am afraid to leave Angela alone with the baby. She isn't making good decisions," I confide, as we start our three-block walk to Joey K's diner.

"I know, Mom. She has been so mean to me. I am so worried about her. It's like the last time she was sick all over again. She only gets this way, when she is about to go over the edge," she says, as her voice begins to falter.

I take her hand in mine and squeeze it, as we make our way down the crowded sidewalk. We are surrounded by people in costumes, laughing and drinking, unaware of the hell our lives have become. It's the weekend before Fat Tuesday. The biggest party weekend of the year. It's still nice to do something normal, like eating a meal in a restaurant. I miss normal.

We head back after our meal, as we promised. I am relieved that Garry finally made it to the apartment. As we come in, he jumps up and heads out the door, promising to return around 7 p.m. Angela is busy taking things out of the living room closet. There is a stack of Christmas decorations in the corner getting larger, as she continues working. Jason is rocking Lottie Mae, quietly watching her work. Susan returns to her apartment, leaving us with our two patients.

As dusk draws near, Angela announces she is going to get ready for bed. I have given up on straightening up behind her. Garry calls to tell us traffic is too heavy, and he can't make it back for 7 p.m. I feel so let down and angry. I don't ask much from him. He only lives a few blocks away. How can he not get here? I feel so helpless. Jason is here but has zero influence on her. She steamrolls right over him.

Angela comes back in the living room dressed in cowboy boots, a black and white poke-a-dot furry robe, make-up, and a red flower in her hair. I have seen her rummaging through her things all evening, leaving stacks of her belongings scattered from the living room to her bedroom. It is obvious she is ill, but for the moment, she is home and sitting on our couch. I leave her with Jason and Lottie Mae to take my bath and get ready for bed.

I just settle in for a long soak, when I hear Jason yelling from the living room. I can't hear what he is saying, but I know I need to get out and see what is happening. I jump out, dry off and speed dress. My heart is pounding out of my chest, as I run toward the front of the apartment to find Jason standing at the open front door.

"What's going on?" I ask, out of breath.

"She's gone," he says, staring down Magazine Street.

"What?" I ask, in shock.

"She ran out the front door, jumped on her scooter, and took off," he tells me, still staring, hoping she would come back.

"OH MY GOD!! I am having a panic attack," I tell him, as I start hyperventilating.

"She took her phone. I'll try to track it," he offers, in a dazed voice.

"I'll call Susan and Garry," I offer. It's the only thing I can do. I run get my phone and start calling. Susan is the first one I get.

"Hey, Angela took off on her scooter. I was taking a bath. Your dad never came back, and she just got away. I don't know what to do," I tell her.

"Chris and I will start looking. Have you called dad yet?" she asks.

"Not yet. He said he couldn't make it back here because of traffic, when I spoke to him earlier. I'll call him," I tell her, before hanging up and calling Garry.

"Garry, Angela is missing. She took off on her scooter. Susan and Chris are looking for her. I need you to help us," I say in one breath, as he answers.

"I'm not home. We are in the Quarter on Decatur Street," he tells me, with the crowd loud in the background, "I'll call Susan."

Click. He hangs up the phone.

I am stunned. I can't believe he lied about not being able to come and help us with Angela. He drove past our house from his home to get to the French Quarter. I am so angry, but that won't help anything, so I let it go for the moment. Jason gives me Lottie Mae to hold, as he begins to get ready to join the search. I rock our precious angel as I pray for her mama, my sweet daughter, who is losing her mind all over again.

"I can track her on my iPad, using the Find My iPhone app," he says, showing me the grid of New Orleans' streets, with a little red dot blinking on the screen.

"I'll stay here with Lottie Mae, in case she comes home," I tell him, as he runs out the door to his scooter.

I rock our little one to sleep and return to the living room to wait for their return. My stomach is in knots as I imagine all the possibilities of what could happen to her, on the streets of New Orleans, during Mardi Gras, by herself, in her mental condition. She blends right in with the party goers, except she isn't intoxicated, she is mentally ill.

Around midnight, the search party comes back to the apartment without her. They had followed the signal, from the Find My iPhone app, to St. Charles Street, but never saw a glimpse of her. The streets are too congested. With heavy hearts, they call it a night. Susan said Garry did show up to help, but they were unsuccessful, so he went home.

I know I need to try to rest in order to have the strength to care for Lottie Mae in the morning, but I can't stop my mind from worrying about Angela. After a couple of hours, I finally drift off to sleep on the futon near Lottie Mae's crib. I don't hear the front door when it opens.

"Why haven't you plugged this in?" Angela demands, holding the humidifier that I had unplugged earlier, because it had started leaking.

I raise up and blink a couple of times. I have only had one hour of sleep. It takes a moment to clear the disorientation.

"Angela, it's leaking," I try to explain, as I realize she has returned.

"Well, I'm fixing it. Don't worry, I know how to take care of my baby," she says, before stomping to the kitchen, humidifier cord dragging behind her. I hear the water running in the kitchen, where she is filling it and I quickly get up and join her.

"Angela, it is leaking and can cause a fire," I say, as I take it out of her hands without her consent. I continue, "Have you taken your meds? Where have you been? We have been so worried..."

"NO! I haven't taken my meds and I'm not going to," she states firmly, ignoring my other question of where she was all this time.

"You need to take your meds and go to bed," I say, knowing I sound like I'm talking to a ten-year-old, instead of my thirty-one-year-old daughter. I don't care how I sound. I need sleep. All of us need sleep. We go several rounds, before she finally gives in, and goes to bed. I lie back down with one eye open to keep track of Angela. It's less than an hour when Jason comes and wakes me. I follow him to the living room to find Angela standing there, shaking, hair in disarray, crying, waking the house.

"I'm having a breakdown," she sobs, "Call dad, Susan, and then call 911."

Treatment in America: Her Life Matters

Chapter Twenty-Three

By the time Garry and Susan arrive it's 4:30 a.m. Angela is restless, pacing up and down the narrow living room. Jason sits quietly on the couch and I position myself in the doorway, blocking her path to where Lottie Mae is sleeping. Finally, the police arrive.

"Hello, I'm Officer Johnson. We had a call for assistance?" the tall pretty young black officer introduces herself.

"Yes," Jason begins, "Angela asked us to call, because she is having a breakdown."

"I'm having a breakdown," she starts out speaking softly. Then she begins to change, pointing at us, "It's because of all of these people."

"Can you explain?" the officer calmly asks, as she joins us, closing the door behind her.

"She's a bad sister," Angela says, pointing at Susan, "He's a bad lover (pointing at Jason), he's a bad father (pointing at Garry), and she's a bad mother (pointing at me)."

"How are they bad?" the officer continues patiently.

"She beat me and tried to hold me here earlier today," Angela says, turning her anger toward me, as she argues her case with the officer.

"I hear what you are saying. I am trained as a professional to observe. First, I feel you are lying. Your mother obviously has not beat you. You don't have any marks on you and from my assessment of her, no marks either. I don't believe you. What I need now is for my partner to come inside, and take statements from the rest of the group," she states, then signals me to join her on the front porch. She opens the door as she speaks into her police radio asking her partner to take over. I join her on the porch, as her partner enters the living room, and begins taking everyone's information.

"I can see your daughter is very ill. I am sorry, but I am limited as an officer of the law. From what she is saying, I don't think she is going to kill herself, or harm others, even though she is obviously mentally ill. We can't do anything unless she is a danger to herself or others. Off the record, if I were you, I would call the Coroner's office. In Louisiana, the coroner has the power to get her admitted into a mental health facility," she sympathetically tells me.

"Thank you. This is something new for us. She was admitted less than a month ago to Community Care Hospital, but she was already at Tulane Hospital with her baby when she became ill. All we had to do was walk her downstairs. I know she needs treatment. She is a danger to herself. She is in danger of getting killed, because of her lack of judgement," I say, doing my best to persuade her to take her to the mental hospital, despite what she just said.

"Our training is very specific. If she isn't verbally saying she is going to kill herself or kill someone else, our hands are tied," she says earnestly.

"Thank you, again. I'll go call the coroner," I say, filled with anxiety. I excuse myself to Susan's apartment to make the call.

I google the number for the 24-hour hotline. The person on call is kind as I tell them what is happening.

"There is a chance that you might can stabilize her, if you can get her back on her medications. She will need to have twenty-four-hour, seven day a week supervision, until it's working. It's Mardi Gras and the chances of getting her admitted tonight are almost impossible," the stranger tells me, giving me no hope. I hang up and return downstairs to report my findings to the group.

The police have finished questioning everyone and have gone. The group is quiet from exhaustion and now hopelessness has set in, as we are left to our own devices to survive this.

"Angela, do you want to go take a bath?" I ask, trying to find something for her to do, so we, her support group, can discuss our next step in getting her help.

"OK," she answers as a child. She seems exhausted, too. She slowly gets up and heads toward the bathroom. I wait until she is inside the bathroom before continuing.

"The officer told me that they aren't allowed to do anything unless she is verbally saying, 'I am going to kill myself,' or if she threatens to kill someone else. She suggested I call the coroner, because they have the authority to admit the mentally ill. They said we might be able to get her stable, if we can supervise her, and get her to start taking the medications again," I convey the coroner's words to Garry, Susan and Jason.

"I don't think we can take care of Angela here, while she is sick. She doesn't need to be in the same house with the baby. It's too much taking care of Lottie Mae and taking care of her as well. I can't get her to take her meds. She doesn't listen to me," Jason tells the group, frustrated and near tears. "Whatever you all decide is fine. I need to go to bed. I have to get up in a couple of hours," he tells us, before excusing himself to his bedroom.

"I feel she is getting worse. She doesn't listen to me either. Look, I don't mean to run out, but I've got to sleep at least three hours, if I am going to make it to work today," Susan apologizes, as she kisses each one of us before heading upstairs, "Let me know what you decide."

"She doesn't listen to me, either. I have tried to get her to take her medications, but I don't have any influence over her when she is this sick. Garry, can you take her with you? She listens to you," I plead with her father, the only one left of our group that can help. He is self-employed as an oilfield production consultant. He has the money and power to adjust his schedule to help care for his daughter.

"Laura's kids are at the house for Carnival. We don't have anywhere to put her," he tells me, speaking about his new wife's family.

"I know you just got married, but your daughter needs you. I asked you to come help with her earlier, because she isn't listening to me. What did you do? You drove past our house to party in the French Quarter," I recount the events to Garry. I am in shock at how he is acting. We have always approached parenting as a team, even after we divorced. His newest wife is a director of nurses for god's sake. Surely, she understands.

"We already had plans, before all this. I have been trying. I'll see what I can do," he reluctantly gives in, "I'm going to have to make a few calls."

As Garry makes his calls, I check on Angela. I help her pack a bag and get her medications organized. She is compliant with my request, as I help her prepare. We get her bags and join Garry in the living room.

"I've been on the phone trying to find a hotel. New Orleans is all booked because of Mardi Gras, but I found a hotel in Houma," he tells us.

"Are you going to stay with her?" I ask, choosing not to confront him on why she can't stay at his house again. I am too exhausted.

"Yes, I will stay with her," he answers, like a child being made to do an unpleasant chore.

"She is so sick Garry. I need to make sure you realize that," I continue.

"I know, I know," he says becoming impatient. He grabs the bags we packed and leads her to his vehicle. I follow them outside.

"Call me when you get settled," I yell as they get inside his truck. I am so tired I can barely think. I go back inside, lock the door, check on our baby. I crash on the futon, where I sleep soundly for the next few hours, exhaustion overtaking my anxiety.

I wake up as Jason is leaving for work. I get up and peek over the railings to check on Lottie Mae. She is awake, staring at the stuffed animals that line her crib. There is my sweet angel. How I wish your mommy was well. I think about the previous night's events that carried into the wee hours of the morning. I check my phone, no calls or text. Well, maybe she is still sleeping, and they forgot to call when they got there. I will call later, after I take care of this little one.

I do our morning ritual of bathing and grapeseed oil massage, dress us both for the day, and proceed to make the formula for her feeding pump. I place her in the portable baby swing, positioned in the kitchen near me, so I can work and watch her at the same time. Lottie Mae smiles as she swings. I am getting concerned, as the day is turning into late morning, with not a word from Angela or Garry. I can't take it any longer and decide to call.

"Hey, are you alright?" I ask, when Angela answers her phone.

"Hey," Angela says, in a sleepy voice.

"Is Garry there?" I ask.

"No, he had to go to work," she tells me.

I feel panic return, as I realize he dumped her alone, in a strange town, in a strange hotel, two hours away. I can't breathe. I start shaking, as I try to remain calm enough to speak.

"Where are you?" I manage to ask.

"I don't know..." she answers, sounding very confused.

"It's OK, sweetheart. I'm going to call your dad. Just try to rest and don't go anywhere," I tell her, hoping she will be able to follow my instructions, but inside I know she isn't hearing me. She is too sick to comprehend what is happening, much less what I am asking. I quickly hang up and call Garry.

"I just got off the phone with Angela. You left her alone. You promised you would stay with her," I say angrily. I'm scared at this point and don't try to take time to speak kindly, "Which hotel are you staying in?"

"We are at the Ramada. I just flew offshore for a few hours. I left her some money. I'll be back before five o'clock," he says like it was all part of the plan.

"YOU IDIOT! SHE IS TOO SICK TO BE ALONE!!!" I scream into the receiver. (Click) He hangs up on me. I am shaking as I rack my brain for what to do next. I quickly dial my sister, who lives in Alexandria, Louisiana.

"Lynn, Angela is having another breakdown. Garry was supposed to take her to his house, but his new wife won't let her stay there, so he took her to the Ramada, in Houma, and left her there, alone. I'm with the baby and can't leave. Can you please go check on her? She is so sick," I beg my sister.

"I'm on my way. I'll get my mother-in-law to pick up my kids. I'll call when I get there," she volunteers immediately.

"Thank you so much," I say, feeling a little better that help is on the way, as I hang up the phone. I feel the overwhelming emotions of the past twenty-four hours rise and consume me. I fall to the floor and cry uncontrollably, shaking as waves of sadness flood my soul. I must compose myself and hold my emotions together. There is an angel in my presence that needs me to care for her. I rise up and see her sweet tiny face. No time for tears.

I go to the bathroom and wash my face with cold water, push my hair back behind my ears, and go tend to Lottie Mae. She grunts, as I gently pick her up and balance the feeding pump backpack on my other shoulder. We make our way to the living room. I settle into the gliding rocker and stare at this little one I love so much. I look at her little innocent face and wish I could make her well, her mommy well, all of us well. I try not to look at the clock. It will take a while for my sister to reach my other grown baby. I pray again for God to intervene. I wonder if he hears me anymore. Three hours later the phone rings.

"I made it to the hotel, but Angela is not here. I went to the front office and asked the guy at the desk if he has seen her. He told me the room number they are staying in, but he hasn't seen her," my sister informs me. "Wait, I think I see her. There is someone walking this way. I'm not sure if it's her. Whoever they are, they are covered in mud, and missing a shoe…Angela?"

"Is it her?" I ask with hope. I hear sirens getting louder in the background.

"Jamie, I need to go. I'll call you right back," Lynn tells me, then click, she's gone.

Chapter Twenty-Four

I wait for what seems like an eternity, before receiving the call back from my sister. I answer the phone and hear her sobbing, as she tries to collect herself.

"Hey, it is Angela," Lynn says, then begins telling me the events she just witnessed. "She was walking toward me. I didn't recognize her at first. I had to say her name twice, before she would even look my way. She walked right past me, like she was in a trance. Then a truck comes flying into the parking lot sideways with rocks flying. This farmer gets out cursing and yelling at me. He thinks I'm Angela, until I explain that I am her Aunt. I also told him that she has a dying baby and she is mentally ill. He finally softened his tone and began to apologize, just as two police cars, with sirens wailing, come sailing in the parking lot. The farmer tries to explain to the officers what is going on and that he doesn't want to press charges, but they ignore him. They proceed to grab Angela from her room, place her in handcuffs, and then tell me they are taking her to Lafourche Parish jail and that's where we can find her."

"Oh my god! Why are they arresting her?" I ask, in shock.

"The farmer told me that his cattle farm backs up to this hotel. Evidently, she went behind the hotel, climbed his barbed wire fence, got on one of his tractors, then drove over a cow and a dog, and tore down his fence. He said she did around thirty thousand dollars' worth of damage," Lynn tells me.

"I begged Garry not to leave her alone. He is offshore. Left her some money and took off. Now what are we going to do?" I ask, feeling sick inside.

"I'm going to go back in her room and pack up her things. She has twenty-dollar bills and clothes covering the floor," Lynn conveys her plans.

"I'm going to call Susan and Jason to let them know what's going on. I will get there as fast as I can," I reassure her.

"OK, be safe. I'm going to head to the sheriff's office and see if they will listen to me," she tells me, hoping to shed light about Angela's condition, so the police will have mercy on her.

Still shaking, I hang up and call Susan. I tell her what's happening and that I am getting ready to head to Houma, but I need Jason or her to stay with the baby. While we are on the phone, Susan ask her boyfriend, Mike, to stay with Jason and the baby, so she can ride the two-hour drive with me. She is afraid I am too emotional to go alone. Truth is, I am too emotional, but I know I must go no matter what. I am glad she is going with me.

We stop to fill up with gas, grab some coffee, and head to the Lafourche Parish jail. At least she is alive, I tell myself. I was so afraid I would be getting a different call from the police. She is so vulnerable in her mental state. So easy to become a victim. This is the complete opposite of her normal. How do I tell these people, this is not her? How do I make them see it's her illness? I can't stop crying and I pull the car over to the side of the road.

"Mom let me drive, please," Susan asks, as I get out and throw up on the side of the road.

"OK," I say and trade seats with her.

We finally reach the sheriff's office, where Lynn is waiting in her car. We pull up beside her. We all jump out and hug and cry.

"I tried to talk to them (she points toward the police station), but they think she is drunk. They told me they are transferring her to the women's prison," my sister tells us, frustrated by their lack of concern for the truth.

"OK. Thank you so much for being here. I'm going to go in and see what I can do. Maybe they will listen," I say and head toward the door.

I press the intercom and ask to speak with the sheriff. I hear the click releasing the magnetic locked door and I step inside. I see Angela. Her hair is disheveled, her eyes are wide open, but blank. She looks past me without recognition. She is handcuffed to a railing in the holding cell. She is out of her mind, crouching down, squatting, leaning backwards, pulling on her restraints, working to escape as she continues tugging, ignoring that I am here. There are other inmates in the holding cell that are sitting quietly watching the show.

I am met by an older officer that appears to be in charge. I explain in detail about Lottie Mae, Angela's recent hospitalization, and the bipolar disease that she is obviously suffering from. How, before she had PTSD trigger the Bipolar, she was just as normal as he and I.

"Do you have any children? I am begging for mercy," I ask, all pride removed.

"Well, it's not my decision. It's the arresting officer's," his stern face softens slightly as he answers.

"May I speak with him?" I ask, composed except for the tears flowing down my face.

"Wait here," he instructs, and exits behind another set of locked doors.

I wait as asked. A few minutes later, a young policeman appears. He looks like a baby, barely twenty-one years old.

"I'm Officer Brown," the young uniformed man introduces himself.

"Hi, I am the mother of Angela McMillin," I say, then begin telling him each step of our heartache. He listens with a narrow frown and hardened eyes. I try to let him have a glimpse of what can make a mother lose her mind. I end my story asking, "Would it be possible for her to have a psychiatric evaluation?"

"She knew what she was doing. You can bond her out at Thibodaux Women's Prison later, after we transfer her," the young heartless Barney Fife mentality officer declares. It is like he hasn't heard a word I am saying.

"I don't think you understand," I continue in desperation, "she is mentally ill, because she can't accept her six-month-old baby is dying. If you have a compassionate bone in your body, you will help me get her evaluated. She needs help!"

"Lady she knows right from wrong. She is going to Thibodaux, where they have a nurse that will evaluate her, when she gets to the prison," the ignorant officer states.

"You can help us. You don't have to send her to the prison. You can send her to the hospital," I say, heartbroken as I come to realize he is not going to change his mind. I am filled with anger that this man is not even listening to what I am saying. This anger is building inside me, coming from the pain of me not being able to protect my child. I feel the hot tears begin to come. I tell the arrogant idiot, "I have been living a horrible nightmare. First with my granddaughter's terminal diagnosis and now trying to get help for my daughter...I don't know what to do. (I start to cry, then sob uncontrollably) I guess, I'll have to go to Thibodaux."

"I wouldn't bother going over there. They aren't going to let you see her," continues the heartless bastard.

"Well, you are not a mother. I don't expect you to understand," I say knowing it's a waste of breath.

After he leaves through the locked door, another officer that was observing from a distance comes and joins me.

"Would you like to see your daughter before you leave?" he asks kindly.

"She is so sick. I don't know if it will do any good, but yes. Thank you," I tell him for his small gesture of kindness. The middle-aged officer leads me back to the holding cell I passed earlier on my way to speak to the arresting officer.

"Angela, this is your mother. I love you baby. I am going to try to get you some help," I strain to utter. Our eyes meet and we hold our gaze a couple of seconds before she turns away and resumes pulling on the handcuffs without saying a word or showing any sign that she recognizes me. I can hardly bear to see her in this condition, but I will not turn away. If no one will help me here, I will go and find help.

As I exit the small police station, I join Susan and Lynn and try to speak. The words won't come out. I collapse at their feet, moaning and crying heartbroken tears as they wrap their arms around me.

"They won't listen to me. They are sending her to a prison in Thibodaux," I finally choke out. My thoughts are racing. What can I do? Then I remembered what the Coroner's office had told me in New

Orleans. I grab my phone and google Lafourche Parish Coroner's Office. Maybe they will issue a Physician's Emergency Certificate to get her help. I hurriedly make the call.

A kind woman answers and addresses herself as the coroner on duty. I explained the events that are taking place and ask if she might intervene for us. I worry about what might happen to Angela at the prison in her condition.

"If you will wait there, I am going to call and speak with the Sheriff to see if they will reroute her to a hospital. I'll call you back, when I find out where they are sending her," the kind voice tells me, giving me hope.

We wait together in my car still parked in front of the Lafourche Parish jail. We talk about the past forty-eight hours of events leading us here as we wait. A half hour passes before my phone rings.

"Hello, this is Janice from the coroner's office. I am so sorry to tell you this. I did call and speak with the arresting officer. He would not waver on his decision to send her to Thibodaux to the Lafourche Parish Detention Center. I recommend you go there and ask to speak with the nurse on duty. Maybe when she completes her evaluation, she can get her transferred to a hospital," the kind voice on the phone tells me.

"I appreciate all that you tried to do. Thank you so much. I guess I am heading to Lafourche Parish Detention Center in Thibodaux," I say and hang up.

"Hey Sis, I need to get back home. I wish I could go with you to the prison, but I have to work in the morning and it's after 9 p.m. already. Even leaving now, I won't be home until after midnight," she says looking at her watch. She works as an ER nurse at St. Francis Cabrini hospital in Alexandria, three hours away.

"Of course, I understand. You will never know how much I appreciate you coming to check on her for me. Imagine what could have happened if you weren't here. We wouldn't even know where to find her," I tell my sister, as we get out of the car to hug.

(CLANK)

We turn to see the doors of the small second-rate facility open. Two policemen exit the station, dragging our Angela to a patrol car. She is still shackled, struggling as they usher her into the back seat of the squad car.

"DON'T FOLLOW US! IT'S AGAINST THE LAW FOR YOU TO FOLLOW! WE WILL ARREST YOU IF YOU DO!" yells the young heartless arresting officer toward us.

"I'M NOT EVEN IN MY CAR!" I yell back, fueled by heartache and now acting crazy myself.

We three stand there, hand in hand, frozen, staring, as they drive off into the darkness. They are fools if they think I'm not following them. We say our good-byes to my sister, set the GPS, and we are off. An hour and a half later, we are lost. It's so dark without streetlights on this South Louisiana rural highway.

I pull into the first gas station we see and google the prison number. I put the phone on speaker so Susan can hear. My call is routed to the warden's office. Thankfully, the warden's office transfers us to a very compassionate nurse. She listens intently as I tell her about Angela's history and where we are, lost in Thibodaux at a gas station.

"You are almost to the prison. If you keep going West on LA-3185, we are just a mile down the road on the left. When you turn in, park in front. Follow the walkway through the barbed wire fence to the front door. Ask the receptionist to page me. I would really like to talk to you, so I can get a complete history. I have assessed your daughter already and I can tell she is deeply disturbed. I am going to give a call to a doctor that I know. He can help us get her evaluated," the merciful voice instructs us.

By the time we make it inside the prison, it's nearing midnight. The kind nurse meets us as promised, along with the Warden and a guard. I share our story from the beginning. I tell them that until a month ago, Angela has been normal. She is a college graduate that lived overseas. She teaches school, and owns a business, a wine and cheese bar. I tell them about our Lottie Mae and how Angela's break happened when she was told Lottie Mae is terminal at the last family conference with Lottie Mae's doctors. It's been less than a month, since she was first hospitalized for this new condition of bipolar, but we haven't been able to get her to take her medications. They listen intently as we recount our story of sorrow.

"I have some good news. We are going to send her to Chabert Hospital in Houma. The ambulance will drive slowly so you can follow them," the kind nurse tells us. It's the best we can hope for. We thank them before leaving. I will never forget the kindness of this nurse.

"Why don't you sleep while I drive," I tell Susan, as we walk back to our car. I check my watch, 2:35 a.m. "We might have to drive back to New Orleans later and one of us needs to be rested."

"OK Mom. If you get too sleepy, please pull over," she agrees, with this one condition.

We get in, put our seatbelts on and wait to follow the ambulance to Chabert Hospital in Houma, Louisiana. I am feeling a little bit of renewed energy as I cling to hope. I see the ambulance coming and I fall in line behind the red lights. We reach the futuristic looking building made of concrete and glass at 3:15 a.m. I park and wake Susan, as the ambulance proceeds to the Emergency Room entrance.

Susan accompanies me to the freezing cold emergency room waiting area. The nurse on duty tells us the doctor won't be in to evaluate Angela until the morning, possibly by 9 a.m.

"Sweetheart, do you think you can sleep better in the car? I am afraid I'll miss the doctor if I sleep in the car," I turn to Susan and ask.

"It's freezing in here. Why don't you come with me? We can both wait in the car," Susan asks, reluctant to leave me.

"I have a coat and blanket in the back of my SUV that I use at Jenny's soccer games. I'll be fine. I'm afraid I'll miss the doctor when he comes in," I say, explaining why I can't leave.

"OK Mom, I understand," she concedes.

I walk her to the car and grab my winter gear before returning to wait inside. The hours pass slowly. I finally fall asleep, just before the janitor wakes me, and forces me to move. He is determined to mop under the row of chairs where I am resting in the vacant waiting room. Six hours later I am approached by a short man in a white coat.

"Hi, I'm Dr. Smith," the young doctor says, as he extends his hand.

Treatment in America: Her Life Matters

Chapter Twenty-Five

I try to wake up as I shake hands with the smiling doctor.

"Hi, I am Jamie Thornton. My daughter, Angela McMillin, was transferred here earlier," I begin unsure of how much information he has about our circumstance.

"Yes. Would you like to come to my office so we can talk?" he offers.

"Yes, thank you," I answer, as I stand and try to regain feeling in my lower extremities, after resting in the fetal position in the freezing waiting area for hours.

I follow him a short distance to his office and take a seat across from his chair behind a large oak desk. I feel lightheaded from only four hours of sleep in the past forty-eight hours of our latest nightmare.

"I see from the nurse's report from Lafourche Parish Detention Center, that she was hospitalized a month ago at Community Care Hospital in New Orleans for Bipolar Disorder?" the doctor asks, as he takes out a large yellow legal pad and grabs a pen from his white coat pocket.

"Yes. She became ill shortly after a family conference about her six-month-old daughter that has Zellweger Disorder. They told her that the baby is terminal, not expected to live past her first birthday. They only kept her a week before sending her home. The medications weren't working fully yet. Then, when they started working, she started complaining of no energy and stopped taking them, without us knowing it. By the time we started seeing the signs that she hadn't been taking them, it was too late. She got to a point where she could not fall asleep at all. After a couple of days without sleeping, she was too far gone from reality to even listen to anyone. We tried getting her help, but the police informed us if she doesn't say, 'I'm going to kill myself or I'm going to kill somebody,' they can't detain her. Those seem to be the magic words that need to be spoken, before anyone will help us. She becomes so delusional and her thoughts so irrational that she is a vulnerable adult, who is in danger of becoming a victim. She is overly friendly and trusting with strangers. We lost her on the streets of New Orleans as she started spiraling down, losing her sanity. We are lucky she even returned. We didn't know what to do, so we called 911. However, they couldn't help us because she wasn't saying, 'I'm going to kill myself.' I don't understand why we can't get help when we beg for it. She is mentally ill, making her at risk to herself. This is so frustrating. If she were an elderly dementia patient or a stroke patient that has cognitive issues, there would be accountability for not protecting her from herself," I say, getting emotionally worked up, rambling and losing my train of thought from lack of sleep.

"I understand your frustration," he answers patiently. "I have had some success with treating Bipolar Disorder. I had a challenging patient, very manic, much like how you describe your daughter. He was having difficulty taking his medications orally and keeping on schedule. In this case, I gave him injections, once a month, replacing the oral medications. He finally became stable after two months of inpatient care and is doing fine still."

"Well that gives me hope," I say, exhausted and grateful that this kind doctor is offering us hope. "Thank you for helping us. We love her very much. She is a wonderful daughter and mother when she is well. I hope you can get her stable and strong enough so she can be with Lottie Mae. I'm afraid she won't ever get over this, if Lottie Mae passes without her being there. So far, our little one is maintaining, and she is doing OK for now. I hope you can at least keep her long enough for the medication to work. If you could get her on injections once a month, that would work well. Hopefully that would eliminate the noncompliance with her oral medication schedule."

"I will do my best. I must tell you that we can only keep her fifteen days," Dr. Smith tells me.

"Do you think that will be enough time?" I ask, wondering why it's only two weeks and a day, instead of two months, like the one successful Bipolar patient story he just told me about.

"We will get her stable on a medication schedule, before we send her home," he reassures.

I head back to where Susan is sleeping in my SUV, parked in the emergency room parking lot. I am feeling relieved for now. The heavy weight of keeping Angela safe lifted for at least two weeks.

"Hey Sweetheart, I saw the doctor. He's going to keep her for fifteen days. He said he has successfully treated Bipolar cases before. I think we can head back now. There is nothing more we can do here for now," I tell Susan, as she sits up, rubbing her eyes, trying to wake up and listen to the update on her sister.

"I am so happy that they are going to help her. I'll drive us. I've slept for a few hours and I feel alright. I'll find some coffee in a drive thru," she says, with renewed energy.

I am happy to let her drive. I don't think I could have made it by myself. I am nearing total physical and emotional exhaustion. I need to call Jason to update him, before I crash in the back seat. I get my phone out and search his number. I'm having a difficult time finding his number. The fatigue is hindering my coordination and concentration. Finally, it's ringing.

"Hey, how's Angela?" Jason answers anxiously.

"We finally got her admitted to Chabert Hospital in Houma. I was able to speak with her doctor and give him her medical history. He said he has had success treating Bipolar, so that is hopeful. She is going to be here for at least a couple of weeks. Susan was able to rest a little and is driving us back. We should be there around noon," I tell him the short-abbreviated version.

"That's good news. My mother came over and will stay with Lottie Mae today. She said for you to not come by the apartment, but to go upstairs to Susan's and sleep. She has everything taken care of here and she is worried about you," he relays Dana's message.

"That is so kind of her. I will take her up on that. Kiss Lottie Mae for me. I'll talk to you later," I say, then hang up. I have one more call to make before I can rest. I must call my office to tell them of my schedule change. Best to just rip that bandage off fast and make the call.

"Hi Mrs. Joyce," I begin, but can't speak as the wave of emotions are too big to suppress.

"Hi Jamie," she begins, "Is everything alright?"

"No," I say, struggling to be professional. I try not to cry, but I can't control it. I begin crying as the words are stuck in my throat.

"What's going on?" she softens her voice.

"My daughter is sick, again. I have been up all night trying to get her help. She has been admitted to Chabert Hospital in Houma. I am calling to let you know I won't be able to see my patients today," I finally get the words out thru the tears.

"Will you be able to see them later this week? I am having trouble finding another therapist to help out with your schedule," she asks, more concerned with covering my schedule. I miss my old office and sympathetic boss.

"Yes, I will be able to," I say, with fake confidence. I don't know if I will be able to keep my word, but I put up a strong front. Truth is, at this point, I don't know what will happen next. I need my job. I can't afford to drive back and forth, pay my mortgage or have enough to eat without working. I will not give her a reason to fire me. It seems that she is more concerned with her company reports, than the hell I'm going through. As soon as I say I'll cover it, she hangs up.

I sleep a little on the two-hour ride back while Susan drives. We go straight upstairs, as instructed by Dana, to Susan's apartment. Susan takes her shower first and passes out. I take my shower next and join her, but my thoughts are hard to turn off. So much has happened, my brain is trying to process it all. I try progressive relaxation techniques, but they aren't working. I'm so keyed up from the adrenaline caused by the events of the past twenty-four hours. I get up slowly, trying not to wake my sweet daughter that has been by my side through this rescue mission for her sister. It's another hour, two cups of sleepy time tea, and a little cannabis, before I can fall asleep.

I wake up to find the sun has been replaced by the moon. I hear the familiar sounds of city traffic flowing outside on Magazine Street. For a moment, my mind does not remember where I am, or the recent events with Angela. I stare at my surroundings until I realize I'm at Susan's and her bed is empty where she was sleeping next to me.

Despite sleeping for six hours, I feel like I have been run over by a train. I try not to dwell on how I feel and get out of bed before I change my mind. I quickly dress and pack my things and head downstairs to check on Lottie Mae. I use my key and let myself in. I hate ringing the doorbell not knowing if I'm waking our baby. To my delight, Susan is in the living room rocking her, while Granny Dana prepares the formula for the next day in the kitchen.

"Do you want to hold her?" Susan smiles and offers.

"Yes, please. I need some sweet love," I say and set my things down by the front entrance. I am careful to arrange the tubing from her feeding pump as I take her from Susan.

"I'm going to help Dana with the formula," Susan says, as she leaves heading toward the back of the apartment to the kitchen.

I begin to sing to Lottie Mae. She smiles widely. I tell her that her mommy is sick, but sends lots of kisses, and she loves her very much. As I look down on her beautiful face, I feel love and peace for a moment.

Treatment in America: Her Life Matters

Chapter Twenty-Six

The next morning, I drive back to Mississippi to see my patients. I do my best to compartmentalize my feelings as I gather my OT bag and clip board from the back seat of my SUV. Before I reach the door, I see a familiar face emerge from my first patient's home.

"Hi Vicki," I greet my coworker. She is the nurse assigned to my patient. I smile and ask, "How is Mrs. Smith doing?"

"Good. She seems to be doing well with her pain medications and is making progress. How are you doing? I am so sorry to hear about your grandbaby and that your daughter is also sick. A few of us tried to donate our vacation hours to you, but Mrs. Joyce said it must go into a pool for everyone. We can't elect who we give it to," the kind nurse from my original office tells me. She and I are both still adjusting to the new office location and manager.

"Thank you so much for even trying," I say, giving her a big hug, "We are hanging in there, one day at a time. Sometimes, it's more like one hour at a time. My daughter is back in the hospital. I still have to work. Thanks for the update on Mrs. Smith. I better get in there and get started." I try to keep it short so I can stay strong. I'm afraid if I share too much with her about all we are going through, I won't be able to contain my emotions enough to make it through the rest of the day.

I stay focused and see all the patients on my schedule. As I fax my paperwork from my home office, I get a call from my sister.

"Hey Sis," Lynn begins. "I went to see Angela. That place reminds me of when I had my breakdown."

"How is she doing? I really appreciate you going and checking on her," I say, hating that I can't be there.

"She is still not doing too good. She was agitated and wanting to get out," Lynn went on, "Listen, I don't think I can go back to see her while she is there. I had a panic attack."

"Oh no," I respond, as I remember what she went through. Five years prior, she had her first breakdown while she was at work. I took off work and stayed with her and took care of my three nieces. In her case, it required two hospitalizations before we could get her stabilized. She has recovered and has even returned to work as a nurse, but she still has false memories about her experience. She still blames us for locking her up.

"When I went behind the locked doors, I felt like I was a patient again and they weren't going to let me out," she went on to explain, as her voice begins to faulter. "I flashed back to that time..."

"I understand. You don't have to go back. I am going to finish my work week while Dana is staying with Lottie Mae. I'll go see her this weekend. She will be fine. Don't worry about anything. I love you," I tell her, trying to console her.

The next few days, I continue working my home health job. Every evening, I call Dana for updates on Lottie Mae. Susan calls me every day. She told me Angela had a rough first week, refusing to take all her meds, and there were episodes where she had to be given injections of Ativan to calm her. I drive straight to Houma after work on Friday. I need to speak with the nurse face to face. If Angela hasn't been taking her medications while they are treating her, maybe the doctor will keep her until she does comply. I get to the hospital a few minutes before visitation hours and sign my name on the clip board placed in the waiting area of the locked unit on the seventh floor.

A tall, thin nurse from the locked unit comes and takes the clip board. There are two other visitors waiting to see their loved one. They have already signed in and taken a seat in the designated waiting area.

"Mrs. Thornton?" she asks, looking across the room.

"Yes, I am she," I answer.

"Can you come with me? I have a few questions I need to ask," the nurse asks softly.

"Yes," I immediately answer, and get up to follow her through the magnetic locked door.

"Your daughter signed the HIPPA consent form allowing me to talk to you about her progress. We have been having a difficult time getting her to take her medications. She refused to take the Lithium the doctor prescribed for her bipolar the first five days she was here. She took her first dose, yesterday. We also had to give her Haldol by injection, to help calm her, and keep her from hurting herself," she informs me.

"Yes, her sister told me that she was fighting the medications," I confirm that I am aware. "The doctor initially said he was only going to keep her for fifteen days. Do you think he will keep her longer since she hasn't taken the lithium long enough for it to work fully?"

"I don't know. So far, I haven't heard of a change on her discharge date," the nurse says.

"Please tell Dr. Smith that I am asking him to keep her longer, so that the medicine has time to reach its effective dose. Lithium needs to be taken over a period of several weeks, before it's fully working," I say wondering if this nurse knows what the term effective dose is. She will never be stable, until the medication is working fully, and she is compliant taking it as prescribed.

"I will tell him," she affirms.

"Because she just started taking the lithium yesterday, it will only be one week that she has been taking the medication, if he sends her home after only fifteen days here. That clearly isn't long enough for the medicine to work," I say, feeling my breath begin to quicken, and panic start to rise as I repeat myself. I am desperate to make them see Angela needs more time to heal, before sending her back out in the world.

"I promise, I will tell him your concerns. Would you like to go visit with Angela now? They have let the others in. They are in the dayroom," she says, redirecting my attention, pointing toward the room next door that has a wall of glass windows facing the nursing station. A large muscular orderly holding a clip board stands post at the entrance. Inside the cubed space is a long rectangular table. Patients are seated on one side and the other side host their visitors. As I walk toward the door, I see Angela get up and walk toward me.

We hug until the orderly interrupts.

"No touching please," the young man instructs, "you can take a seat on this side (he motions Angela towards the row of patients on the right side) and you can sit across from her."

I nod and take my assigned seat. This is a little different from Community Care. I sit and lean forward with my hands extended toward her. She seems giddy, considering her surroundings.

"Hey Sweetheart, how are you?" I ask cautiously, knowing she hasn't been taking her medications.

"We can't hold hands. I hate this place. It is better than Community Care though," she says, as she looks around the room. "You see that guy over there?"

She nods her head toward a young man with dirty blond hair, visiting with a woman seated across from him, at the end of the table.

"His brother was murdered by a serial killer. That's why he's in here. He went completely nuts after," she whispers across the table.

"I spoke to the nurse," I say, trying to change the subject. I know it is common for patients to be noncompliant with medications, because the meds dull the "on top of the world" feeling they get from the mania. Also, heightened sexuality is another symptom, and completely the opposite of Angela's character when she is well. I try to soften my tone as I go on, "She told me you just started taking the Lithium, yesterday. Is that accurate?"

"I didn't want to take it at first. I hate all the side effects. I did something funny and now they are all mad at me," she says, changing the subject and starts talking like a small child.

"What happened?" I ask.

"I saw they had a camera on the ceiling in my room, so I climbed up on my bed where I could reach it and tore it down. I saved all the metal pieces and took them to the dayroom. Then, my friend, she motions toward the young man still visiting with his family member at the end of the table, helped me play tricks on the nurses. We took turns throwing the nuts and bolts at the nurse's station. They didn't know what was happening," she starts laughing as she tells her story. It is painfully obvious she is way off kilter mentally.

"I think Jason is coming to see you tomorrow while I watch the baby," I say hoping to get her mind off this new person. Why can't they provide separate units for men and women?

"I need some more clothes. Do you think if I make a list, he can bring them to me?" she asks, reminding me of how she was when she stayed at Community Care. She doesn't ask about Lottie Mae. It's a nightmare we are living. Our sweet baby has lost her mind. She is in a state of delirium.

"I'll see what we can do. Well, my darling, I need to go so I can get to the city before it gets too late. I need to get back so Jason's mom can go to Lake Charles for a few days. I love you," I say, as I accept the fact that she is too sick to have meaningful conversation. I ignore the orderly's instructions and give Angela a big hug and kiss on the cheek, before the nurse comes to escort me through the locked doors.

Treatment in America: Her Life Matters

Chapter Twenty-Seven

The doctor will not extend Angela's stay. On day fifteen, she is discharged into the care of Jason. So much for Dr. False Hope. When I asked the doctor why he was giving her oral medications instead of injections, he said it's because she won't agree to the injections. I asked why does that matter? Why aren't you making that decision for her? I told him she isn't well enough to make those decisions. I compared her vulnerability to that of a stroke patient that needs intervention to stay safe, but it fell on deaf ears. How can this doctor say she is stable, when he can't even get her to take her medications long enough for them to work? Now he is sending her back to the same environment that she was in, before she came under his care. The same situation that resulted in her not taking her meds and ending up at his hospital.

I continue working my home health job three days a week, then drive back to the city to stay for four days. Dana and I are a good team. We have become friends, sharing the responsibility of caring for Lottie Mae, and now also caring for Angela. I arrive to take over for her Thursday, just before 10 a.m. Angela has been home for only one day and I am anxious to see how she is managing.

"Good morning," I greet Dana, as I drag my large rolling suitcase over the threshold.

"Good morning," Dana says, as she smiles and continues working on her iPad. Lottie Mae is in her swing in the living room, just a few feet away from where Dana is reclined on the couch. Dana pauses from her home shopping and says, "Angela is still sleeping. So far she has been doing OK."

"I'm glad she is OK. I've been worried if she would be alright. She just started the lithium a week ago," I voice my main concern, before redirecting my attention, "How is this little angel doing?"

"She is having a little constipation. PT Patty came by yesterday. She showed me a massage for her belly. It is supposed to help stimulate her bowels to move. OT is coming at 1 p.m. I also wrote on the calendar when the nurse is coming," she tells me, as she gets up and starts gathering her things.

"Thanks for organizing the appointments and being here. I don't know how we'd make it without you," I say sincerely.

She hurriedly packs her belongings and heads out the door, back to her family in Lake Charles. I go and wake Angela up gently.

"Good morning," I whisper, as I gently nudge her shoulder. "I am about to take our little one for a stroll. Want to come with us?"

"Hi Mama," she opens her eyes and answers, as she stretches her arms above her head, "that sounds good. Give me a minute to get dressed."

She is talking in her soft sweet voice. Maybe she will be alright. I go get our little one from the swing and get her dressed for strolling. The air is a little cool this morning. I pick out her beige knit cap with yellow bow and matching sweater, grab her baby sunglasses with soft foam straps and start getting her ready. Some sunshine will do us all some good. Angela dresses quickly and joins us. We start out walking west on Magazine Street.

"How are you feeling?" I ask, as we navigate the sidewalk, avoiding holes and cracks so that the ride is smooth. The Garden District of New Orleans is gorgeous, almost two-hundred-year-old suburb of the French Quarter and the Central Business District. The streets are lined with beautiful live oak trees that are older than that, but their roots wreak havoc on the sidewalks.

"I feel so tired all the time. I am so sorry for how I talked to you mom. I couldn't make it without you," she tells me, sounding more like her old self.

"I know it's the illness that has you confused and saying things you don't mean. I wish I could make everything better," I say, as I link my arm through hers. Lottie Mae smiles as the sun light warms her face.

We are quiet as we continue walking, enjoying doing something that is not related to a hospital.

"Oh, I almost forgot to tell you," Angela begins, "Dad and Laura have sold their house and are moving to Ponchatoula, Mississippi."

"What?" I ask in shock. They live less than a mile away. I can't believe he would pick now to move farther away, "Are you serious?"

"It will be a month or so before they move. I think they have already made an offer on a farm," Angela shares.

"I am so angry with him. He used to be different. It's like he lost his mind and fell into a vagina," I vent, "I haven't gotten over how he just left you alone when you were so sick."

"Mom, please don't get mad," she asks, oblivious to the heartache his negligence has caused me or the danger he put her in.

"I'm sorry, sweetheart," I apologize. Her memories are clouded as I continue trying to explain, "I don't mean to upset you. When you get sick, you become unreasonable and lose your ability to recognize danger. He is the only one you listen to. I blame him for what happened while you were sick this last time. He is the one that left you unsupervised and I am the one that spent all night trying to keep you out of prison and get you help."

"I can't take it right now. Please stop talking about him. I'm sorry I brought it up," she says, defending him and visibly becoming upset.

"OK, I'll try," I say, giving in. We continue walking the familiar route. We see a few homeless people sleeping under the trees in the park as we make our way.

"Do you think we could make some snack bags to hand out while we walk?" Angela asks.

"What kind of bags?" I ask.

"Snack bags," she says, and begins to explain, "We have extra water, packages of peanut butter and crackers, and fruit. We can make snack bags to hand out to the homeless."

"I think that is a great idea. Let's do it," I agree, with measured optimism that maybe she is doing better. Thinking of others is certainly an improvement from before. The parents of her former students, and a few of my tennis friends from back home, have continued bringing food and groceries. We have built up extra supplies of water and snacks that we can share. Our little one is sleeping by the time we make it back.

I feel hopeful as we fix lunch and get ready for the Occupational Therapist.

Patty arrives right on time. We have two therapist that visit regularly each week. One for Physical Therapy and one for Occupational Therapy, both named Patty. OT Patty was one of my instructors from the University of Louisiana at Monroe, four hours north of New Orleans. What a small world. She is very talented and very kind.

"I brought a string of lights today. These rope lights don't get hot to the touch and they are just the right size in diameter for her to hold them," she excitedly tells us, as she laces the long rope of lights in and around the baby bouncer. She takes Lottie Mae's little hand and gently opens it and places it around the plastic lighted rope. "She is getting good positioning opening up the web space between her thumb and palm and the lights stimulate brain activity."

Angela and I sit at attention, while Patty demonstrates how to position our baby's little fisted hands. Angela is involved and trying. I am grateful she is feeling better.

The next morning, Angela and I decide to make our snack bags for the homeless. Each bag consists of one bottle of water, one package of peanut butter and crackers, and a banana or apple. It's not much, but hopefully it will give them a little nutrition and it will allow us a little time to not think of ourselves or the pain we are feeling. We pack the zip lock bags of snacks into a large shopping bag, get Lottie Mae strapped into the stroller, and we are off. We hand them out as we make our route. Some bags we leave sitting beside the sleeping homeless, without waking them. It's the first time we have felt happy in a while.

Angela's first week home is uneventful. I feel cautiously optimistic when I leave. The second week after leaving Chabert Hospital, Angela seems to become even more energetic and back to her old self when I return to the city.

"Jason is going to make some home-made sausage for St. Patrick's Day. He's going to grill them while we watch the parade," she tells me of their plans as I walk in the door, returning for my four day weekend to help with Lottie Mae.

"How many people are you expecting?" I ask, hoping that it's not too many. We don't need Lottie Mae exposed to germs in her condition. I wish we wouldn't have a party at all. I'm not feeling it. Angela and Jason have always had parties and a big social life. For them, this is their normal.

"Just a few friends and family. I have the cutest little outfit for her," she excitedly tells me, as I follow her to Lottie Mae's room. "I picked this up yesterday." Angela holds up a two-piece outfit that has green four-leaf clovers on the top, with matching green bloomers.

"That is adorable," I say, admiring the festive costume.

"I also got me something to wear," she says, smiles and leads me to her closet. She pulls a bag from the over filled space, dumps the contents on her bed. "I am going to wear this pink Marie Antoinette wig, with this 'Kiss me I'm Irish' shirt, and green tutu. What do you think?"

"It's festive," I say, feeling a little awkward not knowing how I should react. In previous years before Lottie Mae and before this battle with Bipolar, I wouldn't second guess it. While I want her to enjoy life and be as normal as possible with Lottie Mae, I worry if the excitement is too much for what we just went through and might trigger the mania. I choose my words carefully, trying not to upset her, "Lottie Mae is susceptible to illness. Maybe we shouldn't have a big party."

"It will be OK, Mom. Jason really wants to do this," she reassures me. I let it go. I must remind myself that it isn't really my home. It is theirs. I am only here to help.

The day of the parade, I find myself taking over with Lottie Mae as the crowd begins to grow outside our apartment. People begin to line the sidewalk of Magazine Street. It's reminiscent of Mardi Gras. Jason is working the grill, as Angela begins to dance around in her pink hair and green costume. Some of their friends are here drinking beer and waiting for the parade to begin. I sit with Lottie Mae on the front porch and people watch. The main one being Angela.

I decide to take our baby and go to the back of the house. The music and noise are building to the point that I can still hear it from behind closed doors. I try to stay in the moment as I rock our little one. Her face is beautiful and relaxed as she drifts off to sleep in my arms. I continue rocking her as strangers come through the narrow apartment every now and then to use our bathroom. I can't wait for this day to pass.

The next morning, I get up early and pack my things so that I can make it to my Monday morning work meeting. It's still dark outside as I tiptoe to leave. I don't bother trying to clean or pick up from the night before. It wasn't my idea to have the party and I am exhausted from trying to keep Lottie Mae away from the noisy crowd. Jason is taking off work to be home, until his mother gets here later this afternoon. I'll let him clean it.

Two days later, I get more bad news.

"Hey Miss. Jamie. My mother has been admitted to the hospital. Her appendix ruptured," Jason tells me, as I answer the phone.

Chapter Twenty-Eight

I hang up the phone and sit down on my bed and start to cry. I have been depending on Dana so much. She has been taking turns staying with Lottie Mae, allowing me to continue working, just enough to keep our heads afloat. I don't know how we are going to make it without her help. I call my sister, but she won't answer her phone. She hasn't answered her phone when I've called and left messages for the past two weeks.

I fall to the floor and pour out my heart to God. I ask for mercy and forgiveness. I tell God no matter what, I will not turn from him. I feel like Job from the bible. I lie there prone, shaking from despair. How are we going to make it through this? I feel hands on my shoulders, lifting me up.

"Jamie, what's going on? Are you alright?" Lance asks, as he helps me off the floor.

"No. I'm not all right," I manage to squeak out. He holds me in his arms rocking back and forth as he tries to soothe me.

"Who was on the phone?" he asks.

"It was Jason. His mother's appendix ruptured, and she is in the hospital. They performed emergency surgery and she is in recovery. Looks like she will be out for several months. She won't be able to lift anything over five pounds while she's healing. There will be no one to help with Angela and Lottie Mae," I tell him, and begin to cry again as I recount our fate.

"Why don't you ask them to move in with us. We can take care of them here," he offers, trying to fix things.

"That won't work. Lottie Mae's specialists are all at Tulane. She doesn't need to be two hours away from them. Not to mention, Jason's work is in the city. He can't run Salutations from Brookhaven. Besides, it's not my decision. It's Jason and Angela's decision. It's all out of my control," I explain.

"You have a teenager still at home that needs you. You haven't been to but a handful of her games this year. It's not fair to her for you to stay gone all the time," he reasons with me.

"Why are you adding more pressure to me? I'm about to explode already and I don't need this shit. I give my attention to the child that needs it the most and right now Angela needs me more. I'm going to have to take a leave of absence from my job and go take care of them," I say, feeling anger begin to give me strength.

"So, you are just going to quit your job, leave your teenage daughter and go live with Angela," he clarifies angrily.

I pull away from his arms and head to my closet.

"I need you to go away from me, before I say something I can't take back," I stop to say, looking into his eyes.

"Say it. You have made up your mind anyway. You don't care how this affects us," he continues.

"I hate you at this moment. I want a divorce. I can't take this shit anymore. I haven't been happy in years, but I have kept trying. Now, when I really need you the most, you want to add pressure on me, when I'm already at my limit. News for you. That's not love," I say boldly, not caring anymore as I pull the largest suitcase I can find out of storage.

"You are being selfish. I have loved you and when I married you, I told you I would never divorce you," he says, as he follows behind me

"GET AWAY FROM ME!!!" I scream, unable to keep calm any longer.

He retreats to his spot on the large couch in the living room. I am happy Jenny isn't home to hear us fighting. She is spending the afternoon with her best friend. I continue packing with shaky hands. I cannot give in to fear now. I will call and talk with Jenny on my way to her sister's house. Jenny has shown great maturity understanding the sacrifice we all are making.

I call my boss before heading to New Orleans. She seems happy that I am taking a leave of absence. I am told to expect one of the human resource specialists to call within the next few days. I do have short and long term disability insurance. Maybe we can survive this. Even if quitting work to be with Lottie Mae means losing everything, I don't care. I must go.

I finish packing and head back to New Orleans. Angela seems to be maintaining during our crisis with Granny Dana's appendix. She can help care for Lottie Mae with me or Jason nearby. Jason's brother calls to say he, his wife, and their three children, are coming to visit. His brother is a preacher that has an inner-city ministry in Memphis, Tennessee. They want to help while Dana is out. Saturday, they show up with a huge dish of lasagna and smiling faces.

"Hi, I'm Rebecca," the young thirty-something says, as she hugs my neck.

"Hi, I'm Maemo. It's so good to meet you. Jason tells me you are a sweet sister-in-law," I tell the beautiful lady, wearing a long casual maxi skirt with a simple cotton top and hair tied up in a scarf.

"We are only going to be in town for a week. We are going to be staying at my sister's house not too far from here. She's going to watch my kids, so I can come over and help out," she says smiling.

"Thank you, so much! How good are you with computers?" I ask, as we make our way to the kitchen to store the lasagna.

"Not too good. I can turn one on," she laughingly tells me.

"Well, I want to set up a website for Lottie Mae," I begin, "I have taken a leave of absence from work and thought I'd start a blog to raise awareness about Zellweger and to help us raise money for all the medical expenses and basically to just survive this."

"I don't know what to do, but I'll help any way I can," Rebecca offers.

It takes us two days using iPage and Weebly Block and Build to construct the website. We also spent hours with tech help. In the end, we were successful in its launch. I start posting updates every evening. The blog is meant to give a glimpse into a day in our life. Besides educating the public on Zellweger Disorder, it gives opportunity for our friends to donate money.

By the time Rebecca and her family leave heading back to Memphis, we are beginning to see Angela become increasingly agitated. I begin to suspect she isn't taking her medications once again. I get a call from Susan shortly after they leave. She is also noticing subtle changes.

"Yesterday, I asked her if she was still taking her medications and she lit into me," Susan shares, "I only asked because she has been shopping online and spending money she doesn't have."

"I have noticed that she's been asking me to watch Lottie Mae more. She's been complaining about Jason not helping her. She seemed like she was doing better last week. She wasn't staying in bed as much. She was taking care of Lottie Mae more. Now, I am a little worried she isn't sleeping enough. I'm afraid that she hasn't been honest about her meds," I say, sharing the same concerns.

"I've called and talked to dad," Susan confides.

"Well, I will never call him again to help. If you want to call him, that's between you and him," I say, trying not to pressure Susan with my anger at her father for leaving Angela alone the last time I asked him to help.

"He's going to come pick her up and take her to see Dana," she goes on to tell me their plans. "Dana has been calling him, asking him to spend some time with her. Jason has also been calling him, telling him how Angela is beginning to be mean to him again."

"OK. I'll tell her to get ready," I say and hang up. I don't know why the others aren't angry with Garry for abandoning her at that hotel in a strange city the last time. I go to tell Angela that her dad is on his way. She is already packed and says she's going to wait on the front porch, so she can smoke a cigarette.

A few minutes later, she pokes her head inside.

"He's here. I'll call later to tell you how Dana is doing," she yells down the hall, toward Lottie Mae's room. She closes the door and runs to get inside her father's pick-up truck. I know she is sick now. When she is well, she kisses her baby and kisses me good-bye.

The house is quiet. Just me and Lottie Mae. I am grateful that I can be here taking care of her. I try to stay present in the moment. I spend the evening preparing her formula, giving her a bath and massage with lavender scented grape-seed oil. While getting her dressed, I find myself praying for God to help us through this. I pray for Angela to get the needed help to heal. As tears start rolling down my cheek, I feel little Lottie Mae's hand on top of mine as I rest it beside her on the changing table. I am startled because she lacks the ability to move her arms voluntarily. When I look up, she is staring right at me. I bend down as I take her little fisted hand in both my hands and give her soft butterfly kisses from her hand up to her face. I love this angel so much. She helps me bear the pain of watching her mother's heart break.

The next morning, I get a call from Susan.

"Mom, Angela is back at Chabert Hospital. She had another breakdown last night," her sister tells me heartbroken.

Treatment in America: Her Life Matters

Chapter Twenty-Nine

I am not in shock that Angela is back in the hospital. She had just started the lithium when she was discharged. They didn't keep her long enough to see if she would be able to comply with her oral medications. Looks like I was right. She stopped them without warning. Why won't the doctors listen?

"Dad took her to see Dana in the hospital. While they were there, she called one of her old friends from college, Allen, to pick her up. Dad let her go with him. I get a call around 1:30 a.m. from her asking me to take her to Chabert. She was crying, saying she was having a breakdown," Susan recants the events.

"I am glad you were able to get her to go. Who is Allen?" I ask.

"Someone she used to see on and off a long time ago," Susan tells me.

I hang up the phone and go back to our angel. It's quiet in the house as I rock her in the living room. I hope Jason is OK. As Angela becomes sick, she starts turning on each of us, one at a time. She has been hard on him. Now salt will be added to the wound with this Allen friend.

When Jason returns from visiting his mother, he comes and finds me as I am folding clothes. Lottie Mae is content in her bed watching her musical mobile.

"I want to ask you if you can help me with something. I am worried about Angela taking Lottie Mae and running off when she is sick like this. While she is in the hospital, I want to file for protective custody," he tells me solemnly

"I understand. I will help you under one condition. I want you to promise me that you won't keep Lottie Mae away from her when Angela is well," I offer.

"I promise. I will never do that," he agrees.

We have already set up appointments for Lottie Mae to see the audiologist, ear nose and throat specialist, along with her pediatrician at Tulane for Monday, Jason's day off. We decide to go to the courthouse the following week to complete the custody paperwork. I struggle with this decision, but I feel it is necessary.

I feel so weighted down with sadness. It's hard to do anything extra outside of taking care of our little one. Cleaning the house has become taxing. I finally address the stack of mail growing larger on the dining room table, where it has been collecting the past couple of weeks. The Family Leave of Absence paperwork package is in the mix. I complete the stack of forms and send them overnight to meet the deadline.

During the night I wake up as Lottie Mae is coughing and spitting up. I jump up and turn the feeding pump off, grab the suction bulb and begin clearing her airway. She gasps as she takes a big breath, then begins crying with a weak wet voice. I quickly change her clothes and pick her up. Jason runs in to check on us, as I finish washing her face.

"I think she is OK for now," I tell him, as she begins to relax in my arms.

"I heard her choking..." Jason says. His voice trails off as he returns to his room next door.

I am worried about Lottie Mae. She is having trouble with constipation and it seems to make her start throwing up as her system gets backed up. I make a mental note to let the nurse know what is happening. I rock her for the next thirty minutes, before she can fall asleep again.

Nursing and both therapists continue their weekly visits as I try to keep up with it all. In the evenings, when Jason comes home or when Susan comes by after her workday, I take a couple of hours of alone time to write and post the blog. People are beginning to send in donations and messages of encouragement. Later that week, Lance and Jenny drive down to see us.

"I'm sorry about pressuring you. I love you so much," Lance begins, as we sit down to visit. Jenny has already come in to kiss me and then heads to the back patio to hang out and phone her friends.

"It's OK. I love you, too. We are all under pressure," I say, wanting everything to be better. I can't handle any more pressure. No more confrontations for the moment.

"How's Angela doing?" he asks, as we sit on the couch to catch up.

"Since she is back at Chabert, I have only spoken to her a couple of times. She calls, asks for me to bring stuff, gets mad, hangs up. It's so frustrating. I have been reading a lot about bipolar disorder. Each time she has a break, she is less likely to return to her old self. I don't know how I can tell the doctor anything I haven't said already to make him give her injections, instead of oral medications. I don't know what else to do. Now I have started writing the blog for Lottie Mae and it's hard to know how to address Angela's illness," I tell him.

"You can't write about everything. She will still have a life after Lottie Mae. People judge so harshly about mental illness. It might make it hard for her to get a job," he says, worried about Angela's future.

"I have to say something. I will try to choose my words carefully. How's Jenny doing?" I ask.

"She has been OK," he continues. "We miss you."

"I know. I'm sorry. I feel I must be here. There is no one else left," I say, beginning to tear up as I defend my decision to stay.

He and Jenny spend the day with us. We go strolling down Magazine and loop through the park on our way back. We share a meal and keep things light. I miss being there to see Jenny play ball. Our lives have changed so much. The visit goes well despite the huge argument we had the last time I saw Lance.

Susan and her friend, Angie, ask me to ride with them to visit Angela at Chabert. Jason volunteers to stay with Lottie Mae when he gets off work at Breaux Mart, since Salutations is closed during the week. Angie is a tall, thin red head that has been working with Susan on the set of Treme, an HBO series based in NOLA. She is usually quiet, my favorite thing about her.

"I just love your family," Angie announces, as we leave New Orleans headed west to Houma. "Thank you for letting me go see Angela with you. I just finished setting up Lottie Mae's Facebook page and wanted to ask if there was anything you might want me to post?"

"It's nice of you to do that, Angie. I am going to start sharing the post from the blog. You can handle posting for the fundraiser that some of Angela's former student's parents are organizing," I tell the eager new friend of Susan's.

"My parents were hippies. They were so dysfunctional. So different from how loving your family is," the naive girl shares, "I am so glad to have met you all."

I think she must not be too bright, if she thinks we are functional. What's wrong with being a hippie. She is clueless. I just smile and nod.

"When my twin brother died, he left his life insurance proceeds to me. I moved to the city and have been working as a model and just started doing some acting. I met Susan on the Treme set," she continues to talk about herself with confidence. I try to be polite and listen. I have so much on my mind that I choose not to share with this person. She wouldn't understand.

We finally make it to Chabert Hospital after two hours of hearing about every detail of Angie's life. As we sign in on the visitor's log, I notice that there is someone already signed in to see Angela. I scan the room to see if I recognize who might be visiting her. There is an elderly couple sitting together on the far right side of the visitor's waiting room and sitting near them is a young man, dressed in a worn out t-shirt, shorts with frayed hem, dirty tennis shoes, and a black skull cap. He vaguely looks familiar.

"Susan, is that guy here to see Angela?" I whisper in her ear, as I nod toward the young man.

"I think that is the guy she met when she was hospitalized here the last time," Susan informs me.

"Shit, that's just great," I say, shocked and angry, "What are we supposed to tell Jason?"

"I don't know. I'm not going to tell him. It will kill him," Susan says.

We are interrupted by the nurse unlocking the metal doors. She enters taking the clip board and reviews the list of names.

"We are going to start visitation. Who is here for Angela McMillin?" the nurse asks.

We all stand, including the stranger we have been guessing about. Susan and I look at each other, as this unfortunately confirms he is here to see her too.

"You can go first," new crazy boyfriend offers politely, with a delusional expression on his face. He's smiling at us like we are his future extended family. His unkept appearance tells me he can't even take care of himself. The kindest thing I can do is not respond.

I follow the nurse along with the elderly couple through to the locked unit. As the nurse begins reading the rules that I am all too familiar with, I see Angela waiting for me, holding a stack of crayon colored pictures. We file into the designated visitors' room and take our seats across from our loved ones.

"Hi Mom, when do you think you can get me out of here?" she starts asking.

"Well, Angela, you weren't taking your medications and you are very sick again. You need to get well, before you come home," I say, taking the straightforward approach.

"I need to get back home to my baby," she begins, with tears beginning to swell in her eyes.

"When you were home, you didn't do your part taking your meds. In fact, you not only didn't take your meds, but you were starting to do everything you could to get away from Lottie Mae. I think you need to stay longer," I say, laying it all out on the line. I have been timid the first two times she had a breakdown and that approach has not been effective.

"You are the reason I'm here. If you would just let me have a break every now and then, I wouldn't need to get away," delusional Angela lashes out.

"I love you, sweetheart, and I have tried to give you breaks, but you are not well..." I start explaining, but before I can finish, she cuts me off.

"GET HER OUT OF HERE. I HATE YOU!" She stands and screams.

I get up and head toward the exit. Her nurse meets me as I try to leave.

"Can you ask her to sign the consent for release of medical information?" the young nurse ask, as she escorts me to the nurse's station.

"I think it's too late for that," I tell her, wondering if she missed the yelling.

"I want to talk to you about her medicines," the concerned nurse adds.

"Maybe next time," I say. I am sad and feeling defeated. What else could I possibly tell them, that would make them help us, that I haven't said before. I return to Susan and Angie in the waiting room. They take turns visiting with Angela while I wait and cry silent tears.

On the drive back, we share our conversations with her. We agree not to mention Angela's fourth visitor, even though she says he's just a friend. We don't want to hurt Jason. We know that this behavior will end when she is taking her medicine.

"Maybe, if you didn't talk about the medications, she would have talked to you more," Angie tells me, trying to help.

"Angie, this is your first experience with Angela while she's ill. This is the third time she has been hospitalized, because she stopped taking her medication. Maybe, if we address the problem of her not taking the medications, while she is in a safe place, we can get her stable enough to return to Lottie Mae," I say measured, trying to contain the anger as I explain to this idiot my reasoning. "I would appreciate your silence, if you feel the need to give me any more advice. You don't have a clue what I've been through with her."

We make the rest of the drive back in silence. Later, I told Susan that Angie is never to ride with me again to visit Angela. I have to draw boundaries with any negativity in my life in order to be strong. I am beginning to understand how important that is, if I am going to make it through this with my own sanity.

Chapter Thirty

Jason and I coordinate our schedules. Tuesday mornings Jason doesn't have to be at work until 10 a.m., so I pick 8 a.m. to schedule my weekly counseling appointments, allowing him to stay with Lottie Mae. I have so much on my mind. I choose walking the short fifteen-minute hike, instead of driving, to my first counseling session this morning. The cool air makes me quicken my steps as I near my destination.

The office is in a residential, light purple, Victorian, two story home. I enter the wrought iron fenced yard and ring the doorbell marked "office." I am greeted by a middle-aged, balding, man dressed in khakis, a plaid shirt, and bow tie.

"Hi, I'm Tom Miller. I have some paperwork for you to fill out," the soft-spoken man says, as he hands me a clip board, "I'll be with you in a few minutes."

I take the clipboard and choose a seat in the waiting area, just inside the entrance. It's not long, before he returns to retrieve the completed forms and leads me into the formal office on the ground floor.

"I know I spoke to you on the phone, but this is our first face to face meeting. What I would like to do is start by letting you tell me what brought you here today," he begins, as he settles into his chair with note pad and pen. I take a seat on the couch across from him. There is a large box of tissues on the side table next to it.

"Yes. I'm Jamie Thornton. I'm living in New Orleans, just a mile from here, helping to take care of my granddaughter, who is terminally ill. Lottie Mae, my grandbaby, has been diagnosed with Zellweger Disorder. Zellweger is a biogenesis cell disorder. She is missing enzymes, in every cell in her body, that affect the ability for absorption of nutrition and the ability to remove toxins. She is almost nine months old, functioning at the level of a three to four-month-old. She is not expected to live past her first birthday," I say, as I introduce myself and tell him about the foundation of our heartache.

"I'm so sorry you are going through that," he says sympathetically.

"Her mother, my first born, Angela, became mentally ill, after we were given the results from the genetic testing and prognosis. She was diagnosed with PTSD onset of Bipolar Disorder. Since then, she has been hospitalized three times, all within thirty days of each other. She is currently in the hospital in Houma," I tell him.

"You certainly have a lot going on. Do you have any support from other family members?" He asks, as he makes notes on his yellow pad.

"At first we had lots of support, but recently they are dropping like flies," I say, thinking of all the unfortunate events leading to me caring for Lottie Mae almost solo.

"Go on," he encourages.

"Lottie Mae's other grandmother, Dana, had been splitting the week with me caring for her. She has a special needs daughter in Lake Charles where she lives. Dana was coming for three days, then I would come for the other four days. This allowed Dana to care for her daughter and allowed me to work my home health job while spending time with my youngest child, who is sixteen and still living at home. My husband is taking care of her while I'm here. Now Dana's appendix ruptured, so she won't be able to help for a few months. My mother decided to have shoulder surgery. Jason, my common-law-son-in-law, is working two jobs. Susan, my next to oldest, that lives next door, has increased her work hours, leaving me to manage alone," I say, crying at this point.

"You have a lot to deal with," he affirms. He offers me tissues and a glass of water as he patiently waits for me to compose myself.

"Now, with Angela sick, she is the opposite of her normally sweet, refined self. She is overly friendly with the opposite sex. She keeps saying that I don't give her a break, when I'm the one doing most of the housework, taking care of Lottie Mae, and organizing the ton of doctor's appointments, and home health visits. Jason, Lottie Mae's father, is also hurting and beginning to lose his patience with her. I know it's the illness causing her to act so different. He can't see that it is the illness. I can't blame him for being hurt. I am just afraid he's going to punish Angela for all that she's doing while she's sick. I've begged the doctors to help me with her. She won't take the medication like it's prescribed. They won't change from oral medications to injections. I don't know what to do," I say, as I begin to sob uncontrollably.

He listens patiently and lets me vent all the brutal details of Lottie Mae's illness and the fears and frustrations of caring for an adult child with mental illness. He lets me talk freely without judgement and I am grateful. After the session, he writes a reminder for our next appointment and assures me he will help me through this.

"My cell number is listed. Please feel free to call me if you are having a crisis. I am available," the kind therapist says, as he hands me his personal business card.

I walk the mile back to our apartment taking time to be present in the moment. The sun has risen above the tall buildings of the city and a gentle breeze blows the hair from my face. I try not to think about the long list of stressors I just listed to my new therapist. I leave it all behind for the next fifteen minutes. When I walk through the door to Lottie Mae's, Jason is waiting for me in the living room.

"How did your therapy session go?" he asks.

"Good. I like him. He was easy to talk to," I share.

"There is something I want to talk to you about," he begins.

"OK," I say with dread and take a seat on the couch.

"I am worried about how Angela will react if she comes back here. I think it might be better if she stays somewhere else, until she has been taking her medications longer. It's too much of a risk for Lottie Mae," he tells me.

"Where is she supposed to go? I can't depend on Garry to stay with her. She must have twenty-four-hour, seven days a week supervision when she is sick," I adamantly say, feeling defensive.

"I've talked to Garry and he said he could take her to your mother's house for a week. They want to discharge her Friday," he conveys their plans.

"She's not going to listen to my mother," I blurt out, as I try to think of any alternative.

"We don't have any other choice right now. She can't come back here," he states firmly.

I do not have the energy to debate on what to do with Angela. I barely have enough energy to do all that is necessary to make it through today. I let it go for now. It is out of my control.

"I have another appointment tomorrow at 3 p.m. for the psychiatrist. Do you think you will be able to watch Lottie Mae?" I ask, changing the subject.

"I go into work at Breaux Mart at 6 a.m. and get off at 2 p.m. That will be fine," he agrees.

The next afternoon, I make it to my doctor's appointment and get prescribed antidepressants, valium, and a heavy-duty sleep aid. He diagnosed me with PTSD with severe depression. I ask him if he thinks I will have a breakdown, but he is reassuring telling me that if I haven't had one already, I am going to be fine. He is worried about my weight loss. So far, I have lost thirty-five pounds without trying. It's hard to remember to eat when so much heartache has stolen my appetite. I talk with him about strategies for eating and agree to start drinking protein shakes as supplements. That way, I can line them up in the refrigerator and count how many I've drank in a day to make sure I'm getting enough nutrition. I'm beginning to have bruising and signs of anemia.

"Hi Mom," Susan says as she comes in to visit after her long day on set. "How did your doctor's appointment go?"

"Good. I've got enough pills for my own medicine organizer now," I joke, trying to lighten the mood. "How's your work going?"

"It's OK. Jason said that he talked to you about Angela going to grandma's when they discharge her?" she asks, as she goes to peek at Lottie Mae in her bouncer beside me.

"Yes, he told me. Why isn't she staying with Garry and his wife?" I ask, knowing the answer before I ask it.

"Laura does not want her there. He says he must do what his wife says. He called grandma and asked if she could help by letting her stay there, while he figures out where she can go," she explains, beginning to become agitated.

"This makes me so angry. I'm sorry, I don't mean to upset you. Do you mind watching Lottie Mae for me while I write the blog? I just need a couple of hours," I ask, and stop myself from going on and on about her father putting his new wife above his daughter's needs.

"Sure, I don't mind. I need to take a shower and grab something to eat and then I can take over," she offers.

It's nearing dusk as I settle into my chair on Susan's balcony. I have my laptop and a glass of wine with me. I take a few minutes to gather my thoughts. It's been so hard to write and not tell of our worries about Angela. I open my computer and see a notification from one of my post. It's a message from another grandmother who lives in Australia. Her granddaughter has recently been diagnosed with Zellweger and she has been reading my blog. She gives me encouragement to keep writing and sharing. She tells me how it helps her. I feel the love and compassion, from thousands of miles away, lift my spirit. I take a sip of wine and with renewed hope begin writing.

Treatment in America: Her Life Matters

Chapter Thirty-One

Angela was released from Chabert Hospital, after only one week of treatment. She stopped having the medical staff call me and routed the discharge planning to her father. I am feeling hopeless for her recovery. It doesn't matter if I point out the scientific facts. Her medications haven't been working, because we can't get her to take them, yet they continue oral medications instead, of injections. I wonder if Angela being uninsured is part of the reason, she is not receiving proper medical treatment.

"Hi mom, how is Angela doing?" I ask anxiously.

"She is sleeping right now. They made it here around 6 p.m. I made some soup and cleaned out the extra room so she can rest," my mother tells me. "I was just reading my bible."

"Well, I was just checking," I say. "I'm worried about her not taking her medications. They take a few weeks before they are working fully. She might try to run away."

"She was a little confused. She's like a little child. It's so pitiful. She will be OK. I have prayed and given it to the Lord," she optimistically states, convinced her faith alone is strong enough to cure Angela.

"Call me if you need me," I say, not wanting to have a discussion on the Lord. My mother is the kind of religious person that feels anyone that believes differently from her beliefs is going to spend an eternity in hell fire. She has managed to bring a little hell on Earth to some of us, even before we die.

I am feeling discouraged as I hang up the phone. No matter how I explain to Angela's different medical teams at the different hospitals, or how much I explain in detail to my family, and to Jason's family, no one is listening to me. It's all I can do to push my worries aside and focus on Lottie Mae. I do love her so much. She seems more like my own child than just my grandbaby.

My two best friends come to visit again and take me to hang out down the street at Tracy's Irish pub, while Jason is home watching Lottie Mae. I have a two-hour window, before he has to leave to open Salutations.

"How are you doing? Still wearing the green fingernail polish on your toes" Suzy asks.

"Yes, still wearing it," I answer, as I stick my right foot out and show my painted green toenails through my sandals. "It's been so hard. Angela went to my mother's to recover from the last hospitalization. I can't get the hospitals to keep her long enough for the medicine to work. Jason doesn't want her staying here while she's sick. He thinks it's too much to care for the baby and her. Dana is out recovering from appendix surgery. Susan has been working longer hours, sometimes fourteen hours on set. It's been just me cleaning and taking care of Lottie Mae."

"Why don't you make them help you clean?" Betsy asks.

"We are all under so much pressure. I'm afraid to ask them anything. They aren't too happy that I want Angela to come back to the apartment with us. They aren't even comfortable with her staying upstairs in Susan's apartment," I share.

"You are giving up your life to come here and help them. They should do whatever you ask," Betsy tells me, encouraging me to stand up for myself.

"Just make a list of things you want them to do to help out," Suzy chimes in. My two best friends are strong independent women accustomed to fixing problems. They each are the boss at their place of employment and in their homes.

"I will speak up and ask for help. It's not so easy. I'm also afraid that Jason might limit my time with Lottie Mae, if he gets too upset," I tell them my darkest fear.

"Just do it!" Betsy encourages.

I thank them for coming to spend time with me. I am grateful for their friendship. I want to take their advice, but my intuition tells me to proceed with caution. Later that evening, another tennis friend and her husband stop by. They bring us groceries and laughter with their visit. My spirits are lifted by their kindness at a time when I need it the most.

The next night Susan stops by after work, a little before 8 p.m. The wine and cheese bar is closed tonight. Jason is home and is rocking Lottie Mae in the living room when she arrives. I just finished writing the blog and posted it from Susan's balcony. I head downstairs and join them.

"Hey, now that I have you two together, there is something I want to talk to you about," I venture, taking my friends advice.

"Sure, what's up?" Susan asks, as she takes Lottie Mae from Jason. He gives her his seat in the rocker. He moves to the couch and takes a seat on the opposite end from where I am sitting.

"I have been falling behind with cleaning the house. With Dana out sick and Angela in the hospital, I can't seem to keep up. Do you think we can divide the chores?" I ask. There I said it. Now I hope they don't get mad.

"Just tell us what you want us to do and we will do it," Susan curtly replies.

"All you have to do is ask and we will help," Jason chimes in.

"It's hard for me to ask for help. Maybe if we write out a list of things that need to be done, it will make it easier," I suggest, not wanting to ask them for help chore by chore.

"Are you OK, Mom?" Susan asks, "You seem to be stressed out."

"I am worried about Angela staying at my mother's house when she's still so sick, but other than that I'm OK. I have been the only one cleaning the apartment and it's getting harder for me to keep up without help. That's all," I say bluntly. I regret asking for help immediately.

"When my mother comes back, I want you to take a break," Jason interjects, as he becomes annoyed.

"I'm OK. I just thought I'd ask for help cleaning the apartment. That's all," I soften my request, as I try to control my emotions. I want them to just say, OK we'll help. Instead, they are defensive. I was afraid of this. I don't need them telling me I need a break. I just need them to help a little more. I wish I would not have listened to my friend's advice. They can't imagine how sensitive we all are in this situation.

After one week at my mother's house, Angela is begging to come back. I am torn between needing to care for her and needing to care for Lottie Mae. Granny Dana has recovered from her appendix surgery and is finally cleared to resume helping with Lottie Mae. Things have changed with Lottie Mae since she was here last. She has been battling constipation and more spitting up. The doctor lowered the rate on her feeding pump. Her digestive system is slowing as the disease progresses. Dana's return is helping somewhat. Jason asks to have another team Lottie Mae meeting the second night after Dana returns.

We gather in the living room. Lottie Mae is in her swing, Jason and his mother are on the couch, Susan is sitting in the rocker by Lottie Mae's swing, and I take a seat on the straight back chair across from them.

"We have been talking and want to let you know how we feel," Jason says, taking the lead. "We love you, Maemo. We want you to continue helping us with Lottie Mae. We don't feel it's good for Angela to be around Lottie Mae while she is sick. I can't have her staying here," he calmly tells me, speaking for the group.

"I understand your concerns," I say. I also know he is angry with her for her overly friendly behavior with her former hospital mates. I offer a compromise. "Why can't she stay upstairs in Susan's apartment? I can be with her at Susan's at night and she can help me with Lottie Mae during the day."

"I don't think it's a good idea for her to be there," Susan states, as she looks toward Jason and Dana. I realize they have been discussing this without me.

"It's just that I don't have anywhere else for her to go. If she stays upstairs, I can take care of Lottie Mae and be there for Angela," I desperately plead, hoping to change their minds.

"You have been doing so much while I've been out. Why don't you go home and spend time with your family? I'm back now so you can take a break," Dana offers, trying to change the subject from Angela returning to the apartment.

"I don't need a break. I am not leaving this baby. I have happily stepped in to help. I have been paying the rent, utility bills and groceries here with the donations from my friends and what the blog is bringing in. I am just asking for a little help cleaning the apartment and for Angela to be allowed to come back home. Now you want me to go back to Mississippi for a break and Angela can't return to her own home," I say feeling the blood begin to boil in my veins.

"We aren't trying to upset you," Dana says, trying to smooth things over.

"I can't talk to you right now," I say, stopping myself from saying anything else. I see that I am outnumbered. This meeting was an ambush. They had already made up their minds.

Treatment in America: Her Life Matters

Chapter Thirty-Two

After a week staying with my mother, four hours from Lottie Mae, Angela returns to New Orleans. Jason, Dana, and Susan voted three to one, against me, to not let her come back to the apartment. I wish Garry would let her stay with him at his home. She needs someone with her, but his new wife won't allow it. Instead, he takes his old camper trailer and sets it up in a trailer park across the river in Harvey for her to live in. I am so scared that it's just a matter of time, before we relive the same "she's off her meds" nightmare, again.

"Thanks for letting me pick you up," Angela says, as I enter her Honda CRV.

"Did you want to come inside and see Lottie Mae?" I ask.

"Jason asked me to come by when he's not there. He said I can come by after 10 a.m." she explains.

"I didn't know. How are you and he doing? Have you been able to talk to him?" I ask. I haven't talked to him much since he has taken the position of keeping Angela away. I understand why he is hurt by her. I wish he could understand, it's not her doing this. It's part of her illness.

"A little. I try to talk to him, but he doesn't want to see me right now," she tells me, as she drives us toward the Westbank.

"It's hard for him. You say and do really mean things, when you are sick," I gently tell her, "You don't seem to remember any of it."

"It's all blurry to me, Mom," she says softly, and I believe her.

"How far is it to your new place?" I ask, changing the subject, not wanting to upset her any further. I am learning the limits of my ability to influence her. She really can't help that she has an imbalance of chemicals in her brain. She has lost herself under the pressure of Lottie Mae's diagnosis and suffering.

"It's not too far," she tells me. We make the twenty-minute ride to the industrial area of Harvey. The trailer park is lined with small RVs. There are a few work trucks speckled in the driveways of the rough looking park. I don't see any sign of families. No children's bicycles or swing sets. No trees or flowers. Just a place where workmen stay, while working temporary jobs at the shipyard.

"Whose camper are you staying in?" I ask, as we pull into the small parking space allotted between the second and third trailer, of the eight-camper trailer park.

"It's one dad uses when he works out of town sometimes. This is it. It's not much. I think I can make it cute after I get it decorated," she says optimistically.

I get out of the car and stare at the place her father has sent her to live. Nothing but men staying here at this work camp. She is isolated from everyone. How is she going to manage, without someone here to help her?

"Why aren't you staying at your dad's home?" I ask.

"He thought it would be better if I had my own place. He gave me some money to go shopping. I want to get some outdoor lights to hang and maybe a little table and chairs to sit outside. I can make it cute," she says, with enthusiasm that seems out of place considering our circumstances.

My heart is sinking. The small camper is brown. Brown plaid cushions on the banquette. Brown couch and brown wood siding. It's not the drab colors or lack of landscaping, it's the lack of people that love her here. She is too sick and vulnerable to be left here to her own devices.

"Are you scared staying here? Do you need me to stay with you?" I offer.

"I'm fine. I want to come back to the apartment. Do you think Jason will change his mind?" she asks.

"He says he wants to make sure you have been taking your medications, before you come back. It's hard on me too right now. I begged them to let you stay. I asked if you could at least stay upstairs in Susan's apartment, but they shot that down. Are you taking your medications?" I ask.

"Yes, I'm taking my medications," she says, as we tour the small trailer, "I'm going to talk to Jason. I'll show him I'm doing better."

She is functioning for now. She can drive her car, do her own grocery shopping, and outwardly seems OK. She shows me her pill organizer and bag of medications. The same as the other two times, right after discharge. I recognize the potential for harm and her vulnerability in this environment and it makes me feel sick inside.

"Let's head back. By the time we get there, it should be after 10 a.m.," I suggest.

We gather her things and head back. Dana is with Lottie Mae when we get there. I am still upset with all three of them for voting to keep Angela away, but I hold it in, and put a forced smile on. I must be diplomatic, if I want to be allowed to care for our angel.

"There's my little baby," Angela says, in baby talk voice as she goes to where Lottie Mae is resting in the bouncer. Dana is seated in the rocking chair, knitting while she watches TV.

"You can have my chair Angela," Dana offers kindly, as she gathers her yarn and needles and places them into the large bag on the floor beside her.

Angela gently picks up Lottie Mae and sits in the rocker. Lottie Mae opens her mouth wide as Angela gives her little kisses on her cheeks. My heart is happy when they are together. I sit on the couch quietly as Angela continues talking to Lottie Mae as they rock. Dana excuses herself and leaves us to enjoy our little one.

Our visit goes well and flies by. I walk Angela to her car. I wait and watch her car until it disappears in traffic, heading to her temporary home on the Westbank. I return inside to go over my plans with Dana for the evening.

"You know, I love your daughter like she is mine," Dana begins, "I am glad she seems to be more like her old self."

"I think she is trying really hard," I say, with measured optimism.

"Are you going to that play tonight?" she asks.

"Yes. Patty, OT Patty, is picking me up around 6 p.m. She's the one that taught me at Louisiana State University at Monroe and is now one of Lottie Mae's therapist. It's so nice of her to go out of her way to cheer me up. We are going to see Million Dollar Quartet at the Mahalia

Jackson Theater for performing arts. It's a musical about Jerry Lee Lewis, Elvis, Carl Perkins and Johnny Cash," I tell her my plans.

"I'm glad you are taking some time for yourself. You need to take more breaks," she tells me.

"I don't feel like going anywhere. She was kind to ask me, so I'm going," I say, a little annoyed with Dana. Lately, she says I need a rest whenever I disagree with her about the direction of Angela's care. She is coming from the perspective of protecting her son. I get it. We have different priorities.

"It will be good for you to get out," she goes on.

"OK, well I better start getting ready. What time are you wanting to leave tomorrow?" I ask, so I know when to come down from Susan's apartment and take over.

"If I leave by noon, I'll be good," she says.

"OK, I'll see you tomorrow before noon," I say, confirming our plans for scheduling the care of Lottie Mae. I go and check on our little one that has been sleeping since Angela laid her down. She is propped on an incline, supported by pillows to aid with her breathing. She doesn't roll or try to turn over. Her disease has her movements limited as the abnormal increase in muscle tone keeps her immobile. I bend down over the rail and softly kiss her forehead, before heading upstairs.

I went to the play. It was wonderful. I felt strange getting dressed up and going somewhere happy people go. It was a kind gesture from Patty to give me this distraction from our pain, if only for a couple of hours.

For the next two weeks, Angela continues to visit when Jason is at work. I see subtle changes that make me suspect this cruel bipolar disease has tricked her into stopping her medications. My proof of her noncompliance with oral medications comes when my phone rings.

"Mom, I got a call from Bill, the owner of Feelings," Susan begins, "He said Angela is there with two men taking things from the restaurant and putting them into her SUV."

Bill and his partner have been like two fathers to Angela and Susan since they moved to New Orleans. Bill gave both Angela and Susan jobs at Feelings, before their careers advanced. He leased the space above Feelings to Angela and Jason, for their wine and cheese dive. His own partner suffers from bipolar disorder and he recognizes the signs.

"What?" I ask in shock.

"He said she seems pretty confused. He wanted to let us know what's going on," she tells me.

"Have you talked to Angela?" I ask, hoping that she is still in contact with her.

"I called her earlier, but she's not answering," Susan says frustrated.

"OK, sweetheart. I'll be here with Lottie Mae, waiting by the phone," I say as I hang up. My mind is starting to race. I told Garry that Angela needs to stay with someone and not be dumped in that man camp. Why are they treating her like her life is disposable?

I spend the evening trying to keep busy. I do laundry and play where's the baby game with Lottie Mae. I place her bouncer on the bed where I fold laundry. I take a towel as I prepare to fold it and shake it, so it falls over her face, then slowly pull it down as I say, "Where's the baby?" as her face becomes uncovered. She opens her mouth wide, in her adapted smile way, letting me know she enjoys the interaction. I try to keep busy to keep from worrying.

Two hours later, I get another call.

"Mom, she has been arrested in Sulphur, Louisiana," Susan says, as she starts to cry.

Treatment in America: Her Life Matters

Chapter Thirty-Three

It is a long night of tossing and turning. I wake up every few hours, check the baby, check my phone, and then wait some more. Just as the sun is coming over the horizon, my phone rings.

"Hey Mom, I can't deal with her anymore. She called me last night after she was arrested. I told her it would take a while before I could get there. I had to call and arrange to be off work. You know how hard that is right now. Then it's a three-and-a-half-hour drive one way. By the time I get there, she has already been released. She is still in the parking lot of the police station, but she won't come with me. She is with some guy named Sam. He is the brother to Mark, the guy that she met while hospitalized at Chabert, in Houma. She's been calling and talking to Mark, since she left the hospital. The two brothers drove to New Orleans and went with her to Salutations. They took the tip jar, left from the night before, and several bottles of wine, according to Bill. From what I can tell, they had a fight after leaving Salutations, and left brother number one, Mark, in the French Quarter. She and brother number two, Sam, then went to Sulphur, Louisiana, where she was arrested. Now, she says they are heading to the beach in Texas," Susan tells me exasperated.

"The beach in Texas?" I ask puzzled.

"Yes. I know it doesn't make sense. Yesterday evening I got a call from Margaret, the parent of Angela's former student, that has been bringing meals to us. She saw Angela with a strange man buying supplies at Whole Foods. Angela told her she was heading to the beach for a vacation. She was very worried about Angela, because she could tell she wasn't her normal self. I tried talking to her, Mom, but Angela is back to that manic state, where she doesn't listen to anyone," her sister tells me, as her heart breaks.

"Oh my god," I say, as I feel my heart sink, "where is she now?"

"They peeled out, throwing rocks all over my car, heading west," she says, "I am done."

"Thank you for trying so hard and going down there to help her. I don't know what to do anymore. Have you called your dad?" I ask, feeling like I could scream inside.

"I called him. He's on a job offshore right now," she says defeated.

"I told him this would happen. I don't know why I can't get anyone to listen and help," I vent angrily.

"I can't hear this right now. I have to go," Susan says, sounding overwhelmed and frustrated. She hangs up.

I sink to the floor and start praying. I lie there prone as my body shakes, convulsing as I cry uncontrollably. I can't believe this is happening. My poor baby has lost her mind, and no one will help us. I pull myself together and check on sweet Lottie Mae. She is still sleeping peacefully. I try not to dwell on the hundreds of scenarios in my head, the tragic possibilities that can happen to a person in a vulnerable state.

I keep busy cleaning the apartment, taking care of Lottie Mae. I can't write the blog tonight. I am too worried about Angela and I don't want to share with the world about the challenges of her illness per my family's request. People judge so harshly.

The next evening, I get a phone call.

"Hi Mama, I'm in the hospital," Angela tells me.

"Where are you?" I ask, happy that she is alive.

"San Antonio, Texas," She replies.

"What happened," I gently ask.

"I needed a little break. My friend, Mark, and I were heading to the beach. We stopped in San Antonio and got into a big fight. I ran away and met a guy named Jefferson. He was so beautiful. Somehow, I lost Jefferson, but I could hear him singing. I followed his voice to the Alamo and tried to break in, but the security guard caught me. They sent me here," Angela says, sharing her strange sequence of events.

"Thank God you are OK. I need you to ask them to give your medications by injection, so that you don't have to remember to take them every day. Can you ask them?" I ask, desperate to change the behavior causing us to lose her to this damn disease.

"I don't need this shit!" she defiantly shouts and hangs up on me.

The next day, I get a call from University Hospital, San Antonio Texas.

"Hello, I'm Silas. I'm a medical student at University Hospital. I have been assigned to your daughter, Angela. She gave me permission to call you. Can you tell me about her history?" the young intern with a foreign accent begins.

"Yes. She was diagnosed with PTSD onset Bipolar Disorder four months ago, after receiving the news that her baby is terminally ill. This is her fourth admission for treatment since then. She has not been successful managing her illness with oral medications. She needs her medications given by injection for her to be compliant. Not taking her medications properly is a symptom of her illness. I hope you can help her," I say, trying to stress the most important reason she keeps relapsing is because she is not taking her medications as prescribed.

"I will tell the doctor your concerns. Thank you for talking to me," he says, trying to exit the call.

"Wait, how long do you think you will be keeping her?" I ask, hoping Texas has a better healthcare system than I've seen in Louisiana for caring for their mentally ill.

"The doctor will keep her until she is stabilized," he says, giving me the rehearsed answer.

"Please, ask the doctor to keep Angela, until the medications have reached their effective dose. We can't keep her safe without it. She has been released each time too soon," I plead.

"Yes ma'am," he politely answers and hangs up.

The next day, the student doctor calls again to tell me that they are only keeping her for one week. I panic. How can they be discharging her so soon? Didn't they listen? I rack my brain for anything I can do to make them see how she needs help. I google the hospital and find the name and email of their CEO. I send a detailed letter of Angela's history and beg him to intervene. I am not a litigious person and bringing a lawsuit against anyone would be the last avenue I would ever resort to. I hope he gets the message that I won't let this go if he doesn't help me.

The next day he writes back:

> Mrs. Thornton,
>
> We appreciate you taking the time to inform us of your concerns regarding your daughter and her inpatient stay at University Hospital. I understand this is a stressful time for you and your family. Your concerns have been discussed with your daughter's healthcare team. Treatment decisions are based on what is in the best interest of the patient. Your daughter is able to make decisions in conjunction with the healthcare team regarding her inpatient stay as well as following up care. We must respect your daughter's autonomy and right to make her own healthcare decisions.
>
> Providing the highest quality of care and services to our patients and their families is our number one priority. Again, thank you for bringing your concerns to our attention.
> Tom Briggs, FACHE
> CEO, University Hospital

As I read this letter, a heavy blanket of hopelessness begins to cover my spirit. I don't know what else I'm supposed to do to get help in keeping my daughter safe. How can she make her own decisions in this mentally vulnerable state she is in?

Chapter Thirty-Four

"Ms. Jamie, this is Stephanie. I used to work with your daughter, Angela, when she worked at Covington Middle School in Austin, Texas. I am sorry to be calling you, but I don't know what else to do. Angela started calling me at 3 a.m. this morning. She left a bizarre message about needing me to pick her up from University Hospital, in San Antonio. She then started calling every hour, on the hour, ten more times. She threatened to cut off my head, if I didn't start answering her calls. What is going on?" the stressed-out woman asks.

"I'm sorry, Stephanie. I don't know if you have heard, but her baby is terminally ill, and Angela has had a breakdown. She is not herself right now. I have been on the phone with the staff at University Hospital. I told them she is too sick to be discharged. They are ignoring my pleas. Now, they are trying to send her home with anyone. I haven't spoken with her today, but I'll see what I can find out," I say, trying to explain Angela's state of mind.

"I don't care what the problem is. Tell her not to call me ever again," the young acquaintance of Angela angrily demands.

"She is very sick right now. I am sorry she called you, but keep in mind, it's not her, it's the illness," I say, trying to make her understand.

"She was screaming at me on the answering machine that she was going to kill me, if I didn't answer the phone. I never want to talk to her again," she adamantly states.

"OK, thanks so much for understanding," I say sarcastically. I hang up the phone and digest what she just said. I call University Hospital and ask to speak with Angela, but she has already been discharged. How can they just put her out on the street with no one there to pick her up or care for her? I feel sick inside. How are we going to find her?

I send Susan a text, asking if she has spoken to Angela, and to call me whenever she hears anything. She is working, so it may be a while before she can respond. I try to center myself by concentrating on Lottie Mae. I don't worry about cleaning the apartment or laundry. I just need some pure love from our sweet baby. I spend the rest of the day rocking her, bathing her, and singing to her as I show her pictures from her Thomas the Tank Engine sing-along musical book. I continue to pray silently throughout the day for Angela's protection and for a miracle.

Late afternoon, I get a call from Susan.

"Hey Mom, sorry I couldn't call earlier. I spoke to Angela. They released her this morning to herself. They just put her on the street! She hitched a ride to Austin from some stranger. She is heading to Polly's house. Polly taught with her at Covington Middle school," Susan says, sounding shell-shocked.

"Oh my god! I can't believe they just put her out on the street. I had a disturbing call this morning from a lady named Stephanie that also taught school with her in Austin. She was so angry. Angela had called repeatedly last night, every hour on the hour, threatening to cut her head off, if she doesn't answer the phone. Does Garry know what is going on?" I ask, wishing there was someone else that could help.

"I talked to him earlier. I will call you, as soon as I hear anything. Call me, if she contacts you," she says, trying to be strong and proactive.

"OK, I love you," I tell her.

"I love you too, Mom," Susan tells me.

It's getting dark outside. Jason gets home from his job. We don't say much to each other. It has become awkward. I do tell him briefly what is going on with Angela. He is so angry with her, that I only share what is necessary. I feel like I'm on a tight rope walk in this house. If I take the wrong step, I'll fall, and that will be the end to my time with Lottie Mae.

I leave Lottie Mae in Jason's care and go upstairs to Susan's apartment. I grab a bottle of wine and a corkscrew from the rack and proceed to pour a large glass of Pinot Noir. I take my journal and head to the balcony. The sky is fading into a dark grey, with a trail of pink left behind, as the sun slips below the horizon. I write about the things I can't talk about and find a small release of the emotions flooding my head. The wine relaxes me as I cry and write like a mad woman. It's nearing 7 p.m., when my phone rings.

"I have some good news. Angela's friend called to say she was taking her to a halfway house to spend the night. Dad said he will have someone go pick her up and bring her back, tomorrow," Susan tells me.

"Halfway house? Where?" I ask confused.

"It's in Austin. I still have three more hours, before we finish shooting tonight. I'll call you tomorrow, after I find out more," Susan says, trying to keep it brief.

"OK sweetheart. Thank you. Love you!" I say, as I hang up.

The next morning, Susan calls to tell me the arrangements. Garry is sending Sam, the guy that she ran off to San Antonio with, to drive Angela's Honda CRV to pick her up. Susan said that Garry had worked offshore with Sam's older brother and knew him enough to ask a favor. I am not surprised, as much as I am disappointed, that he is not going to get her himself. He said they should be getting back to New Orleans late tonight. I busy myself with Lottie Mae's care, trying to calm the emotions that are churning inside.

The wind picks up as the day turns into evening. It begins raining heavy, with loud claps of thunder, and bolts of lightning flashing, lighting up the sky. Lottie Mae is sleeping in her crib, despite the loud sounds of the storm. I am still waiting to hear from Susan of Angela's arrival. The National Weather Bureau issued a warning of severe thunderstorms with a potential for producing high winds and hail. Finally, the call comes.

"Hi Mom. She made it to Dad's, but we are about to leave. Dad was cooking dinner. Angela asked if she could take a bath, so she could change into clean clothes. That's when the shit hit the fan. Laura told her, under no circumstances, could she stay here, or take a bath. Dad just does whatever she tells him to do. Now, we must get out in this storm and drive eighty miles to Uncle Thomas' house, in Venice, to spend the night. Then we have to get up and drive eighty miles back to New Orleans for her doctor's appointment. We don't even have any medications for her, so we also have to go to the pharmacy when it opens tomorrow. Laura is such a bitch," Susan says, angrily describing the heartlessness of her new stepmother.

"That bitch! He needs to get his priorities in line and grow a set of balls. Can you put him on the phone?" I ask, as I prepare to tell him how I feel.

"OK," she says, then takes the phone to where her father is working in the kitchen.

"Garry, why won't you let Angela stay at your house?" I ask, trying to remain calm. He still lives only one mile from Susan and Angela's apartment. This is ridiculous.

"Laura is not able to have Angela stay with us at this time," Garry says, repeating what his wife told him to tell me.

"Well Garry, it's already late, it's storming outside, and it's too dangerous to drive anywhere in these conditions. That is your home and you decide who stays there. This is your daughter we are talking about," I say patiently, trying to reason with him as I try to control my anger.

"You don't understand. This is Laura's home, too. She has a say in this," he says, defending his wife's decision.

"Are you choosing that bitch over your daughter?" I angrily ask, all patience lost at this point.

Click. Conversation over. Nothing but dead air on the phone and between his ears.

Chapter Thirty-Five

It was a little after midnight last night, when Susan called to say they had finally reached her uncle's house in Venice. This morning, as Jason is heading out the door, he asks if he can talk to me about something, when he gets off work, this afternoon. He didn't ask about Angela. Lately, he doesn't come back to the apartment, until two or three in the morning, on the nights he runs the wine and cheese bar. Between working and staying out late, Jason hasn't been around much lately. My thoughts of the worst scenarios he might want to discuss are interrupted by my phone ringing.

"Hey Mom, we finally got her to the doctor and got her meds," Susan tells me, sounding exhausted.

"How are you? Did you get any rest?" I ask, concerned Susan is stretching herself too thin.

"Not much. I am going to try to get a nap before I head to work. I just wanted to let you know what was going on. How is Lottie Mae?" Susan asks.

"She is sleeping now. She had a good night. Do you know where Angela is going to stay?" I ask, knowing that it's not where Laura is.

"Dad said he will stay with her at the camper in Harvey. We need to see if we can find a private hospital or center that can help her," Susan says, sharing my concerns.

"I looked online at a few hospitals. They are so expensive. She doesn't have insurance. I will keep looking. Are you sure he is going to stay with her?" I ask, doubting her father's follow through.

"That's what he said. I don't know. I'm just exhausted and too tired to worry about it now," Susan says, nearing her limit. "By the way, before I forget, Angie, my friend that went with us to visit Angela at Chabert Hospital, along with Margaret and Julie, the parents from Lycée Francais, are coming to the apartment this evening at 6 p.m. to finalize the plans for the fundraiser at Calcasieu restaurant next week," Susan informs me.

"OK, I had completely forgotten about that. Tell Angela that I will visit after she settles in, next week. I hope you can rest, sweetheart. I know it's hard to unwind after all that," I tell her. I worry about her wellbeing, also.

"OK, Mom. I love you," Susan tells me, ready to get off the phone.

"I love you, too," I echo, before hanging up.

I am exhausted but press on. I need to get the house ready for this evening's meeting. I keep thinking about my Angela and what Einstein is presumed to have said, "The definition of insanity is doing the same thing and expecting different results." It seems we keep doing the same things with Angela and keep getting the same result, failing to protect her in this vulnerable mental state.

I manage to function doing menial tasks, preparing the house for the kind souls that are helping us so much. The day flies by with PT, OT and Nursing visiting. Lottie Mae gets good reports from all three. So far, we are successful in keeping her from losing weight, and are managing her pain.

Julie arrives with a large casserole dish of shepherd's pie. Margaret and Angie show up five minutes later.

"I think we have everything ready. The first part of the night, we have the Siren Sisters and Rob Hudak that will be performing during the silent auction. We have had so many donations. It's really turning out to be quite a lot," Margaret shares enthusiastically. She and her husband, a chef, are the owners of Calcasieu.

"I will be in charge of taking pictures, posting on Facebook, and available to help wherever needed," Angie states her role. I try to be patient with her and look past her lack of judgement the last time she tried to give me advice, when we were visiting Angela at Chabert. I am grateful that she is helping none the less.

"That sounds good. I may need you to check with me during the night. I made a tentative schedule of events for the fundraiser. I will coordinate the performers and announce the results of the auction," Julie says, telling her part of the event.

"Thank you so much for all you do for us. I am so grateful. I don't know how I can ever repay you for all the kindness you've shown," I say, trying not to get emotional.

"We are grateful we can help," Margaret shares, "How is Angela?"

"She is still very sick. It's been a nightmare trying to get her care. She is with her dad right now. It's been too stressful for her to stay here now," I say, leaving out the drama of Lottie Mae's team voting against me and not allowing her to stay here.

We wrap up the meeting after an hour. Lottie Mae has been content in her portable baby swing, in the corner of the living room, while we review the details of the fundraiser. Jason arrives home as the trio are exiting. I am anxious about our scheduled talk.

"Hey, how is Lottie Mae?" he asks as he takes her out of the swing and settles into the rocking chair.

"She has had a good day," I begin, as I sit on the couch across from him, "the nurse said she hasn't lost any weight. OT and PT also came. She had good sessions with them. Margaret, Julie and Angie you saw leaving. They came over to review the details for next week's fundraiser at Calcasieu's."

"That's good. I want to talk to you about something. I am not getting back together with Angela. I can't take the way she talks to me or how she is acting. That said, I want you to know I still want and need you to help me take care of Lottie Mae. I have started seeing someone else, Tina, the one that has been helping at Salutations. I thought I'd let you know. The neighbors that own the bed and breakfast next door have a small cottage they rent out, not far from here on 3rd street. They offered to let me stay there sometimes, when I need a break. I'll try to let you know in advance, if I have guest over," he awkwardly tells me.

"OK," I manage to say, as I am stunned at his admission. I know Angela has been carrying on with other people, but it's different, because she is mentally ill and not herself right now. Jason is not sympathetic to her mental state. He is abandoning the mother of his child, the love of his life by his own declaration, at a time in her life that she desperately needs his support the most.

"I will stay with her while you go write your blog, if you want to go up to Susan's," he offers.

"Thanks. I'll go do that now. Oh, before I forget, I have some errands to run in the morning. Can you watch Lottie Mae and I'll be back to take over around noon?" I ask.

"Sure, no problem," he answers.

"Good deal! I'll be back in a few hours," I say, before grabbing my computer and heading to Susan's.

A week passes without any major changes. I plan, coordinating my schedule with Jason's, so that he can stay with Lottie Mae. I head across the river to Harvey. Angela is expecting me.

"Hey Mama, I'm so glad you are here," Angela says bubbly.

"Hey sweetheart, how are you doing?" I ask, as she leads me inside the small camper.

"I'm doing good. Laura is such a bitch. Did Susan tell you what she did when I asked to take a bath?" Angela asks.

"She told me. What did your dad do?" I ask.

"He said he has to do what she says. So, we had to pack everything back up, get in the car, and head to Uncle Thomas' house during a monsoon," Angela says, telling the same story Susan told.

"I can't believe a person, who is a mother, and a fucking nurse for god's sake, could be so heartless. What is worse is that your dad is willing to put her wants, over his own children's needs," I angrily point out.

"I know. I do like my little trailer though. At least, I have my own place," she says innocently.

"Is your dad staying here with you?" I ask.

"He stayed the first couple of nights I was here. Now he just calls to check on me," she answers.

"So, you are staying here by yourself now?" I ask, realizing once again she is unsupervised.

"Yes, but I'm OK. Do you want to see what I bought yesterday?" she says, smiling and pointing to the large stack of shopping bags piled in the corner of her small living room.

"Sure," I concede sadly, thinking the stacks of bags are an indication the mania is returning.

Angela starts with the largest bag.

"I bought these (she holds up a box of tall red, white, and blue candles) to go with this tablecloth that I found for ten dollars. It will be perfect for the Fourth of July," she excitedly tells me. She continues taking item by item out, explaining where she bought it, and what she is going to do with it. She has bought a large assortment of non-essential items. After showing me her purchases, I redirect to see how she is managing her medications.

"Where do you keep your pill organizer?" I ask, instead of asking are you taking your medications.

"It's over on the counter," she says, pointing to the plastic box sitting on a stack of mail.

"The fundraiser at Calcasieu is next week. Margaret and Julie came by to go over the details, last week. Angie is going to help do the Facebook posts about it. I am hoping you will be able to come," I say, informing her of the fundraising event, planned by her former student's parents to help us.

"I was hoping Jason would take me," she says, as she settles down from showing me her latest purchases.

"There is something I need to tell you. Jason is dating someone," I say cautiously.

"Who?" Angela's mouth drops open as she asks.

"The girl that has been helping at the wine bar," I blurt out.

"Tina? The one that I hired to help with the wine bar that is an idiot? The one that I said I could train to be another version of me?" she asks in shock.

"Yes," I say and wrap my arms around her, "I'm so sorry."

"I still love him, Mom," she says, as she starts to cry.

"I know, sweetheart," I say continuing to hold her as she cries.

I try to comfort her with words. I don't think I'm getting through. I stay a little longer, before I pull myself away, and head back to Lottie Mae. I hate leaving her alone. I cry all the way back to Magazine Street. I see her so vulnerable and on the edge. I see the handwriting on the wall, but it doesn't matter. No one else seems to see it.

Two nights later, while Jason is at work, and I am alone with Lottie Mae, the doorbell rings. I get up from the rocker and answer the door with her in my arms.

"Are you Angela McMillin?" the tallest of the two New Orleans police officers asks.

"No. I am her Mother, Jamie. This is her daughter (I nod toward Lottie Mae cradled in my arms). Angela is not here. May I ask what this is about please," I ask.

"We found her car abandoned, on the off ramp of I-10, on the Esplanade Street exit. She hit a taxi car and left the scene on foot," the officer tells me.

"My daughter became mentally ill, when Lottie Mae was diagnosed as terminally ill," I begin explaining, but he cuts me off.

"Here is my card. Please call if she returns home. There is a warrant out for her arrest," the police officer says, before turning and leaving.

Chapter Thirty-Six

I toss and turn all night with my stomach in knots. I try to tell myself that bad news travels twice as fast as good news. If something bad has happened to her, I will hear about it soon enough. No need to worry about it before hand. If only I could relay that message to my hurting heart.

Susan calls the next morning.

"Mom, Julie called. She said they were setting up for a birthday party in the park and saw Angela sleeping next to the dog fountain. She was cuddled up with some homeless person. I told her to call the police so they can take her to the hospital," Susan conveys the shocking news.

"Oh my god," I say in disbelief.

"I also got a call from Jimmy. He worked with Angela at Feelings Restaurant, before she opened Salutations. He saw her in the French Quarter last night wearing a pair of cut off shorts and a bikini top. He gave her his shirt and tried to get her to go with him, but she ran off. He said she was very confused and out of her mind. He didn't know what to do," Susan tells me.

"It's a miracle she is still alive," I say, grateful that she survived the night on the streets in her vulnerable condition.

"I will call you back later, when I find out more," Susan says, before hanging up.

I hang up the phone and fall on my knees and thank God that she is alive. I busy myself with our morning routine. I bathe Lottie Mae and take her strolling. Then I let her nap while I clean the apartment and prepare her formula for the day. Late in the afternoon, Susan calls back.

"They took her to Community Care. At least, she is in the hospital," Susan tells me, relieved for the moment that her sister is safe.

"OK, sweetheart. Thank God she is alright. Are you going to be able to go to the fundraiser at Calcasieu tomorrow?" I ask, knowing her work is demanding and it is hard for her to take off.

"Yes, I had already made arrangements last week. I am just so sad about Angela, Mama. Is she ever going to be OK again?" Susan emotionally asks.

"I don't know. I'm sad, too," I say honestly. We keep our call short. Susan is still working, while juggling the phone calls to keep everyone updated.

Jason's mom, dad, and sister arrive at the house the morning of the fundraiser. Lance and Jenny drive down that afternoon. We agree to take turns staying with Lottie Mae, while the others attend the function. I don't want to seem ungrateful by not attending, but I really don't want to go anywhere. I just want to curl up into a ball and avoid human contact. I push my feelings aside, get dressed, and go make an appearance.

The restaurant has a private ballroom used for catering special events. Tonight, they have an easel at the entrance with pictures of Lottie Mae and an announcement for the fundraiser. Inside, a bar is set up with specialty drinks, a table of hors d'oeuvres, and seven tables of donated items, including a Drew Brees' autographed football, paintings, and jewelry for the silent auction. The music is lively as people mingle in the large open room. Margaret takes me around and introduces me to several of the guests. I answer questions about Angela with the prepared short response I rehearsed beforehand, "She is very sick and in the hospital." By the end of the night, several thousand dollars have been raised, bringing total funds to over fourteen thousand dollars.

After the fundraiser, Lance, and Jenny drive straight back to Mississippi. I stop by to kiss Lottie Mae and tell the LeBlanc family good night. Dana and her family stay at Jason's, while I retire to Susan's upstairs. I head to the balcony with a large glass of wine and my laptop. I prepare to write the blog. Just as I finish writing, Susan arrives and joins me.

"Hey Mom, mind if I join you?" Susan asks, taking a seat beside me while holding a Miller Genuine Draft, "I brought my own beer."

"Perfect timing, I just finished," I say, closing my laptop.

"We had a good turnout, don't you think?" Susan asks, referring to the fundraiser.

"Yes, it was packed. I hardly knew anyone," I admit.

"Most of the attendees were Angela's friends from Lycée Francais," she shares.

"I wish she could have been here for it. I am going to start looking for a private facility that can keep her until she is stable, now that we have raised some money," I say, thinking out loud.

"I think that's a good idea. They probably won't keep her very long at Community Care," Susan points out, referring to the last two times they treated her and released early.

We sit quietly sharing a smoke and a drink, staring at the city lights, as the moon rises higher in the night sky. We both are feeling the strain of not knowing what to do next to help Angela. At least, we have a tentative plan and she is off the streets.

The next day, between bathing and caring for Lottie Mae, I start calling the hand full of facilities I have found via google. The average cost for staying at a private facility is over thirty thousand dollars for just thirty days. I don't let that stop me from calling them and telling them our circumstance. I am optimistic if we offer fourteen thousand dollars in cash, they will at least admit her, and give us payment options for the rest of the bill. I was wrong. No one will take her.

Just when you think things can't get worse, I get bad news when I check the mail. I find a notice for a court date from her arrest in Sulphur. I call a tennis friend back in Mississippi. She is an attorney and I hope she can give me some direction.

"Hi Denise," I begin, "I'm so sorry to bother you. I need your advice. Angela has been sick as you already know. She's back in the hospital again. When she was off her meds, she got into some trouble."

"I'm so sorry you are going through this. What happened?" She asks.

"She was arrested recently in Sulphur, Louisiana, for public intoxication. She wasn't taking her medications and was not drunk. Just very ill and mistaken as drunk. She has a court date for the tenth, but she is still in the hospital. What should I do?"

"Can you fax me the paperwork you have, and I'll see what I can do. In the meantime, can you put together a binder with all of Angela's medical and arrest records? This will make it easier if another episode happens. You can show the police and medical staff the binder and they will see what you are dealing with," She instructs me.

"I will get started on that. I appreciate you so much. Thank you," I tell my sweet friend.

I follow her advice and start getting the paperwork together for Angela to sign, allowing release of her medical records. She has been at Community Care for three days and they are already wanting to discharge her. We still haven't found a place that will take her when she leaves Community Care. I am so desperate to get Angela help, that I call Susan to ask their father to help. He has the money to fund her hospital stay. I know, because I left over three hundred thousand on the table, just so he would grant me a divorce. I hang up the phone and lay down beside Lottie Mae and wait for Susan to call back.

"Mom, Dad found a place for her," Susan tells me, as I answer the phone after one ring.

"Where?" I ask, confused after calling every place within a five-state radius.

"Bethel Colony South, Women at the Well," Susan tells me.

"Where is that?" I ask.

"It's here in the city. It's a place for drug addicts and alcoholics. I think it is sponsored by a church group. It's free," she says, giving me the brief description.

"It's not for treating mental illness?" I ask.

"No. He had her tell them she has a problem with alcohol," Susan explains.

"She has never had a problem with alcohol. That is not true. She is the most prudent one of all of us, when it comes to drinking responsibly. He just didn't want to help us pay for treatment in a proper facility," I say, questioning the appropriate placing of Angela. A charity set up for the homeless, by a church, cannot be the best situation for her illness.

"I know she doesn't have a drinking problem, but no other place will take her," she says frustrated.

"I just don't understand your father anymore. He has more than enough money to pay for her medical treatment and never miss it. We used to be able to talk about you girls and do what's best for you. I'm sorry I get so upset. I'm at my wits end trying to take care of everything with Lottie Mae and also take care of Angela," I vent.

"At least we have somewhere to take her. I'm worried too, Mom. I better get back to work. I just had a little break and wanted to call. I love you," Susan says, before hanging up.

I dial my sister. I really need to talk to her. I hear the phone ringing, then go to voice mail. I don't understand why she won't answer her phone. I have been there for her countless times over the years. This is the last time I will ever try to reach out to her. This I promise myself.

The next day, I resume taking care of Lottie Mae, as Dana and her family head back to Lake Charles. It's a nice quiet day after the busy hustle of yesterday's fundraiser. I do the laundry, clean the apartment, and spend many hours rocking and singing to our little one. I find peace holding her in my arms.

Just as I lay her in her crib, Jason comes home with his new girlfriend, Tina. She is an attractive, small framed girl, with thin, short, blond hair, wearing a summer dress, with sandals. I am surprised by her visit, even though he has been talking about seeing someone for the past week.

"Hi, I'm Jamie, also known as Maemo, Lottie Mae's grandmother," I say, extending my hand to the young lady replacing my daughter. This is bizarre.

"Nice to meet you. I'm Tina," she shyly says, shaking my hand.

"We are just going to hang out down here. Stay as long as you like," he smiles and tells me.

"OK. I'm just going to write the blog. It probably will take me two to three hours. I'll text, before I come down," I say, embarrassed by the whole situation. I am not in a position to criticize or say anything that might jeopardize my time with Lottie Mae.

The night air is cool. I set my computer on the table and take my seat on the balcony. I love this space. I am high enough off the street not to be bothered by those who pass by, and still close enough to people watch, while enjoying being outdoors. I write about the little things in Lottie Mae's day. I video her enjoying a sucker, while working on her ability to close her lips, so that she doesn't have dry mouth, from mouth breathing. She was so cute when she taste it and sighs. I upload the video and do another read through of the post, making sure I catch all the edits before I call it a night. I text Jason, letting him know I am about to head downstairs.

I wait five minutes and finish my wine. It's nearing 11 p.m. and I want to go to sleep, so I will be rested in the morning for taking care of our little one. I send another text, just to make sure he knows I'm about to come back. No response. Damn! I don't know what to do. I wait another five minutes, before I just forget about courtesy, and head downstairs.

I use my key and open the front door.

"Hi, I'm back," I yell down the hallway, as I enter the apartment. No one answers as I pause and listen. I close the door and turn the lock, as I hear footsteps running down the hall, to the bathroom from Jason's room. I freeze and debate on whether to continue to Lottie Mae's room. It's a shotgun apartment and the only way to get to Lottie Mae is walking right through his room. I don't know if I should continue or retreat. I hear the bathroom door close. I decide to go for it. As I pass through, I see someone completely covered by sheets, head to toe, lying in the bed. I hasten my pace, until I reach my futon bed, next to Lottie Mae's crib. I quickly take off my shoes and jump into bed with my sweatsuit on. I'm mortified. How the hell can he judge Angela, when he is carrying on with this girl, while his baby is in the next room and his ex-common-law-mother-in-law is coming to babysit, and he is supposed to be fully mentally stable?

Chapter Thirty-Seven

The next morning, I wake up still thinking about the night before. I am going to pretend it didn't happen and mind my own business. I push the disturbing images out of my mind and busy myself cleaning the kitchen. Lance and Jenny are coming to visit today, and I want to get things ready for their arrival.

"Well, it looks like you caught us," Jason says sheepishly to me, upon entering the kitchen as I take dishes from the drain rack and place them into the cabinet.

"I sent you two text and called out from the front door, but you wouldn't answer. I'm so sorry," I apologize nervously, thinking he should be the one apologizing.

"We are going to have to get a system. I could hang something on the doorknob next time," he awkwardly offers, as he nervously laughs.

"Lance and Jenny are coming to visit today." I say, changing the subject and wishing I could disappear through the floor at this moment.

"That will be good. I am about to head out," Jason says, as he pours coffee into his Yeti stainless steel cup.

"Is your mother still coming on Sunday?" I ask. Our schedules have changed, now that I am staying in the city full time.

"Yes, she should be here around 9 a.m. tomorrow," he says, before leaving for work, "I better get going. Bye."

"Bye," I say, relieved that he is leaving. I don't know how much more awkwardness I can take.

Lance and Jenny arrive a little before noon. I need some emotional support right now. Jenny has been playing ball and going to school. She never complains but seems sad. We are all sad. I miss her so much. Lance has been taking care of our home and her while I've been away. I am grateful for his help. I am too tired and worn out to be angry with him, anymore. It's hard for two strong willed people to compromise. We both think we are right.

"Hey sweetheart, how are you holding up?" Lance asks, as he kisses me hello.

"I've been better. How are you?" I ask, as I kiss him back.

"Missing you. Where's the baby?" He asks, as he comes in.

"She's in her crib," I say, pointing down the hall. "I thought Jenny was with you."

"She's coming. She fell asleep on the way down and is just slow getting all her things out of the car," Lance says, as he heads to see Lottie Mae.

I step out on the front porch and lean over the railing. I see her digging things out of the back seat of our Honda Element and go to help her.

"Hey, my baby girl," I say, tapping her on her back as she gathers and stuffs items into her duffel bag.

"Mommy," she says, as she twirls around and gives me a baby bear hug.

"Let me help you. Want to take Lottie Mae strolling, after we get your stuff in?" I ask, as I start grabbing the bags stacked outside the car that are ready to be taken inside.

"Sure. I have missed you, so much! How is Lottie Mae?" Jenny asks.

"She's a little fighter like her Aunt Jenny. She has been having some trouble with her little tummy, but she is having a good day today. How is your ball playing going?" I ask my athletic teenager.

"We just finished soccer this week. Our softball games start in two weeks. Do you think you might be able to come home to see me play?" Jenny asks, as we carry her bags into the house.

"I wish I could be there. I hate missing your games. It looks like I am going to be here for a while longer to help with Lottie Mae," I say gently.

"I understand. I was just asking," she kindly tells me, as we join Lance inside.

"What's our girl doing?" I ask, leaning over Lance's shoulder as he plays with Lottie Mae.

"She's smiling at her Paw-Paw," he says proudly.

"She misses her Aunt Jenny," Jenny says, peering over Lance's other shoulder.

"I'm going to get jealous! Let's get the stroller and go for a walk, if you are up to it, Paw-Paw," I suggest.

"That sounds good," Lance agrees.

"Can I push the stroller?" Jenny asks excitedly.

"Yes. Give me five minutes and I'll have everything ready," I tell them, as they continue smiling and awing over the baby.

I unfold the stroller, pack the diaper bag, get Lottie Mae strapped in, and attach her feeding pump backpack to the handle. We start out heading west on Magazine Street. Jenny pushes the stroller, as Lance and I follow behind. It's a typical day in New Orleans. The sidewalk is crowded with tourist shopping and local people heading to stores and cafés that line the street.

"How are things going with you?" Lance ask cautiously. He has been patient while my heart has been breaking. The more I push him away, the more he keeps trying.

"I feel like my life keeps getting worse. Jason brought a girl home last night and I walked in on them," I tell him about my awkward night.

"What? Do you want me to whip his ass?" Papa bear asks.

"No. It's crazy though. He's doing the same thing she was doing. Except he doesn't have a diagnosis, yet. I can't say anything to him, if I want to continue taking care of Lottie Mae. I'm afraid he will make me leave," I confess.

"He better not try," Lance says angrily, "Jamie, Jason has abandoned our daughter at the time she needs him the most. He is a weak, pitiful little excuse of a man. He has no honor. Don't give his actions another thought, my love."

"Also, I have more bad news. The nurse had to decrease the rate on the baby's feeding pump when she was here. Lottie Mae's digestive system is slowing, causing her little stomach to distend, and she is having trouble with constipation. I am worried we are starting to see signs that she doesn't have much more time with us," I say, sharing what I am most concerned about.

"You think she is getting worse?" he asks, as he puts his arm around my shoulders.

"Yes. I just want to get Angela well, so she can be strong enough to be here, before the end comes. I am afraid, if she can't be with her baby while she is dying, it will devastate her after Lottie Mae is gone. She may never recover from that. I can't lose both Lottie Mae and Angela," I share, through my tears.

"We won't lose her. When do you get to see Angela next?" he asks, as he tightens his grip around my shoulder to comfort me.

"I'm going tomorrow. She invited me to come and asked me to bring Lottie Mae. They are having a church service and she is getting baptized," I tell him.

"You are a wonderful mother, Jamie. I know you will do everything possible to help her get well, so she can be strong enough to be here," he consoles me.

"I appreciate you saying that. We better head back. It looks like it might start raining," I say, looking up at the dark clouds starting to thicken above our heads.

We make our way back to the apartment, before the rain starts. We spend the afternoon visiting and taking turns rocking Lottie Mae. I feel better having talked to Lance about the episode with Jason and his new girlfriend. Lance and Jenny leave as the sun sets, heading north, the two-hour journey home.

At 8:15 p.m. I get a call.

"Hi Mommy. I am just checking to see if you can still come to my baptism tomorrow?" Angela asks, in her soft voice.

"Yes, sweetheart. I'm planning on it," I tell her.

"Are you going to bring Lottie Mae?" she asks anxiously.

"I'm going to bring her. How are you doing? Are you feeling any better?" I ask cautiously.

"I feel so bad. I miss her so much," she says, beginning to cry.

"I know baby. Just hang in there. Keep taking your medicine. I promise I will do everything I can to bring you back home, when you are well," I say, encouraging her to keep trying.

"Thank you, Mama. I better go. We have lights out at 9 p.m." She tells me.

"Ok, Good night. See you tomorrow," I say, before hanging up.

Sunday morning comes and I get up early to prepare to meet Angela at Bethel Community Baptist Church. I did not tell Jason, the atheist, of my plans. Better to ask forgiveness than permission. He leaves for work at 8 a.m. Dana arrives at 9 a.m., right on schedule. I tell her I am taking Lottie Mae to church for Angela's baptism. She doesn't question me, and I am relieved. I am anxious driving across town by myself with Lottie Mae, but I make it there without any problems.

I park out front of the large brick church, get the stroller out, place Lottie Mae in, shove the diaper bag underneath in the carriage storage compartment, and attach the feeding pump backpack. I am nervous as we head into the sanctuary. Men are seated on the left side of the center aisle and women are seated on the right. I see Angela seated on the back row and she waves at me as we enter. We take a seat next to her at the end of the aisle, so the stroller stays beside us. She kisses me and Lottie Mae as we settle into our seats.

I sit and listen as they sing hymns, followed by preaching. I don't share the same beliefs, but I do like listening to one of the speakers, Pastor Mel. He seems most authentic and humble, as he shares his life story of transformation. During the service, he baptizes Angela and six others. I speak to him after church and thank him for providing a place for my daughter to heal, when no one else would help. After speaking to the pastor, they allow Angela to visit with us for a few minutes to say our good-byes.

"Do you think we could do something for Lottie Mae's birthday next week?" she asks humbly, as we get Lottie Mae ready for the trip back home.

"Well sweetheart, what did you want to do?" I ask.

"I was thinking we could do a Barbie theme party. Maybe I could make the cake and invite our family and some friends over," she shares her plans, as if everything is normal.

"Let me check with Jason and Dana. I will see what they say. It's been a little strained between us and I just want to make sure they don't mind," I suggest. We have so much going on. I don't want a party, but I will try to make it happen for her.

"Thank you so much! I don't know what I'd do without you," she says, as she hugs me tight around the neck.

"Just promise me that you will continue taking your medicines and get well, so you can come home permanently," I bargain.

"I promise," she tells me.

We kiss good-bye, before she heads back to her group. I place Lottie Mae into her car seat, and we head back toward Uptown. Before we make it to the interstate, Lottie Mae is sleeping soundly. My thoughts are with Angela. How are we going to have a birthday party with our lives falling apart?

Chapter Thirty-Eight

It was decided to go forward with Lottie Mae's birthday party. Jason also wants to celebrate her birthday with friends and family. Angela is doing better each day. She is benefitting from the structured environment at The Well. She has been compliant with her medications there. She came home on pass for a few hours Thursday without any incidents. She helped make Lottie Mae's cake and prepare the apartment for Saturday's party. I can see she is trying very hard.

Friday evening before the party, Susan stops by after work. Jason is home after his workday at Breaux Mart and is rocking Lottie Mae in the living room.

"Hey everybody," Susan greets us, as she enters the front door.

"Hey sweetheart," I say, as I get up and kiss her.

"Hi Susan," Jason looks up and says.

"I just wanted to stop by for a few minutes to go over the plans for tomorrow. I will be able to help as much as needed. I have the whole day off," she offers, as she takes a seat on the long orange couch.

"Good. I need help cleaning the apartment," I say, sounding like a broken record.

"We will help," Jason says curtly, "I think you need to go home and take a break. You seem like you are getting too stressed out lately,"

"I'm fine. I'm just asking for a little help cleaning," I say, feeling defensive.

"What about tomorrow? What do we need to do before the party?" Susan asks, changing the subject.

"Angela is having Garry pick her up for the party. I will be getting Lottie Mae ready. Jason, are you going to cook on the grill?" I ask, looking at Jason, he nods confirming. "That leaves you, Susan, to help decorate and get the apartment ready in the morning."

"OK, that will work. I'm exhausted, I'm going to go ahead and go to Mike's. I'll be back around 9 a.m." she says, as she gets up and kisses Lottie Mae on the top of her head and hugs Jason and me goodbye.

The next morning, I wake up early to get myself and Lottie Mae ready for the party. Susan and Mike come over around 9:30 a.m. and help set up chairs and tables in the back courtyard. Jason's mother, father, sister, brother, sister-in-law, and their three kids arrive. Lance, Jenny and Lance's two sisters arrive from Mississippi. Angela arrives with Garry and his new wife, Laura. The house is filling up with people from the front door, throughout the apartment, to the kitchen's back door. Half of the people streaming in, are ones I have never laid eyes on before. It is overwhelming, as the crowd continues to grow.

I let Jason's mom take Lottie Mae to hold, after she finishes bringing her things inside. The house is already overcrowded. I didn't want to expose Lottie Mae to so many germs. I need air. I excuse myself and go to hide in my car parked on Third Street, around the corner. In the quiet of the car, I begin to cry uncontrollably. I am emotional for many reasons. Lottie Mae wasn't expected to live long enough to see this day. Angela is here, fighting for her sanity to be with her baby. Jason is becoming an asshole. He even invited his new girlfriend here. Then there is Garry and his new bitch wife here. Those two have made everything more difficult and now they are like guest of honor. I have a short self-pity party solo before I pull myself together and hope no one has noticed my absence.

Just as I open the car door to head back inside, I bump into Diane, Lance's oldest sister that I am close to.

"Hey girl, what are you doing out here?" she asks, shocked to see me, "Are you OK?"

"Yes," I lie, "I just needed a little quiet space to clear my head."

"You look like you have been crying," she persist, "What is wrong?"

"It's just been really hard. I have had all the responsibilities of caring for Lottie Mae and the house while Angela has been sick. I don't mind, but I just need them to help. They get upset when I ask. Now we are having this big party and I was feeling overwhelmed and needed a time out. I try to be careful not to make anyone upset, because I'm afraid they will take Lottie Mae away from me," I vent, until my words turn into more tears.

"They better not take that baby from you. You have taken care of her all this time. It's going to be OK," she says, as she hugs me and lets me cry.

I dry my tears and allow her to escort me back inside. There are people standing everywhere. Angela is holding Lottie Mae, rocking in the living room. Garry and Laura are seated on the couch, next to Jason's father, Joe. Lance and Jenny are visiting with a small group in the corner. I make my way through the shotgun apartment, through Jason's room and into the nursery. As I navigate through the dense group, I come face to face with Dana.

"Jamie, I hear that you are getting run down and your health is becoming an issue with taking care of Lottie Mae," she begins her speech.

"No, my health is just fine. I am doing better with drinking protein drinks and have stopped losing weight," I say, forcing a smile trying to keep things light. I think my asking Jason and Susan to help clean the apartment last night, has led to this confrontation. He must have gotten upset and called his mommy.

"Well, I want you to go home, and get some rest. I am going to stay here now, so you can spend some time with your family back in Mississippi," she suggest, before adding, "Jason called me last night and said you were about to have a breakdown."

I begin to feel the hairs rise on the back of my neck. My heart begins to beat faster, as I try to remain calm and pause before responding.

"I am not having a breakdown and I am not going anywhere. I asked him to help with cleaning the apartment, and I asked for a couple of hours in the evening for a break to write the blog, that's all. Maybe you can ask your son, if he could manage not to go out every night of the week and help around here with some of the chores," I clarify.

"Well, that's not what he, or Susan, told me," she smugly states.

"Did he tell you what happened a few days ago, while he was supposed to be watching Lottie Mae while I was writing the blog? Did he mention that I walked in on him and his new lover in the act? Did he tell you that neither he or Susan, have cleaned this apartment even once, or helped with the laundry?" I ask, already knowing the answers.

I see Jason's face becoming beet red, as he comes to stand beside his mother. The room has become deafly silent, as we stare at each other.

"The house smells like smoke when I get home from work," Jason says, jumping into the confrontation.

"I used to smoke sitting at the back door with it cracked open, so I could listen for the baby. I would have waited to take a break when you get home, but that is not until two or three in the morning, lately. No worries, because I quit smoking last week," I say, letting it all out.

"Well...," he stammers, "I still have asked you not to even smoke at the door."

What a hypocrite. He smokes at the door. That is why I decided to quit smoking. I will not give him any ammunition to use against me.

"Is that all you've got to say about me? You are so ungrateful, and living such a joke of a life, during the time you are needed. You judge Angela so harshly, when she is mentally ill, but you yourself are always running away, staying out late, partying every night. What the hell is your excuse?" I say, full mama bear mode, sick of the LeBlanc's being self-righteous.

You could hear a pin drop, as I stare down Jason and Dana. Diane, my sister-in-law, takes center stage, tears rolling down her face as she comes to my defense.

"You all have got to stop this. Can't you see all that this lady has been doing? She alone has been taking care of this baby and house. You all are ganging up on her, it's not right, it's just not right," she says, sobbing louder than I had been, back in the privacy of my car.

We stop arguing and begin putting our arms around Diane, comforting her, afraid she is the one on the edge of a breakdown.

"We love Jamie," Dana says, as she tries to comfort Diane.

"You can't keep that baby away from her," Diane tells her, "She is the only one that baby knows."

By this time, we have made a circle around my sister-in-law forming a ring of hugs. I am grateful for her words and trying to look out for me. I am just mortified about the drama unfolding in front of so many people. I am also afraid of the repercussions. I just want the drama over.

"It's OK, Diane. We all love each other. We will work through this," I say, trying to smooth things over.

"You just got to love each other," she says, crying and repeating herself.

It took a few minutes for Diane to calm down, after her emotional stance for me. The party was over after that. We all hug and make peace. We decide the team, Jason, Dana, Susan and me, will meet in the morning to see what we can do to make things better for all of us. I feel my anxiety level rising in anticipation.

The crowd begins thinning as Lance, Jenny, along with Lance's two sweet sisters give me hugs, kisses and encouragement on their way out. Angela missed the drama between Dana, Jason and me. She was in the living room holding Lottie Mae from the time she arrived, until it was time for Garry and Laura to take her back. As she kisses me goodbye, I feel hopeful she is healing and will soon be back permanently. After telling everyone else goodbye, I head up to Susan's apartment for the night. Dana and her family are staying the night at Jason's below.

I text my therapist.

"Hi, this is Jamie Thornton. I am texting to see if you might see me for an emergency appointment in the morning," I press send. My counselor has been an extraordinary source of strength during this time.

"Yes. 8 a.m.?" Tom, my counselor, responds.

"Yes. Thank you," I text back.

Treatment in America: Her Life Matters

Chapter Thirty-Nine

I manage to write the blog about the party, minus the details of our blow out. It is taxing to push it all aside and paint a picture of what is left with filtered words. Somehow, I manage to focus on the positive aspects of Lottie Mae's birthday. It's quite a milestone, one year old. We weren't sure if she would make it this far, but she is a little fighter. I see her mommy improving and fighting to be present for her as well. I head to bed soon after I finish writing. My spirit and body are exhausted.

I wake up before my alarm sounds. So many thoughts come flooding back into my head. I make a cup of tea and grab a note pad. I sip my tea and begin compiling a list of what I want to talk with Tom about. I have been seeing him once a week for months now and he's been my saving grace. He helps me keep things in perspective and gives me direction on how to respond to all the challenges. Most importantly he listens.

I decide to walk the one-mile sidewalk trip to Tom's office, located on the first floor of his beautiful Victorian home, just off Thalia Street. It's hot and humid, but I don't care. The exercise eases some of the tension I feel. As I pass through the park where the homeless sleep, I see a few I recognize from when Angela and I handed out bags of food. I'm not afraid anymore. My fear has been replaced with empathy. How many of them are untreated mentally ill? Probably all of them. My eyes are open now, as well as my heart.

My mind shifts from the homeless, back to my list of current struggles, as I ring Tom's doorbell marked "office." He opens the door, looks at me, then without a word, opens his arms wide and embraces me, as I begin to cry silent tears.

"What's going on?" he asks, as he releases his hug, and leads me into the parlor.

"Everything," I say, as I grab a tissue off the end table and take a seat on the couch facing his chair. He listens intently, as I tell him about recent events leading up to the birthday party blow out. I explain that I still must go and face the firing squad when I get back to the apartment after our session. "I just need some advice on how to say what I need. Scrudential Insurance canceled my short-term disability this week. I have been raising money with the blog and so far, we have been keeping up paying copayments on Lottie Mae's medical care, all the bills, groceries at the apartment, and still have money left over. I feel if I could have a small allowance from the funds raised, I could pay my insurance premium, continue seeing my psychiatrist and going to my counseling sessions, and have enough to live on, while I take care of Lottie Mae. It's just hard to ask the group for help."

"You have given your life to help them. It's OK to ask for help. You need to ask, so that you can continue helping. It may make it easier if you prepare a list ahead of time of what you want to say," he gently guides me.

"I will do that. I am so afraid they are going to take Lottie Mae away from me. Any time I ask them to do anything, they say I'm too stressed out, and try to get me to leave. It's getting near the end and I don't want to leave her. I can't leave her. She wasn't expected to even live this long. They don't seem to realize that we are on borrowed time," I share my fears.

"It may be challenging, but it will help your stress level to have your basic needs met. Your life matters, too," he encourages.

"I also have to address the topic of when I can bring Angela home. She has been doing better at The Well. She's taking her medications and seems to be more like her true self. The past two times she visited she was attentive to Lottie Mae. I promised Angela I would bring her home, if she will do her part getting well, taking her medications. I intend to keep my promise," I share.

"I understand. How do you think they will respond?" Tom asks.

"I'm afraid they don't want her to ever come back," I admit.

"Prepare the same way for this. Write out a list of reasons supporting why you feel it is very important, even imperative, to bring her home. This may help you say, what you need to say, in a calm manner," he suggests.

After our session, he offers to drive me back home, but I tell him I enjoy the walking. Before leaving, I thank him for seeing me on a Sunday for an emergency session. The strategies he gave me to stay calm, while communicating what I need, run through my head as I make my way back to Magazine Street. I think about what I want to say. I go straight upstairs and begin making my list of things needed to reduce mental and physical stress. I finish and gather my things, preparing for the meeting. I take time to get on my knees and pray for peace and wisdom, before heading downstairs.

I arrive and find Team Lottie Mae is gathered in the living room. Dana and Susan are seated on the couch. Jason is sitting in the rocking chair near Lottie Mae, as she sleeps in her portable baby swing. I enter and go kiss my sweet angel on top of her head, before taking my seat on the straight back chair across from them.

"We have talked about the things you said were bothering you. I'm going to take notes, so we can make a list of how we can work through this," Susan begins, as she assumes lead of the meeting.

"Jamie, we care about you and want to make this work. Why don't you begin by telling us what you need us to do? Susan is going to write a list, so we don't leave anything out," Dana reiterates.

"I'm going to close Salutations. I'm selling the lease. I will just continue working part time at Breaux Mart. I'll be able to help more. What do you need to stay and not be so stressed out?" Jason asks, with a flat affect.

I take a deep breath before I begin. I have repeatedly asked Susan and Jason to help me more with the housekeeping for months now, starting when Dana was hospitalized with her appendix ruptured, but things haven't changed much. I slowly exhale and prepare to ask for help again. This time adding financial help and a timeline for Angela's return.

"Scrudential canceled my short-term disability. Without that, I need help paying my health insurance premium of nine hundred and fifty dollars a month, so I can continue being proactive with my mental health counseling and doctor's visits. I also cashed out both of my 401K retirement accounts months ago to help with expenses, and now I'm broke. If I could have help paying my insurance premium and three hundred dollars a week, I think I can survive financially. I also want to ask for help cleaning the apartment, with the laundry, running errands to the store, and at least a couple of hours each evening watching Lottie Mae for me, so I can write the blog," I finally choke out my request, while looking down at the scribbled notes I had made as instructed by my therapist. When donations started being sent from the blog, we set up a joint bank account with Jason and myself as trustees. Those kind souls that donated money to help us, entrusted me to do the right thing. I treat it respectfully and with accountability to the group. Now, I'm at their mercy.

The group agreed that this could be done. Susan made a list of chores and divided it between us. Dana and Jason agreed to the new financial assistance for me without question. There it was done. I still felt awkward and humbled by the gift of charity. It's hard for me to accept help, but the group makes me feel, that I too, am a part of her care and needed. With the heavy financial talk over, I cautiously broach the subject of Angela's returning home.

"I thought Angela did very well at the party. She has been taking her meds for a few weeks consistently, now. I was wondering, can she come back to be with Lottie Mae?" I ask.

"It's so much stress for her here. I don't want to rush it. I'm afraid she won't be able to handle it," Susan says, remembering all the times before.

"I can't be here when she is here. I think it's way too early to even talk about it," Jason adamantly says.

"Let's see how she does the next couple of weeks," Dana gently suggests.

"I don't want to wait until Lottie Mae is so sick that she is unresponsive. We don't know how much time we have left. Angela needs to have time with her, too," I say, trying to persuade them.

"I think Dana has a good suggestion," Susan says, trying to find middle ground, "If she's doing well around Lottie Mae, and still taking her medicine after a couple more weeks, we should have a better idea if it's too much for her, or not"

I reluctantly accept the groups decision to wait and see how Angela progresses. We make a truce to be better communicators with each other and not let things escalate to the level it had at the party. I also make it clear that I will not be leaving Lottie Mae to go back to Mississippi.

Treatment in America: Her Life Matters

Chapter Forty

A week passes with Angela continuing to improve. I pick her up for a day pass and make it back to Magazine Street shortly before the hospice nurse arrives.

"Come in Maria," I say, as I open the door for the sweet short nurse wearing a smile.

"How's our little one this morning?" she asks, as she sets her medical bag on the couch.

"She's been sleeping a lot this morning," Angela shares, as she stops rocking and starts arranging the baby's feeding tube. She unhooks the backpack holding the feeding pump from its stand and places it on her shoulder. Carefully, she stands holding Lottie Mae and carries her to her crib, so the nurse can examine her.

"She's got a lot of puffiness going on," I add, as we follow Angela down the shotgun apartment to the nursery.

Angela gently places Lottie Mae in her crib and steps to the side to allow the nurse access to her. Lottie Mae has no voluntary movements. Her little arms and legs stay extended, and her hands open slightly with the neoprene soft splints the occupational therapist made. She isn't able to kick or try to roll over. Her facial expressions are limited to faint smiles when she is kissed.

"The most important thing is that we keep our angel comfortable. Since she is not able to tell us she is in pain, we must watch her facial expressions, and for other signs like crying or grunting," the nurse shares, as she methodically examines our baby from head to toe.

"She has been acting like her stomach hurts. She still struggles with constipation and spitting up. Her breathing sounds congested, too," I say, peering over the railing, as the nurse continues her work.

"Is there something we can give her for pain?" Angela asks.

"Yes. We can start giving her Tylenol every four hours. I'm going to call the doctor and see if we can get some oxygen ordered for her. We need to decrease the rate on the feeding pump as well. That may give some comfort with her breathing and the fluid overload," she explains, as she finishes her examination of Lottie Mae.

Angela takes over and begins putting Lottie Mae's gown back on and swaddling her with her pink and green baby blanket. I walk the nurse to the front door, so I can talk to her out of Angela's earshot.

"Maria, I wanted to ask a favor of you, while Angela can't hear me. As you know Angela has been sick, but has been doing better now," I begin.

"She looks a lot better. What can I do for you?" she asks.

"I promised her that I will bring her home permanently to be with Lottie Mae, if she will stay at The Well, take her medications, and get stable. So far, she is doing everything to get well. I am trying to be diplomatic with Jason and his mother. They don't seem to want her back at all. I don't want to push for her back too soon, but I also don't want to wait until Lottie Mae becomes unresponsive, or in a coma. Will you promise to let me know when we are nearing the end?" I ask.g

"I promise, I will let you know. She is going into congestive heart failure and kidney failure, but it is still early. I admire how you take care of your daughter. We will get through this," she assures.

I thank her and give her a hug as she leaves. We decide to take Lottie Mae strolling on our usual route. It's warm and muggy, a typical New Orleans summer day. I feel grateful Angela is doing so well and we enjoy being in the sunlight. I can tell Angela is improving by how attentive she is to Lottie Mae. It's amazing the difference when she has been taking her medications as ordered. I don't understand why the hospitals don't provide the care needed to reach this level of stability.

We have a nice lunch back at the apartment, before loading up to take Angela back to The Well. As we pull up to the dingy building surrounded by chain link fencing, Angela begins to cry.

"Mom, I hate leaving her. When can I come home?" She asks, as tears stream down her cheeks.

"Soon, my baby. I promise. I will see how things go this week and I will bring it up again with Jason, Dana and Susan. Hopefully they will soften, as they see how well you are doing now. Hang in there, sweetheart," I encourage, as tears fill my eyes. It's out of my control. I want to bring her home right now, but I must be cautious, also. If I bring her home too soon and we fail, I fear they may kick me out as well. I kiss her good-bye and drive away with a heavy heart.

Two days later, Dana makes it back from Lake Charles. Things are strained between us, but we both make efforts to show support to one another. After unloading her bags, we review the changes from Lottie Mae's last hospice visit. We are still using the communication board to list all her medications and times to be given.

"The hospice nurse came by. They decreased the rate on her feeding pump again. Her kidneys aren't functioning properly, causing fluid buildup and congestive heart failure. Since she can't tell us when, or where she's hurting, we started giving Tylenol every four hours and oxygen to use at night," I tell Dana, reviewing the nurse's instructions.

"I see she is a little puffy," Dana says, as she looks back at Lottie sleeping in her crib. "I don't like giving her Tylenol though. It's not good for her liver. Why did they want this?" she questions.

"She has been having the fluid buildup and can't say she is hurting. This is so she is comfortable. With pain management, it's best to control the pain, before it escalates to a point where the medication takes longer to work. By giving it every four hours, we can keep her from hurting," I patiently explain to my co-grandparent.

"I don't think she's hurting now," Dana points out.

"Well, that's because I've been giving her the Tylenol. I noticed her grunting more and at times grimacing indicating pain, before we started the Tylenol," I tell her, trying to make her understand. I wish Lottie Mae was my own daughter, instead of granddaughter. That way, I could insist she be taken care of in a way that she is comfortable, without having to explain to anyone.

That evening, I retire to Susan's. I write the blog and head to bed. As I toss and turn, I hear through the hard wood floors, my baby crying below. She never cries out with me. I bet Dana did not give her the

Tylenol. Her cries cut me to the bone. I want to go to her, but I can't. I roll out of bed and lie on the floor, above where her crib is in the apartment below. I pray for God's mercy and to stop her pain. I feel as though I could melt through the floor, as I weep uncontrollably, until I fall asleep.

The next day, I rack my brain for how to fix what happened last night. I already reviewed the medication changes from Hospice with Dana. We have a communication notebook. Maybe if I ask her to write down the time she gives the Tylenol to Lottie Mae, she might be more inclined to actually give it to her, so she doesn't have another night of pain like last night.

"Hi, how is Lottie Mae this morning," I ask, as I enter the apartment.

"She is doing good. I just gave her a bath and now she's enjoying her swing," Dana says, as she continues working on her crocheting, sitting in the rocker beside Lottie Mae's baby swing.

"I wanted to check on her. I thought I heard her crying last night. Did she sleep OK?" I gently prod.

"She had a little spell where she cried," Dana admits.

"How did it go with the Tylenol?" I ask, knowing already she didn't give it to her. I specifically told her to give the Tylenol every four hours and to stay on schedule.

"I gave her some around 10 p.m. I didn't want to give it to her, until she needed it," she says, justifying her noncompliance.

"When I practiced home health, I was trained to educate my patients to not wait until their pain level escalates to take the medications. If you rate pain on a scale of 1-10, you need to take the medications when you are at a level of 3, in order to keep the pain under control. If you wait until you are in intense pain, at a level 8 or 9, you won't be able to find relief for hours," I say, trying to make her understand the importance of a medication schedule.

"I just don't like giving her anything she doesn't need," she says, ignoring my explanations of Lottie Mae's needs, "What are you doing up there all night? I hear you walking around a lot."

"I tried to go to bed early. I couldn't sleep last night, because I heard her crying. Please give her the medicine. Where's the notebook?" I ask, hoping to lead her to a solution.

"The communication notebook?" she asks.

"Yes," I say.

"It's on the kitchen table," she answers.

"Let's start using it to write down when we give her a dose of pain medication. I don't think she will cry out in pain, if we give Tylenol every four hours. Maybe writing it down will help us keep up with it," I say, trying to persuade her.

"Jason won't be here this evening, if you want to spend time with Lottie Mae," she offers, changing the subject.

"Where is he going?" I ask.

"He is spending the night at the cabin the neighbors offered him to use," she says, without elaborating. I don't care if he ever comes back, I think to myself.

"Thanks. I will. I'm going to run some errands and pick up some groceries. Do you need anything?" I offer.

"No, I think we have everything for now" Dana says, as I head out the door.

I run my errands and write the blog early. I don't tell Dana I plan to sleep downstairs tonight. I will not let my baby suffer unnecessarily. After taking my bath, I put on my comfortable workout clothes that have become my new pajamas. It is getting dark outside, by the time I head downstairs to help Dana.

"Good evening," I whisper, as I enter the apartment. I tiptoe through the dark living room, through Jason and Angela's room, and find Lottie Mae sleeping in her bed. Dana is on her iPad, while reclined on pillows on the futon, beside Lottie Mae's crib.

"Hi. She's sleeping. How are you?" she asks, looking over the top of her glasses.

"I can't sleep very good away from her. I thought I'd sleep down here tonight, since Jason won't be here," I say, hoping the practiced response I had prepared will smooth things over.

"I don't need any help. You don't have to stay down here for me," she says, sounding defensive.

I notice the oxygen concentrator near the crib is turned off, as I peer over the railing at our little one. I find little Lottie Mae wide eyed looking back at me. If Dana would get off her iPad, she might have noticed our little one is awake. I want to pick her up, but instead I head to the kitchen. I want to see if Dana has written down when she gave her Tylenol last. I find the notebook vacant of notes.

"Has the baby had any Tylenol tonight?" I ask, as I head back into the nursery.

"She had some around 5 p.m." she answers, still propped up working on her iPad.

I look at my phone, 9:34 p.m. I don't ask permission. I just go prepare the children's liquid Tylenol, measuring it into the small syringe. I take it past Dana and insert it into Lottie Mae's g-tube. As I turn on the oxygen concentrator machine and begin untangling the cannula, Dana stops her home shopping, sets the iPad down, and comes to stand between me and the baby.

"Jamie, I don't think the baby needs the oxygen," she says sternly.

"I need you to step back and get out of my way," I say, looking her directly in the eyes.

"She isn't crying. She doesn't need any of this," she defiantly states.

"I am going to put this oxygen on her and then I'm going to pick her up and rock her. If you don't move out of my way, there is going to be trouble," I threaten.

For a moment, she freezes as we lock eyes. Finally, she relents and moves out of my way. I gently pick up my sweet baby and settle into the rocking chair beside her bed. After hearing her crying out last night under Dana's care, I have lost faith in her ability to keep Lottie Mae out of pain. I am sick of tiptoeing around her.

"I am just trying to do what's best for Lottie Mae. All those medicines are bad for her liver and kidneys," she says unrelenting.

"I'm sorry you are too stupid to understand that she is dying and just needs us to keep her comfortable. I tried to be diplomatic and tell you nicely. The medical professionals have set the schedule for her care. You are either too hardheaded or just too dumb to follow instructions. Whatever the case, I am not going to let this baby suffer because of you!" I say, after being pushed over my limit for patience. I know there will be consequences for standing up to her. At least for tonight, my baby won't be crying out in pain.

Chapter Forty-One

Lottie Mae rested well, sleeping through the night. I had set my phone alarm to wake me, every four hours, to give her the dose of Tylenol, allowing her to rest. After I backed Dana down, she stayed clear of me the rest of the night. The next morning, I get ready to leave and avoid talking to her. As I head to the door, she just looks up from her needle work and nods. I tell her I need to take care of a few things and will text her later in the day. As soon as I get to the privacy of Susan's apartment, I call our Hospice agency and request for the social worker to visit. I hope, with a social worker mediating, we can get on the same page for Lottie Mae's care, particularly the pain medicine schedule. They say they can send someone this afternoon, so I forward the message to Susan, Jason, and Dana that they are coming at 5:30 p.m.

I feel so weighted down. My spirit is so tired. I lie motionless on Susan's bed and stare at the wall. I pray for mercy. I don't have the energy to do anything else. I don't want to talk to anyone or see anyone. No one understands what I am going through. The morning fades into afternoon as I remain paralyzed with sorrow. I have no appetite to eat. I lie there for hours waiting for 5:30 p.m. to arrive.

The nurse and social worker are already seated on the couch by the time I come downstairs. Dana, Jason, and Susan are also settled into their seats surrounding them. I check my phone. It's 5:28 p.m. The atmosphere is somber as I say hello and take the chair from the desk and position it across from the gathered group.

"Thank you for coming. I called and asked for the social worker to come to help resolve the problem with Lottie Mae's pain medication schedule not being followed. I'm glad that you also came, Maria," I say, acknowledging Lottie Mae's nurse being present.

"Hi, I'm Samantha, the Social Worker. I hope I can be of help," the small framed woman says, introducing herself as she extends her hand for me to shake.

"We have started giving Lottie Mae Tylenol, every four hours, and using oxygen at night, to help with her comfort level. I told Dana about the changes, but she doesn't want to give her the Tylenol. She is worried about it hurting her liver. Last night, when I tried to put Lottie Mae's oxygen on, Dana tried to stop me. I thought, if you were able to educate her about the importance of giving the medication on time, it would help to keep us from arguing," I say, trying to be concise.

"Let's tell them what happened," Dana begins, "I was supposed to be taking care of her and you came down and insisted that you were taking over. You got all upset because I didn't think she needed the Tylenol and then you threatened me when I told you she didn't need the oxygen," Dana says, with newfound courage.

"I told you, she must have the Tylenol on time, and not to wait until you think she needs it. The night before last, I heard her crying through the floor of Susan's apartment. I knew you didn't give her the medicine. I cannot bear to hear that baby cry in pain when all she needs is her medicine on time. You were the one that tried to block me from putting the oxygen on, by getting in my personal space. I just told you to back up," I say, angrily looking at Dana.

"You don't need to come here, when it's our time to care of her," Jason interjects.

"What is the problem with the Tylenol?" the social worker asks.

"I just didn't want to give her something she doesn't need," Dana confesses.

"We did add Tylenol to her treatment plan. Since Lottie Mae is nonverbal, we want to be proactive anticipating her needs. Jamie has been good with managing her pain, by giving the Tylenol every four hours, before it escalates to a level hard to manage. As the disease progresses, we will monitor for the effectiveness and change to stronger medications as needed," Nurse Maria says, educating the rest of the group.

"That is fine. I just think it's too much to have her here all the time," Jason tells the social worker, referring to me.

"What do you think would be acceptable?" she asks him.

"This is my house and my baby. She can visit twice a week," he suggests.

"Have you lost your mind? I will visit that baby every day," I say, in shock.

"You can visit, but not stay here at night," Dana clarifies.

"I think that is totally unfair, considering that I am the only constant person that baby knows. Have you forgotten that it's been my efforts paying all the bills here? From the rent to the groceries, I pay it all from money raised by blogging. This is how you thank me? Taking my time away from Lottie Mae when we don't have much time left?" I angrily say.

"It's a compromise, Mom. This way, we can all still help with her and get along," Susan says, trying to be a peacemaker.

"Compromise? I think it's more like punishment," I say, feeling hurt and betrayed.

"What days would be good for you?" the social worker asks me.

"Everyday...whatever days they say, I guess. What about the pain medicine schedule? Are you going to give her the medicine she needs, as scheduled, and write down the times you gave it to her?" I ask the most important thing.

"Yes. I'll give her the medicine," Dana concedes.

"Why don't you come on Monday's and Thursday's. I am only working part time at the grocery store now, so I can take care of her," he volunteers, trying to limit my time.

Before I know it, I am barred from my precious Lottie Mae. This sweet little gift that I had taken care of by myself for so long. My worst fear has come true. I retreat to Susan's apartment after the meeting feeling defeated and heartbroken. I try sleeping, but my brain won't stop replaying the horrible events, leading up to them taking Lottie Mae away from me.

After a restless night, I get up early and decide today I am bringing Angela home. If they aren't going to let me take care of Lottie Mae, then I will take care of Angela. I have nothing more to lose. It's time for Angela to be with her baby anyway.

I get dressed and drive across town to Gentilly, to The Well. I go through the chain link enclosure and knock on the door. I feel a renewed energy and a sense of purpose, as I wait for the door to open.

"Hi, I'm Jamie Thornton. I am the mother of Angela McMillin. I am here to check her out of the facility. Her daughter is terminally ill and it's time for Angela to come home," I say to the young woman, dressed in jeans and a t-shirt.

"Hi, I'm Mary. Come in and I'll go get her for you," the kind woman tells me, as she leads me inside to a waiting area.

After a few minutes she returns with Angela.

"Mom, is everything alright?" Angela asks, shocked to see me.

"Yes darling. Lottie Mae is OK for now. It's just time for you to come home," I say, leaving out all the drama of the past forty-eight hours.

"Oh my goodness! I can't believe it! I'm so happy!" Angela gushes.

Chapter Forty-Two

I follow Angela and the office manager of The Well, down the narrow hallway, leading into the bunkhouse, where Angela has been living the past two months. The room is filled with thirty or more crudely constructed, unpainted bunkbeds, along the north wall and a row of lockers, across from them, lining the south wall. She shows me the bottom bunk, on the third row, where she has been sleeping.

"Miss. Mary, do you have a trash bag or something I can use to put my clothes in?" Angela turns and asks.

"Yes, I'll go get some," Mary says, and excuses herself, disappearing down the hall.

"This is my locker," Angela says, as she opens the unpainted door with rough edges.

There isn't much space for walking in the tight quarters with just the three of us. I can only imagine how claustrophobic it must feel, when the other residents are here.

"Wow. There's not much room in here," I say, thinking out loud. My heart breaks looking at the conditions she has been living in while she heals. I realize that this place is the only place that provides a safe haven, for her and many others, that would be on the street otherwise. For a country that boasts about being the greatest in the world, the richest country in the history of the planet, we sure fail at taking care of our vulnerable citizens.

"It's pretty tight," Angela admits.

"Here you go," Mary says, handing Angela two large plastic trash bags.

We hurriedly pack her clothes and personal items into the two bags. On our way out, we stop by the cafeteria, where the residents have just finished their morning bible study and allow Angela to say her good-byes to the ladies of The Well.

"If I can have everyone's attention," Mary says, raising her voice and speaking to the group as we enter, "Angela is going home today. Her mother is here to pick her up. If you would like to tell her good-bye, please do so now."

The gathered group of ladies breaks out in cheers and clapping at the announcement. Several come to where we are and hug Angela and tell me how sweet my daughter is. They all ask about Lottie Mae and tell us they will be praying for us. I try not to cry as I feel moved by their love for my daughter. This place is doing a good thing, even if the building and location look otherwise.

As we drive back to Magazine Street, I try to get Angela caught up on things without saying too much that can upset her.

"We had a team Lottie Mae conference with the social worker and nurse yesterday. Jason closed Salutations. He and Dana are going to be helping more with Lottie Mae. They scheduled us for Mondays and Thursdays to stay downstairs with Lottie Mae. The other days we are going to be staying upstairs, at Susan's apartment," I explain the new arrangement, leaving out how cruel and hurtful this is to me.

"Only Mondays and Thursdays?" Angela's face drops as she asks.

"Yes, but that's just for spending the night. We can visit every day," I clarify.

"Oh, that's good. I miss her so much. I am so glad you came to get me. I was just praying for God to let me be with her, when they came and got me out of bible study," Angela shares.

"I know sweetheart. I would have been here sooner, but I have to take into consideration what the group requests. Jason acts like you aren't on the lease at the apartment and threatens to not let us ever come back," I tell her.

"The lease is in my name. He cannot kick you out, Mom. You have helped us so much," she says, trying to reassure me.

"Well, that's good to know. Things have been strained between Jason and me. Lottie Mae has been having some changes. We started giving her pain medication, just Tylenol, nothing heavy. Dana and I don't agree on this, but the doctor and nurse set the medication schedule. I feel they are right to start this, because our little one can't tell us if she is hurting. I asked for the social worker to visit and educate Dana and Jason about it. During the meeting, they agreed to give the pain medications, then they requested that I only help on Monday and Thursday nights. Susan says it's a compromise," I say, giving the Disney version of events.

"I can't believe he only wants us to see her on Mondays and Thursdays?" Angela repeats, still trying to understand.

"We can visit anytime. We just won't sleep downstairs and take care of her through the night, except on Mondays and Thursdays," I explain, as we pull into a parking spot in front of our fourplex apartment building. "Let's get your stuff upstairs and then we can come back down and see her. I didn't tell anyone I was bringing you home, so don't be shocked if they are surprised to see you."

We get her bags upstairs and begin putting everything away. I am feeling confident I made the right decision to bring her home. Angela acts timid and a little unsure of herself as we unpack. Other than her hesitant nature, she seems much better, obviously her medications are working. Maybe with me by her side, we can weather the rest of the storm together. She is anxious to see Lottie Mae, so we go downstairs as soon as we finish unpacking.

"Hi. It's Angela. Anyone awake?" she says, as we enter the door with my house key.

"We are back here," Dana answers, from Lottie Mae's nursery.

I am extremely anxious to see how this is going to go. I follow behind Angela down the shotgun apartment to where our baby is.

"I didn't expect you today," Dana says, surprised to see Angela.

"I know. Mama surprised me this morning. How is she doing," Angela says, going straight to Lottie Mae's crib.

"She's doing OK. I just gave her a bath and put a fresh outfit on her. Do you want to hold her?" Dana asks. She is surprised, but still kind to Angela. I am grateful for that. I don't care if she hates me, as long as she doesn't take it out on my daughter.

"Yes, I'd love to hold her," Angela gushes.

I remain quiet and let Angela and Dana do all the talking. Angela gently picks up Lottie Mae and cradles her in the nook of her left elbow, while managing to grab and place the feeding pump backpack strap on the other shoulder. We follow them back to the living room, where Angela takes a seat in the rocker.

"How long can you stay today?" Dana asks, as we take our seats near her.

"We just came for a short visit this morning," I jump into the conversation and say. I don't feel like telling her I brought Angela home to stay permanently, yet. I just want to make it through this visit without fighting.

"How are you feeling Angela?" Dana asks, making small talk.

"I'm fine. I have been missing my little baby girl," she answers, between kissing Lottie Mae and talking baby talk to her.

"Well, if you two are going to be here for a while, I'm going to go make the formula for tomorrow," Dana says, and leaves us to enjoy our little one.

It heals my heart to watch Angela with Lottie Mae. I know how much she loves her and how hard it's been to be away. I have been trying to appease everyone and wait as long as possible for Angela to be stable before bringing her back. Now that she is here, I wonder why I let them talk me into keeping her away. Probably because I didn't know the lease was in her name and he was bluffing. What an asshole.

We stay for a couple of hours with Angela rocking and caring for Lottie Mae, as I watch from the couch. Dana stays busy in the back of the apartment, allowing us alone time. As it nears noon, I suggest we go eat and let Dana take back over watching Lottie Mae. We leave without me having to tell Dana anything about Angela never going back to The Well. I'll let her figure it out on her own.

Susan stops by after her workday later that evening. Angela and I are watching movies on Netflix, cuddled in bed, when she gets here.

"Hey Mom. Hi Angela. What are you ladies doing? Don't you have a curfew?" Susan asks, as she joins us.

"Mom checked me out today. I don't have to go back," Angela tells her sister.

"What? Is that true," Susan asks, looking at me.

"Yes. I went and picked her up this morning," I say, continuing to watch the television.

"I didn't know she was coming home today. We didn't talk about it yet," Susan says, staring at me.

"I know. There was nothing to talk about. She is doing better and ready to be with her baby," I say, measured but firm. I don't feel the need to explain my decision to her. She loves her sister dearly. They are best friends, but she doesn't share the same urgent need to reunite her with Lottie Mae. Mostly, because she fears the stress of Lottie Mae's illness is causing Angela to relapse, over and over. My fear is, if Angela is not with Lottie Mae when she transitions to the next world, she may never get over the devastating loss of not being with her baby in her dying days. I cannot lose both Lottie Mae and Angela.

Susan doesn't say anything else about it. What is done is done. We spend the evening watching movies, and hanging out like we used to do, when they were young. Susan heads to her boyfriend's afterward to spend the night. I feel my anxiety easing as Angela's first day home is without any major drama.

The next week passes with everyone adjusting to Angela's return without confronting me for bringing her home unplanned. Dana is kind to Angela, inviting her to spend the mornings with her and Lottie Mae. Jason was livid when he first discovered Angela was back and living upstairs at Susan's. He demanded she not be allowed in the apartment, when he is home, at first. Now, even he is warming to her being home. Despite that, he and I don't speak to each other since he limited my nights with Lottie Mae. We are all concerned, as the baby continues to show signs of decline. We take turns caring for her and forget about why they kept Angela away in the first place.

Sunday evening, I get a text from my fifteen-year-old.

"Mom. Who is this with Jason?" Jenny text. There is a picture attached of Jason handcuffed to Tina, the girl that Angela hired to help at Salutations, dressed in a belly dancer costume, in the French Quarter.

"Where did you get this picture?" I text back, shocked at the recently taken photo.

"It was on Facebook," she text.

"That's the bitch that took Angela's place at the wine bar, while she was sick," I text back. I am so angry at that little hypocrite and his self-righteous family. I remember back to when Angela was first becoming ill and Jason's father texts me, asking if I could control my daughter. I think I'll text Joe and ask him the same thing.

With a tap on my phone screen and a quick tap to hit forward, add text, "Can you control your son?" and another tap to send, there, done.

In less than two minutes, my phone starts ringing.

"What did you send me?" Joe asks angrily.

"It's a picture of your son, in the French Quarter, handcuffed to a whore," I calmly answer.

"No, why did you send me that picture, asking if I can control my son," he stammers and spits out.

"Have you forgotten how you asked me, if I could control my daughter, when she was becoming ill? Well, I'd like to ask you the same thing. Can you control your son? Looks like he's having a good time out on the town, while his baby daughter is dying," I say, poking him right back.

"He is a good father. You are just trying to start something. Your own family doesn't even like you," he yells into the receiver.

"Well, your wife hates the scheduled sex you make her have!" I say, before hanging up on him. His wife had told me during one of our bonding moments that he's so controlling, that he makes her have sex once a week, per his schedule, regardless of her mood.

Chapter Forty-Three

Hospice Nurses are special people sent from heaven to help us transition. Lottie Mae's hospice nurse, Maria, brings pamphlets that educate us on the dying process. Although they don't call it death. They refer to it as birthing into the next world. I like the sound of that better.

"We are decreasing the rate on the feeding pump and are adding morphine and valium to her pain medication regimen, replacing the Tylenol. You can stagger the times you give the morphine and valium. Give the morphine by itself, then wait two hours and give the valium, so that she is getting something every two hours, around the clock, to help manage the muscle cramps and the crying out from pain," Maria instructs us.

Dana hasn't said a word to me, since I emailed the pictures of her son to her husband and informed him that she hates sex with him. We communicate using Angela as our medium. We both are present for Maria's Hospice visit, allowing us to be informed simultaneously of Lottie Mae's new medication schedule and other changes, without breaking our silence with each other. After the meeting, I retreat upstairs to work on the blog. I leave Angela with Dana to care for our baby, until it's time for bed, then Angela joins me upstairs at her sister's apartment for the night. My phone rings waking me. I glance at the clock, 2:15 a.m.

"Hello, Dana?" I ask, looking at caller ID.

"I can't do this. She sobs. I need you to come and take over," Dana says, crying into the phone.

"I'll be right there," I say, before hanging up.

I jump out of bed, quickly change into a sweatsuit, and put my tennis shoes on. Angela's heavy nighttime medications allow her to sleep through the phone call from Dana. I write a note and leave it on the counter for her to find when she wakes up, grab my house keys, and run down the stairs.

I quickly unlock the door and run through the living room, through Jason and Angela's room, and find Dana crying, holding Lottie Mae in the nursery.

"Hey, I came as quickly as I could," I say, as I join them.

"I've been up all night trying to give her the medicine. I can't do it anymore," she says, crying as she gets up from the rocker, and gently places Lottie Mae into my arms.

"It's OK. I'm glad you called me," I say, feeling compassion for my co-grandparent. I look down at the precious baby in my arms. Lottie Mae is resting quietly now as I hold her.

Dana didn't say another word to me. She just started picking up her things and packing them away. I wasn't sure what to say to her. I wanted to say go get some rest while I take over. Don't leave now in the middle of the night. Instead, I just rock Lottie Mae and let her go.

I didn't sleep the rest of the morning, except for a couple times I dozed off, in between giving the scheduled pain medications. I set my phone alarm to sound every two hours to keep me on track. I place pillows in the middle of Angela and Jason's bed and lay Lottie Mae with her head inclined on top of them. I rest beside her. Angela finds my note and joins me later that morning.

"Hey Mama. I found your note. Is everything OK?" Angela asks, as she slides into bed, on the opposite side of Lottie Mae.

"Yes. Dana called me around 2:15 a.m., asking me to come down and help her. She was crying and said she could not do this, anymore. I don't know where Jason is. He wasn't here when I came down to take over and I didn't ask about him. I just thanked her for calling me. I wanted to wake you up, but I was afraid you were sleeping too hard, with all the medicine you must take at night. I'm glad you found my note," I tell her, as I sit up.

"Have you slept any?" Angela asks.

"I slept some, before she called me. I've been giving Lottie Mae the pain medication every two hours and dozing off in between times," I answer.

"Nanna called. She is on her way down to stay with us. She should be here by 3 p.m." Angela tells me.

"Maybe we can divide our day into twelve-hour shifts when she gets here, so that we can manage her pain medications, and still be able to rest and take care of ourselves," I say, trying to problem solve.

"Susan came by after you went upstairs last night. She said they are about to wrap shooting on Treme this week and then she can be here to help, too," Angela says, giving hope.

"That will help so much. Your brother called the other night. He is taking a leave of absence from the military. He wants to be here and help run errands and give emotional support. He said to expect him before next weekend. He is coming, as soon as he gets all the paperwork processed," I share.

My mother arrives right on time.

"Hey, my babies," Nanna says, as I open the door for her.

I give her a big hug and take her bags from her.

"Come in Mom. I'm glad you came. Is there anything in your car you need me to carry in?" I ask my elderly mother.

"I have one more suitcase in the trunk, if you don't mind," she says, handing me her car keys.

"Sure, no problem," I say, taking the keys.

I hurriedly go and get her suitcase from her car. On the way back in, I check the mail. On top of the large stack of letters is a notice for a court date, from the City of New Orleans.

"This just came," I say, holding up the formal notice.

"What is that?" my mother asks.

"It's a notice for a court date, for when Angela was sick, and had that hit and run, two months ago," I tell her.

"What are you going to do?" she asks.

"I should call her dad and make him take care of this. He is the one that left her alone, time after time, when she was sick. Had he been responsible, he could have prevented her from getting arrested. The only reason I don't ask him to take care of it, is because I don't trust him to do it," I say, anger rising in my voice.

"Why don't you call him. He won't mind," my mother suggests.

"Did you even hear what I just said?" I turn to her and asks. "I am going to call my friend, Denise. She has helped me before. She is the only one that helps clean up the messes Garry leaves behind."

"I just hate to see you get so upset," my mother begins, "If you can pray and give it to the Lord Jesus Christ, he will deliver you."

I ignore her and excuse myself to head to the back of the apartment to text my friend. A few minutes later, Denise texts back, instructing me to take a picture of the notice, and send it to her. She says she will get the hearing postponed, so we can deal with it, when we have more time. I thank her for being so generous with her time and helping us.

We devise a schedule. We will be caregivers in teams of two. Angela and I are one team. Nanna and Susan the second team. We give her the needed pain medication, every two hours, allowing her to rest comfortably. Jason's family tells us they will not be returning. They say it is too hard for them to care for her, as the end pushes closer. I don't question their decision. I am just grateful that I can be with her.

Jackson finally gets his paperwork approved and leaves Tinker Air Force Base, in Oklahoma City and is heading to New Orleans. He calls to say he will be here by morning. I am glad he will be here with us.

We have visitors stopping by every night lately. The families of Angela's former students continue bringing meals. Lance and Jenny come every weekend and stay. We keep Lottie Mae in Angela's room propped up on pillows and take turns resting beside her. Most of the time, the pocket doors separating their room from the living room are slightly cracked open, around twelve inches, or so. Tonight, I am lying next to Lottie Mae, when the doorbell rings, signaling more guest arriving. I lean forward to see Garry and Laura come in and take a seat on the couch.

I feel my face become hot, as the emotions I have held in simmer. I think back to when Garry left Angela in that hotel room in Houma, and the time he wouldn't let his own daughter take a bath in his home, because of that bitch, sitting beside him. I feel the hair rise on the back of my neck and my heart begin to beat fast, like it's coming out of my chest. I think about how he refused to pay for her care, when he has more than enough funds. I think about how he made her lie and say she is an addict, so she can get free help. I can't control myself. I lean forward on my right elbow and make eye contact with Laura through the small gap between the pocket doors. I glance around the room. No one else is looking. Just as I turn back and our eyes lock, I mouth, "Fuck you," as I shoot her the middle finger. Afterward, I slowly recline back down beside Lottie Mae, like nothing ever happened.

Treatment in America: Her Life Matters

Chapter Forty-Four

Within ten minutes of my middle finger salute to Laura, she and Garry stand up, and announce they are leaving. I watch as my mother rises and escorts them outside. I hope she is trying to save their souls.

We fall into a pattern of twelve-hour shifts, two person teams, caring for Lottie Mae. Thank God for smart phone reminders, that ring every two hours, letting us know when it's time to give her a dose of pain medication. She sleeps most of the time now. I just finish giving Lottie Mae her noon dosage, when the doorbell rings.

"Surprise!" Jackson shouts, as I open the door.

"Oh my god! You almost gave me a heart attack!" I say, wrapping my arms around my son's neck.

"Got you! It's so good to be here, Mom," Jackson says, giving me a bear hug.

"Come in. How long did it take you to drive here?" I ask.

"I made it in twelve hours, but I stopped a lot," he smiles and tells me, as he carries his duffle bag of clothes inside and drops them on the floor in the living room.

"I'm going to let you sleep upstairs at Susan's. I bought a folding cot that you can use. We are playing musical beds here, taking turns caring for Lottie Mae," I say, as I sort through the sleeping arrangements in my head.

"That's all good. I don't care where I sleep. The couch is fine. Where's my little niece?" Jackson asks.

"Right through here," I say, leading him through the pocket doors, into Angela's room, where Lottie Mae rests on the bed beside her.

"Jackson, I can't believe you are here," Angela says, raising up from Lottie Mae's side.

"Hey Sis, I wanted to come as soon as I could. Sorry it's taken a while," he says, bending down and kissing his sister on the cheek.

"It's OK. I'm just happy to see you," she says, hugging him tight.

"Can I kiss her," he asks, looking at Lottie Mae.

"Yes, it's alright. She sleeps most of the time now," Angela shares.

Jackson bends his muscular body down and gently kisses his niece on the forehead.

"She's a beautiful little angel," he says to his sister, as he raises up.

"Yes, she is beautiful," I echo.

He spends the day with us as we take care of Lottie Mae, giving her the pain medications every two hours. For the most part, we just lay beside her, surrounding her with love as she sleeps. I read the pamphlet left by the hospice nurse telling us what to expect as the end draws near. Angela and Jackson visit and give comfort to each other as Lottie Mae rests.

"I do have a favor to ask for tomorrow," I say, prepping Jackson.

"Sure. That's why I came. What's up?" he asks energetically.

"I need you to run an errand for me. Want to know what the devil looks like? He's wearing a suit asking you to pay insurance premiums, but never intending to keep his promise of helping in your time of need. My short-term disability from Scrudential has been cancelled. Evidently, they think I'm not under stress and no longer qualify for benefits. I had to get my doctor and counselor to make copies of their notes and fax it to them. I am sending a copy of my medical records appealing their decision. Would you mind running it to Fed Ex and have it overnighted for me?" I ask.

"No problem my sweet mama," he answers, giving me a kiss on the top of my head as he gets up from our circle on the bed.

"That will help more than you know. I can't leave Lottie Mae," I explain.

"No worries. I am just happy to be of help!" Jackson says smiling.

Susan and my mother join us that evening and take over Lottie Mae's care. I take a break to go upstairs and write the blog from Susan's balcony. There is little joy in my heart to write about, as I watch Lottie Mae continue to decline. I am grateful that Angela is holding up under the pressure. She is attentive and gentle as she helps with Lottie Mae's care. As I stare at the pink and blue colors of the evening sky, I take a moment to think about what I want to say. It's hard to write when your heart is breaking. I think about the encouragement I receive from reading the emails sent in response to the blog. These messages, from strangers around the world, are helping encourage us to keep going. I finally get the blog posted and head back downstairs to be with everyone.

Susan, Angela and Jackson surround Lottie Mae in Angela's bed. They turn her side to side and adjust the pillows to help position her when they give the pain medication, every two hours. Lately, Lottie Mae has been showing little signs of restlessness, before the medications are due. Her little belly is also distended and her output almost nothing. I am anxious to talk to the nurse about it tomorrow when she is scheduled to visit.

"How is our baby?" I ask the trio, as I join them on the bed.

"She was grunting and squirming and making a little frowny face like she was hurting, before it was time for her pain medicine. We just gave it to her about twenty minutes ago. She just fell back to sleep right before you got here," Angela tells me.

"The hospice nurse is coming tomorrow. Let's make sure we tell her about the changes. I'm worried that we might have to increase the medicine," I share.

"I'm glad they are coming," Susan adds.

"Where's Nanna?" I ask.

"She's in the kitchen," Jackson tells me.

"Thanks. I'm going to check on her," I say, as I slowly ease up from beside Angela, trying not to shake the bed and disturb our precious baby.

I find my mother drying and putting up dishes.

"Hey, do you need any help?" I ask, as I join her in the back of the house.

"No, I got it. Almost finished. I'm glad you are here. The baby isn't doing too good. She seems like she is hurting, before it's time to give her the morphine. Also, I wanted to ask you if you have thought about where Angela is going to go after Lottie Mae dies?" Nanna asks.

"The hospice nurse is scheduled to come tomorrow morning. I will make sure to tell her about the changes. As far as where Angela is going to go, or who she is going to stay with her after Lottie Mae passes, I am probably going to stay with her, and help her find another place in the Mid-City area. She says Uptown area holds too many painful memories. As soon as she gets on her feet, back working and independent, I'll go back home," I tell her our tentative plans.

"I was talking to Garry the other day and he said she could come stay with him. He has a camper that she can live in, at his farm in Ponchatoula," my mother begins telling me.

"Wait Mom. Don't you remember how he left her alone in Houma at that hotel when she was sick? Or what about the time he wouldn't let her take a bath at his house? He causes more harm than good, when it comes to taking care of his daughter," I say angrily.

"But sweetheart, you are so angry," she says, defending her disloyalty.

"Yes, I'm angry," I admit. "I'm angry because Garry has not taken care of her in the past, and you, my mother, are wanting her to go stay with him."

"I talked to him about it when he and Laura were visiting the other day. I think that he is in a better position to provide for her," she says, trying to justify her position.

"You talked to him about it, before talking to me?" I ask, feeling hurt and betrayed.

"Well, you have done so much already. I thought it would be better for everyone, if she goes to his farm. It sounds like they bought a beautiful quiet place in the country," she adds.

"It's not about the money. It's about him not being around. He just dumps her in a place and leaves her to her own devices. She needs someone with her as she recovers. I need you to support me on this," I say strongly.

"I have to do what the Lord tells me to do," she tells me.

"I want you to look me in the eyes and tell me that you are not going to encourage Angela to go stay with her father after Lottie Mae passes. Can you do that Mother? Can you look me in the eyes right now and tell me that?" I say, as I walk to stand in front of her.

"You need to back up," Nanna says, taking a step back fearing my reaction to her answer.

"I would never lay a finger on you. I just want you to be straight with me. Look me in the eyes and tell me that you will support me as I try to save my daughter's life. I am waiting on your answer," I say, drawing a line in the sand.

"I am sorry, but I want her to go stay with Garry," she finally admits.

I pause and stare at her. She said it. She finally crossed a line of no return. I look at my mother and think about all the other things I have forgiven her for. She didn't protect me as a child. She managed to make me feel I was responsible for being sexually assaulted when I was only four years old. When Jenny's father became violent, he beat me mercilessly, and then held a shotgun to my head, and threatened to kill me and the children. He kidnapped me and I was so afraid I jumped from his moving truck on the Interstate off ramp and hid in the woods. I called my Mother for help, but she said she had to teach Sunday school, and Dad had to preach, so they couldn't come help me. Now, here she is interfering with me caring for my adult child. It would be better, if she never came here, at all.

"Thank you, Mother, for finally telling me how you feel. Now, I am going to tell you how I feel. It's one thing to be a terrible mother to me, but when you come in between me and caring for my child, putting my child at risk, that's when you have gone too far. We can put our differences aside and continue caring for Lottie Mae together, but I swear, if you don't stop encouraging her to go to Garry's house after Lottie Mae passes, I will never forgive you. Do it one more time and you will be dead to me," I say without blinking.

Treatment in America: Her Life Matters

Chapter Forty-Five

Maria, our hospice nurse arrives at 9 a.m. right on schedule.

"Hi Maria, please come in," I say, opening the door.

"How are you today?" she asks, as I close the door behind her.

"It's one day at a time. I am so glad to see you. She has been having some breakthrough pain, in between the two hours we are giving her something," I say, updating her as we walk through the pocket doors from the living room into the bedroom, to where Lottie Mae rests on Angela's bed, surrounded by her mother, aunt and great-grandmother. Angela, Susan, and Nanna sit up and greet our hospice nurse as she enters.

"This disease is cruel in how it affects her ability to absorb the medications. We will have to increase the frequency of the doses, since we can't change the volume of medicine given. Start giving the Morphine every two hours, instead of every four hours, with a staggered dose of Valium, every two hours. This way, she will be getting something for pain every hour. If it gets too bad, you can put the medicine under her tongue to be absorbed quickly. How has her output been?" she asks, unwrapping Lottie Mae's blankets that swaddle her, and begins her examination.

"She hasn't had any wet diapers or bowel movements the last three days," Angela tells the nurse.

"She's been sleeping most of the time, but has started waking up crying, before it's time for her medicine," my mother adds.

"Her little tummy feels distended. We need to completely stop the feeding pump. It is causing more discomfort as her little body cannot process the formula anymore," Maria says, as she gently feels on Lottie Mae's tummy.

"Her skin looks yellowish," Susan adds, as the nurse continues with her examination.

"Her body is preparing for her journey into the next world. You will notice changes in skin color, her breathing patterns, and congestion. It's a natural process that varies with each person. Just as it takes hours of labor to be born, it may take hours and even days before it's time for her transition, or birthing into the next world. There is nothing to fix at this point. We just want to make sure we are keeping her comfortable," she explains, as she continues examining Lottie Mae.

"When should we call you? Do we call you when she is getting near? How do we know when it's near?" I ask nervously.

"It's so hard to predict. You may see a facial grimace or movements of her body as her spirit leaves. You don't have to call me before she transitions. It is not necessary for a professional to be here. You don't have to call me immediately after she passes. I encourage you to take time to prepare her body as you say your good-byes. You can give her a bath and dress her in fresh clothes. Spend as much time as you need before calling me. When I come, I will call the funeral home and arrange for her to be transported," Maria says, giving us our instructions for how to proceed.

After the hospice visit, we continue with our comfort measures the next four days without incident. On the fifth day of no nutrition from the feeding pump, her breathing changes to shallow breaths, interrupted with episodes of loud crying outbursts. It cuts to my soul causing hot tears to swell in my eyes as I try to keep it together. I call the nurse.

"Hi, this is Jamie Thornton, Lottie Mae LeBlanc's grandmother. Can you have her nurse call me? Lottie Mae is having increased pain," I say quickly, trying not to cry.

"Yes, Mrs. Thornton, I will have her call you shortly," the hospice answering service operator tells me.

I leave Lottie Mae with Angela, Nanna, and Susan and go into the living room to wait for the nurse to return my call. I lie face down on the cold hardwood floor and begin to pour my heart out to God once more.

"Please God, have mercy on us. Dear creator, master of my soul, my love, I cannot endure her suffering any longer," I pray out loud, as I cry uncontrollably, "Please be with us now and please take her pain away. I can't stand it when she is hurting."

My prayers are interrupted by the phone ringing.

"Hello," I answer, as I compose myself.

"This is Maria Sanchez, your hospice nurse," the kind voice says.

"Yes, Miss. Maria, Lottie Mae has been squirming and crying out. The pain medication doesn't seem to be giving her relief," I tell her.

"We need to change the frequency to giving the morphine every hour and the valium every half hour," she instructs.

"OK, I understand. I will do this, but I'm afraid she won't make it through the night," I say, as I begin to cry. "Are you sure you want me to give her a dose of Morphine every hour and on the half-hour give her a dose of valium?"

"Yes. You must be strong now. Lottie Mae needs you to not let her hurt. We are not saving her life. We cannot save her life. The only thing we can do, is make sure she is not in pain. Her little body is absorbing less and less. All we can do is increase the frequency and hope she is able to absorb enough to ease her pain," nurse Sanchez explains what I already know, but need to hear again from her, in order to follow the instructions that will allow our angel to have relief.

"OK. I will do it," I say.

"When she passes, you don't have to call me right away. Take time with her to say your good-byes. You may bath her and put a clean gown on her. Do not call 911. They will not know our prearranged plans. Call me. I will be the one to call the funeral home," she gently explains, before we say good-bye.

I hang up and return to tell the others the instructions from Nurse Sanchez. We prepare syringes with premeasured amounts of Morphine and Valium and place them in a container on the bedside table, to be able to give on time, without leaving her side. The four of us remain with her around the clock now. We give her the first dose. She is still restless. I gently pick her up, keeping the pillow she has been resting on beneath her. The pillow helps cradle her, without putting too much pressure on her tiny swollen body. Angela is beside me, gently stroking Lottie Mae's brow, Susan is on the other side, stroking her arm, while I rock her back and forth, in my arms. My mother is in and out of the room, as she busies herself cleaning in between the administration of meds.

We give her the second dose of Morphine. She seems to relax and has not cried out since we started the increased frequency. Angela gets up to help Nanna in the kitchen and leaves Susan and me with our baby. As we cuddle, rocking her, a wide smile appears on Lottie Mae's face like she is looking at someone. We have not seen her smile in weeks since she has become so weak. Susan and I look at each other and then back to her. She is gone. I lean down and whisper in her ear, "It's OK to go. I will see you again one day my love."

Susan jumps up and goes to get her sister and grandmother. They come running back, and wrap their arms around us both, as I continue holding Lottie Mae. We cry and hold each other with linked arms surrounding our angel. My mother takes over helping Angela take Lottie Mae from my arms. I am in shock. I am still thinking about how she smiled. There is still a sweet slight smile on her face, as they take her to the nursery, and place her body on the changing table.

My mother goes to run bath water, as Angela begins gently undressing Lottie Mae. Susan helps removing her small arms from the tiny sleeves of her gown, one at a time. We take her into the bathroom and gently place her into the warm water. Angela and my mother bathe her, with Susan and I watching them. Afterward, Angela dresses her in the white christening gown that she wore as a baby, during her dedication ceremony. She looks so beautiful and peaceful. We take turns holding her and saying our good-byes, before calling the nurse.

When Nurse Sanchez arrives, she is kind and takes over the task of calling the funeral home and coroner's office. A half hour later, the funeral home attendants arrive with their gurney to take our angel away. Susan stays with Angela and Nanna, as they place Lottie Mae's body on the rolling bed and begin to head toward the front door. I follow them to the front porch with our hospice nurse.

"You need to let go, sweetheart," Maria whispers to me, as she takes my arm and leads me back into the living room. She closes the door and begins drawing the curtains of the front room window shut.

I want to tell her, it's our family tradition to stand on the front porch, and watch our children leave, until you can't see their car anymore, but I am too overcome with grief, as I fall to the floor, and begin to cry inconsolably.

Chapter Forty-Six

A week after Lottie Mae's passing, we meet at the main pavilion in City Park, to celebrate her short life. It's a beautiful sunny day. There are a hundred or more guests assembled, when we arrive with Lottie Mae's ashes. Angela is holding up well, under the circumstances. After placing Lottie Mae's urn by a large arrangement of white roses, positioned at the front of the pavilion, Lance, Angela, Jenny, and I take our places on the front row, next to Susan and her boyfriend.

I glance around the crowd and see a group of my tennis friends from McComb, my counselor, Tom, and several families from the Lycée Francais de la Nouvelle-Orleans, where Angela taught school. The Leblanc family are on the opposite side, along with Garry and Laura. My mother is standing next to them. Missing are my sister and my two brothers.

We had made a tentative schedule for the service. It was to be like my adopted mother's, Allie Mae Jefferson's, funeral. She was an African-American, former patient of mine, who loved me unconditionally for ten years, before her passing. At her service, I was touched by how they had testimonies from person, after person, honoring her life, as they shared their personal stories. Lottie Mae's service starts with Angela's friend singing, followed by testimonials. Jason, the atheist, requested the ceremony to be without any religious speakers.

"We would like to thank each one of you for being here to celebrate the short life of our angel, Lottie Mae Leblanc. Cindy will you come and sing for us?" I say, turning to Angela's friend, Cindy, wearing a white sun dress and carrying a guitar. The small petite lady walks up and takes center stage. She sings the sweet lullaby she sang at the hospital to Lottie Mae, when she was at Children's hospital during Thanksgiving. Afterward, she returns to stand with the gathered mourners.

"As we celebrate Lottie Mae's life, we would like for those that would like to, to come and share how Lottie Mae has impacted your life. I will start us off by sharing how Lottie Mae, in her short time with us, has changed me. A little more than a year ago, we got the happy news that we were having our first grandbaby. We found out within a couple of months of her birth, that our time with her would be limited by a disease we had never heard of. This tiny precious innocent child has touched my heart in a profound way. I have learned what is important in this life and what isn't important. I am grateful that I had the time with her that I had. I will never be the same. I have seen her inspire love in others and unselfishness in strangers that have been touched by her story. They helped us during our darkest of times. I am a better human being for what I've learned from this precious one's pure love. Would anyone else like to speak?" I ask, as I finish my testimony.

Susan walks up and takes the floor. She shares her story of life with Lottie Mae. Then one after another, different ones take turns sharing how their life has changed from knowing our baby. It is heartwarming to hear their stories. After everyone finishes sharing, the crowd begins to disperse. I can't speak to the LeBlanc family. The wound is too fresh. I let go of the pain from my mother's actions and let go of my need to have her in my life at the same time.

The next day, I walk the mile to my counselor's house on Thalia Street. I feel numb and detached from my feelings. I have cried until there is nothing left inside. I reach his house, open the gate and ring the bell for the door marked "office," like I've done, once a week, for the past eight months.

"Come in," Tom says, opening the door. He gives me a big hug before we take our places in the front parlor.

"How are you?" he asks, as he settles into his chair.

"I don't know yet. I feel so empty. I can't believe she's gone," I tell him.

"You have been carrying so much, for so long. It's quite normal to feel this way," he assures me.

"Thank you for coming to her memorial service," I say.

"You're welcome. I noticed that you were the one holding Lottie Mae's ashes, before the ceremony and then after the ceremony, you were the one making sure to take them," he shares.

"I know. I just wanted to make sure they were taken care of," I admit.

"What are your plans now?" he asks.

"I have just enough money to make it one month, before I must return to a fulltime job. I am hoping to help Angela find another apartment across town in mid-city, so she can have a new environment to heal. Uptown has too many memories she says," I tell him.

"Are you going to continue writing?" he asks.

"I wrote the last entry for the blog, yesterday. What I want to do now, is write a book about Zellweger Disorder, to bring awareness and hopefully research. The other thing I want to share, is what I have learned about treatment in America for our mentally ill. This experience has taught me that change is needed so badly. So many of our homeless have untreated mental illness. How can we expect someone mentally ill to work and be able to buy insurance, so they can see a doctor to get well? This has got to be changed. I am planning on using every ounce of energy I have, to tell how my daughter was treated. I plan on channeling that passion into writing our story. I will not let it go, until I scream it to the world. Maybe, if I can show what treatment in America, for mental health, really looks like, then change will occur." I say, from the bottom of my heart.

"I believe you," Tom says, giving me encouragement.

The End.

Epilogue

This coming September will mark the seventh anniversary of Lottie Mae's death. I live in a small town in Mississippi, with my husband, Lance. We have grown from the pain we went through. We are more considerate to each other. I am grateful that we have weathered the storms. Life's trials have created a deeper level of love and understanding between us.

Angela remarried and has a beautiful healthy daughter. She also has four sweet stepsons that adore her. She is still sensitive to medication changes, causing three hospitalizations since Lottie Mae passed. She has improved with compliance taking her medications. When her medications are not working properly, she promptly asks for help. The last time this happened, was after a recent move. She had to change from her regular doctor to a nurse practitioner. The new NP put her on an antidepressant, in addition to her other meds, and it triggered a manic episode.

As her mania started increasing, Angela called me and told me what was going on. She asked her husband to take her to the hospital. She had not been able to sleep for two days. The ER doctor didn't recognize what was happening, despite her telling him her history. He sent her back home, with instructions to take some Benadryl to help fall asleep. I quickly packed a suitcase and drove the nine and a half hours to my daughter's home.

Her symptoms were increasing by the time I arrived. She was pacing around the house and not able to stop talking or chain smoking. When she becomes manic, she can't practice relaxation techniques or take a hot bath to relax. Nothing helps the chemical imbalance, not Benadryl for sure. She became so agitated and restless that she took her pacing outside, to the front yard. It was dark and I was exhausted and worried. I tried talking to her, but she could not fully process what I was saying. She was holding on by a thread, but aware enough to reach out for help. She called 911 and the operator convinced her to go to the ER with me.

Once at the ER, we finally got a room and a young ER doctor saw her. The doctor wasn't warm or reassuring. He seemed skeptical during his examination. It was amazing to me that she could be this ill and still seem lucid to this professional. I waited with her in our curtain cubical.

As we waited, she became increasingly agitated and couldn't sit still. She told me she was leaving and headed toward the exit leading to the parking lot. I followed her and yelled for help, but no one came. She exited the ER and ended up in the parking lot. The security guard that saw us arrive jumped in to help and started talking with Angela. He convinced her not to leave, for the moment.

I was desperate at this point. I raised my voice and shouted toward the ER nurses' station, "I need help with my daughter. She is very sick and in a vulnerable state. She cannot protect herself from predators. If you do not help me, I will call every news station in this country and tell them this is the kind of treatment they can expect for their loved ones at this hospital!"

Finally, I got some help from the director of nurses and she was able to get Angela admitted, but let me tell you, that doctor wasn't happy. This is why I must tell this story. My struggle to get care for her is not over. Her life matters and so does my life. I will always go and be there for my daughter. I love her unconditionally. I desperately need help changing the mental healthcare system we have in our country, not only for my child, but for all the other adult children, that have no mother screaming for their help.

I am very proud of her. It is a sacrifice for my daughter to allow me to tell our story. She is kind and loving, with a beautiful heart. I had my own dark days as I grieved for Lottie Mae. Angela helped me during those dark times. She listened and lifted my spirits. She helped me heal my heart. We continue to talk daily. I treasure our relationship.

My sincere hope is to illuminate the need for improvement in the treatment of bipolar disorder, along with mental health treatment in general. It is also my hope to band together, with other likeminded individuals, to improve the problem of homelessness in our country. I see a direct link between the two problems, because a large percentage of the homeless suffer with untreated mental illness.

It has taken a long time for me to process all these events. I think of myself, and others, whose flaws are like the gold cracks in Japanese pottery. Kintsugi is an art form using gold and other precious minerals to repair the flaws and cracks in pottery, making each piece unique. I like to think that our flaws and struggles form us into something that is unique and beautiful as well. May you never lose hope, and may you find peace wherever you go.

Acknowledgements

I want to thank my family for letting me have a voice and for letting me know that my life matters, too. To my best friend and husband, Jerry Ivey, thank you for loving me like a MF. I love you, too. I am grateful for my counselors, Dee Meux, CADC, NCAC, CCDC, for helping me find my voice, and Terry Mayers, M Ed, LCSW, Licensed Clinical Social Worker for being a light guiding me through the storm. A special thank you to Dunbar Watt for your endless kindness in finding help for us when we needed it most.

About the Author

Jacqueline White-Ivey was born in Jonesville, Louisiana, a small town in central Louisiana. She moved to Buras, Louisiana, at seven years old, and graduated high school there in 1982. After marrying and having her first two children, she graduated from the University of Louisiana, Monroe, in 1993. She worked as a COTA in Occupational Therapy for twenty-six years before retiring to start her own publishing company, Maemo Publishing, LLC. Her website is jacquelinewhite-ivey.com where she post short stories and blogs. All four of her children are college graduates and she is the grandmother of one angel in heaven and one angel still on Earth. She is active in assisting her local homeless shelter and is a tireless advocate for the improvement of our mental health system in America. She currently lives in McComb, Mississippi, with her husband, Jerry Ivey.

www.ingramcontent.com/pod-product-compliance
Lightning Source LLC
Chambersburg PA
CBHW071233070526
44583CB00017B/2160